COLLECTOR'S GUIDE TO

CookBooks

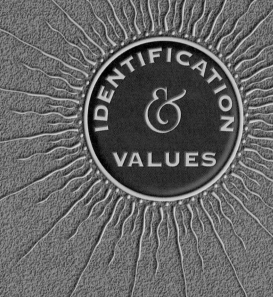

IDENTIFICATION & VALUES

FRANK DANIELS

COLLECTOR BOOKS
A Division of Schroeder Publishing Co. Inc.

On the front cover: *The Pillsbury Cook-Book*, 1913, $20.00; *White House Cook Book*, 1929, $60.00; *Carnation Cook Book*, $3.00; *Royal Baker and Pastry Cook*, 1906, $15.00; *The Shrimp Cookbook*, $12.00; *McCall's Cocktail-Time Cookbook*, $3.00; *Betty Crocker's Talking Recipes*, $30.00; *The Savannah Cook Book*, $25.00; *Cooking in Wyoming*, $6.00; *Newman's Own Cookbook* (hardback), $8.00; *Betty Crocker's New Outdoor Cookbook*, $6.00.

On the back cover: *Meals With a Foreign Flair*, $3.00; *The German Cookbook*, $15.00; *Dishes Men Like*, $10.00.

Cover design by Beth Summers
Book design by Lisa Henderson

COLLECTOR BOOKS
P.O. Box 3009
Paducah, Kentucky 42002-3009

www.collectorbooks.com

Copyright © 2005 Frank Daniels

The current values in this book should be used only as a guide. They are not intended to set prices, which vary from one section of the country to another. Auction prices as well as dealer prices vary greatly and are affected by condition as well as demand. Neither the author nor the publisher assumes responsibility for any losses that might be incurred as a result of consulting this guide.

Searching For A Publisher?

We are always looking for people knowledgeable within their fields. If you feel that there is a real need for a book on your collectible subject and have a large comprehensive collection, contact Collector Books.

CONTENTS

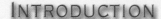

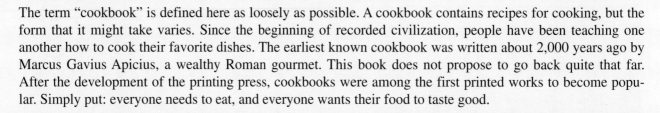

The term "cookbook" is defined here as loosely as possible. A cookbook contains recipes for cooking, but the form that it might take varies. Since the beginning of recorded civilization, people have been teaching one another how to cook their favorite dishes. The earliest known cookbook was written about 2,000 years ago by Marcus Gavius Apicius, a wealthy Roman gourmet. This book does not propose to go back quite that far. After the development of the printing press, cookbooks were among the first printed works to become popular. Simply put: everyone needs to eat, and everyone wants their food to taste good.

The earliest known cookbook that was written in English is *A Noble Book of Royal Feasts*, printed in about 1500 by Richard Pynson (London). It was just 80 pages in length. Following in about 1545 was *A Proper New Book of Cookery*, by an unknown author — a book that appears to feature the first publication of several pastries, including fruit tarts. That book concentrates on American cookbooks, the first of which appears to have been *American Cookery*, published in 1796 by Amelia Simmons (and printed by Hudson & Goodwin of Hartford). Other cookbooks published in the United States before that time, such as *The Frugal Housewife*, were simply reprints of books written in England. Simmons appears to have published the first recipe for what we today call pumpkin pie.

Rather than focus on the rarest of the rare, like Simmons's book mentioned above, of which four copies are known, this "cookbook book" includes recent cookbooks that were published from about 1800 to about 2000 — two hundred years of cookbooks! Most of these are cookbooks that you might have in your own kitchen or might find at garage sales or in bookstores. In the listings, you will also occasionally find notes indicating the importance of a certain author or book. For example, Mary J. Lincoln and Fannie M. Farmer published books and magazines in association with their Boston Cooking School that revolutionized the way people were taught to cook. *The Joy of Cooking* started a revolution of its own, changing the way in which recipes were listed in cookbooks — making them easier to follow.

This book then lists first editions and umpteenth editions, hardbacks and paperbacks, the rarest and the most common. Famous names like *Good Housekeeping* and *McCall's* will appear in the listings, along with obscure authors and publications. The author of this book loves to cook and enjoys finding cookbooks that are artistic, or easy-to-follow, or hard to find, or interesting for any one of a number of reasons. Following Internet sales for the past year, this book attempts to chart actual cookbook sales for the first time.

In addition, this book traces the histories of three important cookbook publishers, hoping to provide a first step towards a complete bibliography from those companies. Enjoy the listings, the photos, and the information provided herein, but most of all, enjoy your cooking and collecting!

About Collectibility

There are several factors that determine the relative resale value of a book. There are thousands of different cookbooks, booklets, pamphlets, and related items produced every year, but few of these are widely collected. Most of these are not particularly interesting or important, as far as cookbooks go. People collect cookbooks for several reasons, any one of which may make a book valuable as time passes. These reasons include:

Relative Importance — Certain authors, such as Catherine Beecher, Fannie Merritt Farmer, and Maria Parloa, have had a lasting impact on cooking in general. Some publishers and/or products, like Pillsbury, Jell-O, and General Mills (Betty Crocker), have attracted a wide following due to their appeal to the population at large.

Content — Some cookbooks are collected due to their unusual recipes or easy-to-follow instructions. Still others are collected because of interesting illustrations or photos that adorn the covers or insides. Sometimes the subject of a book may make it sought-after; for example, cookbooks on chocolate are more widely collected (generally) than cookbooks about beef. All of these elements contribute to the factor of relative importance, and when combined, they increase demand for a book.

Scarcity — When a certain group of books is considered collectible, within that group of books there are always more common items and harder to find ones. If a cookbook is very common, it is usually common because people like to use the recipes; therefore, even common cookbooks can be collectible. Yet for someone trying desperately to locate every book published for Campbell's Soup or by the Delineator Institute, the more difficult to locate books usually sell for higher prices. Some cookbooks can be scarce enough that very few copies are sold publicly each year. Most eighteenth and nineteenth century cookbooks can be quite elusive.

In order to measure the scarcity of books, booklets, and other items found in the specialized chapters, a Scarcity Index has been developed. This index is described in more detail on page 7.

Condition — Even the scarcest books will sell at a considerable discount if they are discolored, ripped, marked up, or incomplete. Therefore, the condition of a cookbook is extremely important. If you have the opportunity to buy one of several copies of a particular book, it is recommended that you purchase the best condition copy that you are able to afford.

Dealers in hardback books typically grade them as fine, very good, or good. On the other hand, magazines and pamphlets are typically graded as near mint, fine, or good. The two sets of terminology mean roughly the same thing. In fact, paperback books are often graded using either scale. In order to be consistent, the single scale with a highest grade of near mint will be used here.

The grade given to a book should be assigned irrespective of its age or collectibility. That is, if two books are graded the same, regardless of age, then they should be perceived as having essentially the same amount of wear. Cookbooks that date before 1940 are seldom found in near mint condition. Cookbooks dating before 1890 are seldom found in very fine condition or higher. Cookbooks that came out prior to about 1850 are often hard to find in any condition, so it is no shame to purchase a good condition copy of a hard-to-find book.

Several different defects (or "wear") affect the grade of a book. Some of these are classified as minor defects, while others are major defects or even serious defects.

Minor defects include mild corner bumps — very slight bends at one or more corners; yellowed (but not brown or brittle) pages; a few dog-eared pages due to recipes being bookmarked; slight scuffing; store stamps; unobtrusive writing (such as an owner's signature); or an owner's sticker.

Major defects include 1" or more of creases, particularly to the front cover; a worn spine; scuffing that removes some of the color from the cover; slight spine roll (so that the spine is not at a right angle to the front cover); slight water damage (pages are not stuck together, but some warping or minor discoloration is evident); more serious writing (such as underlined or circled recipes); or tears (no more than ¼" in length).

Serious defects include a great deal of creases; bumps that warp or crease the entire book; brown pages; obtrusive writing, particularly to the front cover; large tears; missing chunks; tape; obvious water damage; obvious spine roll; loose or missing pages; and loose or missing cover.

Collectors may apply their own weights to these defects. For example, you might not mind a book with a spine roll if it is otherwise undamaged. Then again, you might consider any writing at all to be undesirable. Whether or not you collect books with certain defects is entirely up to you. If you are going to use a book for its recipes, the condition of a book will likely be less important to you than if you plan to display your books.

Combinations of these defects reduce the grade (or condition) of a book. The standard condition descriptions are as follows:

Near Mint (NM): condition of the book or booklet looks bright and fresh, as though it had been printed yesterday. The pages retain their original color. The cover is not damaged or marked up. There are no corner bumps or scuffing. An owner's signature is usually acceptable. Pages are white to off-white.

Very Fine (VF): condition of the item is still very attractive. Although the pages may be yellowing slightly, they still look relatively fresh. The book may have writing in a few places, but the writing is not distracting. The cover may have light wear or corner bumps, but it remains tightly bound to the contents. Generally speaking, a VF condition item sells for about two-thirds of the NM price.

Fine (F): condition of the item is somewhat worn. The pages are probably yellow, and there may be a few short tears (¼" or less) among the pages of the book. The cover has noticeable wear, and the corners are probably blunting. The cover is still bound to the contents, but the binding may not be as tight. All of the minor defects are allowed, but these have not accumulated to the point where the book does not display well. Generally speaking, F condition items sell for about one-half of NM prices.

Very Good (VG): condition of the book is collectible but does not appear new. The pages may be tan to brown. There may be one to three minor defects, but no serious defects. The cover may no longer be tight, but it is still connected to the book via its original binding or staples. The typical used book from the 1930s to the 1950s is in this condition. Generally speaking, a VG condition item sells for one-third to one-half of the NM price.

Good (G): condition of the item is still collectible but no longer retains much freshness. The pages may be tan to brown. There may be tears of up to 1" on several pages, but the book is still useful for its original purpose. The cover may be separating from the binding, but the book is still complete. There may be writing, including distracting writing. There may also be tape. The typical used book from the 1920s or earlier is in this condition. Generally speaking, a G condition item sells for one-fourth to one-third of the NM price. A book in G condition or lower that was printed after 1969 typically has very little collector value.

Fair (FR): condition of the item is often called a "filler" copy, having one or two serious defects. The pages are probably brown or brittle, and some pages may be loose. Tears are easily noticed and may be extensive. The cover is present, but may be torn or split from the binding. Fair condition copies are accepted by collectors for items that are rare until a better copy surfaces, but normally more common books are not collected in this grade. An FR condition book sells for less than one-tenth of the NM price.

Poor (PR): condition of the item is not considered suitable for collecting purposes due to an accumulation of serious defects. The cover may be missing. The pages may be brown, separated from the binding, or written on

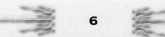

extensively. Chunks or pages may be missing from the interior. PR condition books are practically worthless, even if the books would otherwise have been valuable.

An original dust jacket (dj) is expected to be found with a more common or less collectible book. However, with a rare book, particularly one printed in or before 1920, an original dust jacket is hard to find and may significantly increase the value of a book — especially in top conditions.

About the Scarcity Index:

For each book, booklet, or pamphlet listed in the specialized sections of this book, a Scarcity Index appears in the listings to identify the relative difficulty in locating a copy of the item. The estimate of scarcity is based in part on the frequency with which online sales of the item have been noted. A Scarcity Index of 1 indicates an item for which several copies appear online every week. Items this common are typically not collected in lower grades. SI of 4 indicates an item of average rarity (or commonality). An item with an SI of 7 is rightly called scarce, and there are probably only a few thousand in existence today. By contrast, an item with an SI of 9 is termed rare, and an item with an SI of 10 is very rare. A rare or very rare item appears online less frequently than once per year, and most collections are missing those copies.

About Pricing:

Price values established here are merely guides; these are not necessarily the prices that a collector must pay, nor are they the prices that a dealer must charge. Ultimately, a collectible is worth whatever you, the collector, decide that it is worth. However, these prices represent a sampling of online sales over the past several years. In the case of nearly any item valued at $6.00 or less, it is quite likely that you might see copies selling for significantly less or significantly more, for prices tend to vary widely on more common items. No doubt, you will find books herein that are priced much lower than their scarcity would indicate, but the prices in such cases do represent actual sales. Therefore, we must remember that an item's scarcity is only one of the factors in determining its sale value; for example, a cookbook that is difficult to use may be scarce simply because nobody wants it. Unless otherwise indicated, values given in this book are for items in NM condition.

The cookbooks listed in this section were not made by the specialized companies in the later sections, so this section may properly be termed "general" cookbooks.

Cookbooks, booklets, and pamphlets listed here will usually be shown in the following format:

> *Title of cookbook*
> by Author of cookbook
> Published by the publisher in year of publication
> number of pages, type of book, $value

For example,

Horse Meat Lover's Cook Book (The)
by Ludlow Chevalier
Published by Stable Press in 1951
128 pages, HB w/dj, $6.00

The type of book will be one of the following:
HB — hardback — stiff covers, pages usually bound via stitching
SHB — spiral hardback — stiff covers, pages bound with a metal spiral or plastic comb
PB — paperback — soft covers, pages bound by stitching or stapling
SPB — spiral paperback — soft covers, pages bound with a metal spiral or plastic comb
RB — ring binder
PAM — pamphlet — a single sheet, which may be folded, no staples

The value given is for a copy in Near Mint condition. For values in lower grades, consult the section in this book on grading on page 6.

Order of Listings:

The cookbooks, booklets, and pamphlets in this section are listed in order of title first, with titles that begin with numbers listed first, i.e., *101 Horrible Recipes* would precede *Best Cooking*. If the title begins with "a," "an," or "the," those words are not shown first in the listing. For example, *The Joy of Cooking* is listed under *Joy of Cooking (The)*. If a book has been reissued several times with the words "The New" or "The Revised" added at the beginning of the titles of later copies, those words will be moved to the ends of the titles.

12 Pies Husbands Like Best
  by Aunt Jenny
  Published by Lever Brothers Co. in 1952
  21 pages, PB, $6.00

20 Favorite Recipes of Col. Harland Sanders
  Published by Kentucky Fried Chicken in 1964
  20 pages, PB, $12.00

20 Favorite Recipes of Col. Harland Sanders

20 Minute Cookbook (The)
  by Michael Reise
  Published by Crown Publishing in 1953
  252 pages, HB w/dj, $12.00

20th Century Home Cook Book
  by Mrs. Frances Carruthers, Jeanne M. Hall, and Belle Anderson Ebner
  Published by Thompson, Thomas, & Co. in 1906
  491 pages, HB, $100.00

20 Wonderful Cakes Made by the New Kraft Oil Method
  Published by Kraft in 1955
  24 pages, PB, $3.00

21 "None Such" Mince Meat Recipes
  Published by Borden Co. in 1952
  29 pages, PB, $1.00

38 Answers to What's Cooking?
  by Mary Blake
  Published by Carnation Co. in 1961
  23 pages, PB, $1.00

20 Minute Cookbook (The)

4-Star Way to Increased Cake Sales (The)
  by Sweetex
  Published by Procter & Gamble in 1940
  37 pages, PB, $3.00

50 Delicious Desserts
  by Mary Ellen Baker
  Published by National Biscuit Co., c. 1955
  15 pages, PB, $1.00

50 Wonderful Ways to Use Cottage Cheese
  Published by American Dairy Association in 1955
  23 pages, PB, $3.00

57 Prize-Winning Recipes
  Published by HJ Heinz Co. in 1957
  31 pages, PB, $3.00

38 Answers to What's Cooking?

4-Star Way to Increased Cake Sales (The)

641 Tested Recipes from the Sealtest Kitchens

70 Magic Recipes (Borden's Eagle Brand)

60 Ways to Serve Ham
Published by Armour & Co., c. 1920s
27 pages, PB, $6.00

67 Fail-Proof Recipes
by Mary Lee Taylor
Published by Sego Milk Products in 1941
31 pages, PB, $3.00

70 Magic Recipes (Borden's Eagle Brand)
Published by Borden Co. in 1956
24 pages, PB, $2.00

77 Recipes Using Swiftning
by Martha Logan
Published by Swift & Co. in 1950
34 pages, PB, $3.00

94 Brer Rabbit Goodies
by Ruth Washburn Jordan
Published by Penick & Ford Ltd. in 1929
48 pages, PB, $6.00

365 Luncheon Dishes
by Marion Harland, et al.
Published by George W. Jacobs & Co. in 1902
151 pages, HB, $50.00

500-Plus Ideas for Freezing & Canning
by Elizabeth Henley
Published by Bruce-Royal Publishing in 1964
128 pages, PB, $5.00

500 Recipes by Request
Published by Bramell House in 1948
HB w/dj, $8.00

641 Tested Recipes from the Sealtest Kitchens
Published by National Dairy Products Corp. in 1954
256 pages, PB, $5.00

Abbey Cookbook (The)
by Hans Bertram
Published by Harvard Common Press in 1982
212 pages, HB w/dj, $4.00

ABC of Casseroles
Published by Peter Pauper Press in 1954
61 pages, HB w/dj, $5.00

ABC of Chafing Dish Cookery (The)
 Published by Peter Pauper Press in 1956
 61 pages, HB w/dj, $5.00

ABC of Herb and Spice Cookery
 Published by Peter Pauper Press in 1957
 61 pages, HB w/dj, $5.00

Adventures in Good Cooking
 by Duncan Hines
 Published in 1952
 23rd printing
 PB, $3.00

Adventures in Good Cooking
 by Duncan Hines
 Published in 1955
 26th printing
 PB, $3.00

ABC of Chafing Dish Cookery (The)

Agate Iron Ware Cook Book
 by Agate Iron Ware
 Published by L & G Mfg. Co. c. 1880
 36 pages, PB, $80.00

Agate Iron Ware Cook Book
 by Agate Iron Ware
 Published by L & G Mfg. Co. in 1890
 36 pages, PB, $80.00

Alice B. Toklas Cook Book
 by Alice B. Toklas
 Published by Harper & Brothers in 1954
 288 pages, HB, $45.00

*Adventures in Good Cooking –
1952*

All About Beef
 Published by Idaho Beef Council in 1970s
 PB (folder, handouts), $2.00

All About Home Baking
 Published by General Foods in 1933
 144 pages, HB, $6.00

All Holidays Cookbook
 Published by Ideals Publishing in 1974
 61 pages, PB, $3.00

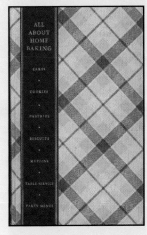

All-Ways Preferable Cook Book
 Published by Malleable Steel Range Mfg. Co. in 1898
 96 pages, PB, $75.00

All About Home Baking

American Cook Book (The)

American Domestic Cook Book (The)

American Woman's Home

Alpha Xi Delta Cook Book
Published by the Marion, IA, chapter c. 1927
100 pages, HB, $100.00

Americana Collection Cookbook
Published by Curtin Productions in 1969
444 pages, RB, $3.00

American Cook Book (The)
by F.L. Gillette
Published by HJ Smith & Co. in 1887
This rare volume became the basis for Gillette's better-known *White House Cook Book*.
521 pages, HB, $350.00

American Cookery Book
by Jennie June
Published by J. Baumann & Co. in 1878
399 pages, HB, $75.00

American Domestic Cook Book (The)
Published by Dr. Herrick & Co. in 1868
32 pages, PB, $25.00

American Everyday Cook Book
by Agnes Murphy
Published by Random House in 1955
HB w/dj, $5.00

American Heritage Cookbook, Vols. 1 – 2
by American Heritage
Published by Simon & Schuster in 1964
371 pages, HB, in slip case, $10.00

American Illustrated Cook Book of Meat Dishes
by Anne Tynte
Published in 1971
64 pages, PB, $3.00

American Practical Cookery Book
by A Practical Housekeeper
Published by John E. Potter Co. in 1859
319 pages, HB, $200.00

American Woman's Home
by Catherine Beecher & Harriet Beecher Stowe
Published in 1869
500 pages, HB, $200.00

America's Cook Book
Published by *NY Herald-Tribune* in 1945
1,032 pages, HB, $30.00

Amy Vanderbilt's Complete Cookbook
> by Amy Vanderbilt
> Published by Doubleday in 1961
> Illustrated by Andy Warhol
> 811 pages, HB w/dj, $6.00

Annemarie's Personal Cookbook
> by Annemarie Huste
> Published by Bartholomew House in 1968
> 336 pages, HB w/dj, $3.00

Annual Cookbook
> Published by Coeur d'Alene Press in 1975
> Newspaper insert, $1.00

Antoinette Pope School Cookbook
> by Antoinette & Francois Pope
> Published by MacMillan Co. in 1951
> 11th printing
> 366 pages, HB, $12.00

Antoinette Pope School Cookbook

Anyone Can Bake
> by Royal Baking Powder
> Published by Royal Baking Co. in 1927
> 100 pages, HB, $15.00

Appledore Cook Book
> by Maria Parloa
> Published by Graves Locke & Co. in 1872
> Reputed to be the first publication of a recipe for tomato soup.
> HB, $200.00

Appledore Cook Book
> by Maria Parloa
> Published by Graves Locke & Co. in 1878
> HB, $125.00

Argo Corn Starch Never Fails Me

Apple Talk
> Published by Northern Pacific RRY in 1931
> 24 pages, PB, $45.00

Argo Corn Starch Never Fails Me
> Published by Corn Products c. 1920s
> PAM, $1.00

Art of Cooking and Serving
> by Sarah Field Splint
> Published by Procter & Gamble in 1927
> 252 pages, HB, $25.00

Art of Grilling, Baking, Barbecuing (The)

Art of Making Bread at Home (The)

Art of Modern Cooking and Better Meals (The)

Aunt Chick's Pies

Art of Cooking and Serving
> by Sarah Field Splint
> Published by Procter & Gamble in 1929
> 252 pages, HB, $15.00

Art of Cooking and Serving
> by Sarah Field Splint
> Published by Procter & Gamble in 1932
> 252 pages, HB, $15.00

Art of Cuisine (The)
> by Henri de Toulouse-Lautrec & Maurice Joyant
> Published by Henry Holt & Co in 1966
> 164 pages, HB w/dj, $40.00

Art of Grilling, Baking, Barbecuing (The)
> by Duncan Hines
> Published by Estate Stove Co.; RCA in 1952
> 64 pages, PB, $3.00

Art of Making Bread at Home (The)
> Published by Northwestern Yeast Co., c. 1930s
> 28 pages, PB, $6.00

Art of Modern Cooking and Better Meals (The)
> by Meta Given
> Published by Geographical Publishing Co. in 1937
> 256 pages, HB, $25.00

Aunt Betty's Cook Book
> by S. Bacharach
> Published by S. Bacharach in 1918
> 97 pages, HB, $27.00

Aunt Chick's Pies
> by Nettie McBirney
> Published by The Chicadees in 1949
> 39 pages, PB, $5.00

Aunt Ellen Booklet on Waterless Cooking
> Published by Griswold Cast Iron in 1928
> 48 pages, PB, $75.00

Aunt Julia's Cook Book
> Published by Esso (Oil Company) c. 1930
> 64 pages, PB, $50.00

Aunt Sammy's Radio Recipes Revised
> by Ruth van Deman & Fanny W. Yeatman
> Published by USDA in 1931
> 142 pages, PB, $15.00

Aunt Susan's Cook Book
    Published by Daily Oklahoman in 1940
    48 pages, PB, $3.00

Aunt Susan's Cook Book
    Published by Daily Oklahoman in 1941
    40 pages, PB, $3.00

Baker's Best Chocolate Recipes
    Published by General Foods in 1932
    60 pages, PB, $30.00

Baker's Weekly Revised Recipes
    Published by American Trade Pub. in 1924
    294 pages, HB, $30.00

Bakery: Cakes and Simple Confectionary
    by Maria Floris
    Published in 1971
    HB, $6.00

Baking Made Easy
    by Margaret B. Baker
    Published by Russell-Miller Milling Co. in 1922
    55 pages, PB, $15.00

Baking Made Easy

Ball Blue Book (The)
    Published by Ball Brothers (Canning) in 1932
    56 pages, PB, $6.00

Ball Blue Book (The)
    Published by Ball Brothers in 1943
    56 pages, PB, $5.00

Ball Blue Book (The)
    by Edition W
    Published by Ball Brothers Co. in 1944
    56 pages, PB, $5.00

Ballet Cook Book (The)

Ballet Cook Book (The)
    by Tanaquil Le Clercq
    Published by Stein and Day in 1966
    416 pages, HB w/dj, $175.00

Barbecue Book
    by Better Homes & Gardens
    Published by Meredith in 1956
    162 pages, HB, $5.00

Barbecue Book

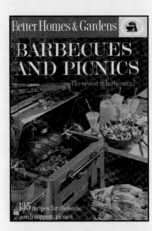

*Barbecues and Picnics
(Creative Cooking Library C8)*

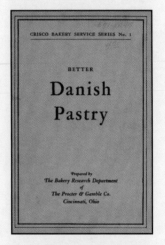

Better Danish Pastry (#1)

Better Meals With Gel-Cookery

Barbecue Book
> by Better Homes & Gardens
> Published by Meredith in 1959
> 162 pages, HB, $3.00

Barbecues and Picnics (Creative Cooking Library C8)
> by Better Homes & Gardens
> Published by Meredith in 1963
> 62 pages, HB, $3.00

Baron's Cook Book (The)
> Published by Paroutand & Watson c. 1900
> 96 pages, PB, $100.00

Beecher's Receipt Book
> by Elizabeth Beecher
> Published by Harper & Brothers in 1855
> 301 pages, HB, $300.00

Beecher's Receipt Book
> by Elizabeth Beecher
> Published by Harper & Brothers in 1867
> 306 pages, HB, $100.00

Bel Canto Cook Book
> by Peter Gravina
> Published by Doubleday in 1964
> 219 pages, HB, $33.00

Best Buffets (Creative Cooking Library, C1)
> by Better Homes & Gardens
> Published by Meredith in 1963
> 62 pages, HB, $3.00

Best War Time Recipes
> Published by Royal Baking Powder Co. in 1918
> 24 pages, PB, $15.00

Better Danish Pastry (#1)
> by Crisco
> Published by Procter & Gamble in 1927
> 10 pages, PB, $10.00

Better Homes & Gardens New Cook Book
> Published by Better Homes & Gardens in 1953
> 416 pages, RB, $25.00

Better Homes & Gardens New Cook Book
> Published by Better Homes & Gardens in 1968
> 400 pages, RB, $20.00

Better Meals With Gel-Cookery
    Published by Charles B. Knox Co. in 1952
    26 pages, PB, $3.00

Bettina's Best Desserts
    by Louise Bennett Weaver & Helen Cowles LeCron
    Published in 1923
    HB, $75.00

Bettina's Best Salads
    by Louise Bennett Weaver & Helen Cowles LeCron
    Published in 1923
    HB, $75.00

Bettina's Cakes and Cookies
    by Louise Bennett Weaver & Helen Cowles LeCron
    Published in 1924
    HB, $90.00

Bible Cook Book
    by Marian Maeve O'Brien
    Published by Bethany Press in 1958
    HB, $10.00

Big Boy Barbecue Book
    Published by Tested Recipe Institute in 1956
    62 pages, SPB, $5.00

Birthdays and Family Celebrations (Creative Cooking Library, C2)
    by Better Homes & Gardens
    Published by Meredith in 1963
    62 pages, HB, $3.00

Blender Cookbook
    by Ann Seranne and Eileen Gaden
    Published by Doubleday in 1961
    288 pages, HB w/dj, $6.00

Blender Way to Better Cooking
    by Betty Solomon
    Published by Odyssey Books in 1965
    208 pages, HB, $6.00

Blondie's Cook Book
    by Chic Young
    Published by Bell Publishing in 1946
    142 pages, HB w/dj, $45.00

Bond Bread Cook Book
    by Barbara Hoyt
    Published by General Baking Co. in 1934
    22 pages, PB, $8.00

Big Boy Barbecue Book

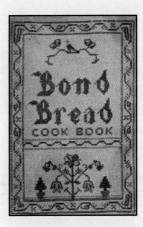

Bond Bread Cook Book –
1934

Bond Bread Cook Book –
1935

Bontempi Cookbook (The)

Book of Merry Eating, M17

*Boston Cooking School
Cook Book – 1905*

Bond Bread Cook Book
    by Barbara Hoyt
    Published by General Baking Co. in 1935
    72 pages, PB, $6.00

Bontempi Cookbook (The)
    by Fedora Bontempi
    Published by Award Books in 1968
    220 pages, PB, $3.00

Book of Cakes and Pies M5
    by McCall's
    Published in 1965
    64 pages, PB, $3.00

Book of Good Neighbor Recipes (The)
    by Maxine Erickson & Joan M. Rock
    Published by Bond Wheelwright Co. in 1952
    403 pages, HB, $6.00

Book of Hors d'Oeuvre
    by Lucy G. Allen
    Published by Bramhall House in 1941
    141 pages, HB w/dj, $12.00

Book of Marvelous Meats M6
    by McCall's
    Published in 1965
    64 pages, PB, $3.00

Book of Merry Eating, M17
    by McCall's
    Published in 1965
    64 pages, PB, $3.00

Booth Seafood Cookbook
    by James Beard
    Published by Little, Brown & Co. in 1954
    460 pages, HB, $6.00

Boston Cooking School Cook Book
    by Fannie M. Farmer
    Published by Little, Brown & Co. in 1896
    This is the first edition of Fannie Farmer's legendary work.
    567 pages, HB, $600.00

Boston Cooking School Cook Book
    by Fannie M. Farmer
    Published by Little, Brown & Co. in 1905
    682 pages, HB, $125.00

Boston Cooking School Cook Book
> by Fannie M. Farmer
> Published by Little, Brown & Co. in 1928
> 808 pages, HB, $100.00

Boston Cooking School Cook Book
> by Fannie M. Farmer
> Published by Little, Brown & Co. in 1930
> 831 pages, HB, $100.00

Boston School Kitchen Text-Book
> by Mrs. D. A. Lincoln
> Published by Roberts Brothers in 1887
> This was a textbook for use by students of the Boston Cooking
> School.
> 237 pages, HB, $200.00

Boston School Kitchen Text-Book
> by Mrs. D. A. Lincoln
> Published by Roberts Brothers in 1891
> 237 pages, HB, $150.00

Bread Basket (The)
> Published by Standard Brands, Inc. in 1943
> 40 pages, PB, $4.00

Bread Winners
> by Mel London
> Published by Rodale Press in 1979
> 362 pages, HB w/dj, $3.00

Breakfast, Dinner, and Tea
> Published by D. Appleton & Co. in 1865
> 351 pages, HB, $300.00

Brer Rabbit's New Orleans Molasses Recipes
> Published by Penick & Ford Ltd. in 1948
> 48 pages, PB, $12.00

Brown Derby Cook Book
> Compiled by Marjorie Child Husted
> Published by Doubleday in 1949
> 272 pages, HB w/dj, $75.00

Buckeye Cookery and Practical Housekeeping
> by Estelle Woods Wilcox
> Published by Buckeye Publishing in 1877
> 462 pages, HB, $150.00

Bread Basket (The)

Brer Rabbit's New Orleans Molasses Recipes

Busy Woman's Cook Book (The)

Cake Making at High Altitudes

Cake Secrets

Calendar of Dinners (A)

Bull Cook and Authentic Historical Recipes
> by George & Berthe Herter
> Published by Herter's Inc. in 1967
> 11th Edition
> 352 pages, HB, $25.00

Burger Book (The)
> by Louis DeGouy
> Published by Grosset & Dunlap in 1951
> 120 pages, HB, $6.00

Busy Woman's Cook Book (The)
> by Ann Williams-Heller
> Published by Stephen Daye Press in 1951
> 342 pages, HB w/dj, $12.00

Cake Making at High Altitudes
> Published by General Foods in 1940
> 30 pages, PB, $5.00

Cake Secrets
> by Frances Barton
> Published by General Foods in 1953
> 64 pages, PB, $3.00

Cake Tour of the USA
> by Frances Barton
> Published by General Foods in 1949
> 32 pages, PB, $5.00

Calendar of Dinners (A)
> by Marion Harris Neil
> Published by Procter & Gamble in 1920
> 16th printing
> 231 pages, HB, $10.00

Calendar of Sandwiches and Beverages
> by Elizabeth O. Miller
> Published by P. F. Volland Co., c. 1930
> 60 pages, PB, $20.00

Calumet Baking Book (The)
> by Marion Jane Parker
> Published by General Foods in 1930
> 31 pages, PB, $6.00

Camp Cookery: How to Live in Camp
> by Maria Parloa
> Published by Boston, Graves, Locke & Co. in 1878
> 91 pages, HB, $75.00

Candy Calendar
Published by Woman's World in 1924
48 pages, HB, $20.00

Canning and Preserving Cookbook
by Southern Living
Published by Favorite Recipes Press in 1972
192 pages, HB, $6.00

Canning, Drying, and Freezing for Victory
by Meta Given
Published by Jas. G. Ferguson & Associates in 1943
48 pages, PB, $12.00

Canoe and Camp Cookery
by Seneca
Published by Forest & Stream Publ. in 1885
91 pages, HB, $60.00

Capitol Cook Book
by F. L. Gillette and Hugo Ziemann
Published by Saalfield Publishing in 1914
Taken from the *White House Cook Book.*
440 pages, HB, $30.00

Carnation Cook Book
by Mary Blake
Published by Carnation in 1948
91 pages, PB, $6.00

Carnation Cook Book
Published by Carnation Co., c. 1950
24 pages, PB, $3.00

Carnation's Failure-Proof Recipes
Published by Carnation Co. in 1957
15 pages, PB, $3.00

Casserole Cookbook M2
by McCall's
Published in 1965
64 pages, PB, $3.00

Casserole Cookery with Protein-Rich Cheese
Published by Kraft in 1946
PAM, $1.00

Catering for Special Occasions
by Fannie M. Farmer
Published by David McKay in 1911
249 pages, HB, $60.00

Calumet Baking Book (The)

Carnation's Failure-Proof Recipes

Carnation Cook Book

Casserole Cookery with Protein-Rich Cheese

Centaur Almanac and Cook Book (The)

Certo Recipes for Making Perfect Jams Jellies and Marmalades

Cedric Adams Cook Book on Fish and Sea-Food Cookery
by Frederic H. Girnau
Published by Kiewel Brewing Company in 1942
96 pages, PB, $15.00

Centaur Almanac and Cook Book (The)
Published by Centaur Liniment in 1886
38 pages, PB, $60.00

Century Cook Book (The)
by Mary Ronald
Published by The Century Co. in 1895
587 pages, HB, $15.00

Certo Recipes for Making Perfect Jams Jellies and Marmalades
Published by Pectin Sales Co. in 1922
PAM, $3.00

Chafing Dish Possibilities
by Fannie Merritt Farmer
Published by Little, Brown & Co. in 1902
161 pages, HB w/dj, $12.00

Chafing-Dish Cookery
by Florence Brobeck
Published by M. Barrows & Co. in 1950
221 pages, HB, $6.00

Cheese and Ways to Serve It
Published by Kraft c. 1920
24 pages, PB, $8.00

Chiquita Banana's Recipe Book
Published by United Fruit Co. in 1958
25 pages, PB, $3.00

Chocolate Kitchen Recipes
by Jane Fulton
Published by Nestle's in 1951
31 pages, PB, $3.00

Choice Recipes
by Maria Parloa
Published by Walter Baker & Co. in 1902
64 pages, PB, $27.00

Choice Recipes
by Maria Parloa
Published by Walter Baker & Co. in 1905
64 pages, PB, $27.00

Christmas Cookie Book (The)
   by Virginia Pasley
   Published by Little, Brown & Co. in 1949
   146 pages, HB w/dj, $15.00

Christmas Cookies
   Published by Wisconsin Electric in 1952
   PB, $12.00

Chuckwagon Cooking from Marlboro Country
   Published by Philip Morris in 1981
   30 pages, PB, $20.00

Clémentine in the Kitchen
   by Phineas Beck
   Published by Hastings House in 1943
   1st printing
   228 pages, HB w/dj, $15.00

Clémentine in the Kitchen
   by Phineas Beck
   Published by Hastings House in 1963
   9th printing
   250 pages, HB w/dj, $8.00

Coast-to-Coast Cooking, M11
   by McCall's
   Published in 1965
   64 pages, PB, $3.00

Cocktail-Time Cookbook, M15
   by McCall's
   Published in 1965
   64 pages, PB, $3.00

Coconut Glamour Desserts
   Published by Baker's Coconut in 1949
   2nd Edition
   23 pages, PB, $3.00

Coffee and Waffles
   by Alice Foote MacDougall
   Published by Doubleday in 1926
   115 pages, HB, $30.00

Common Sense in the Household
   by Marion Harland
   Published by Scribner's in 1881
   546 pages, HB, $100.00

Chafing Dish Possibilities

Chiquita Banana's Recipe Book

Christmas Cookie Book (The)

Clémentine in the Kitchen

Cocktail-Time Cookbook, M15

Cook Book For One

Common Sense in the Kitchen
 by W. A. Henderson
 Published by Hurst & Co in 1870
 HB, $60.00

Company Cookbook M9
 by McCall's
 Published in 1965
 64 pages, PB, $3.00

Complete Electric Skillet-Frypan Cookbook
 by Roberta Ames
 Published by Hearthside Press in 1960
 207 pages, HB w/dj, $3.00

Complete Family Cook Book (The)
 Published by Curtin Productions in 1969
 444 pages, RB, $12.00

Complete Microwave Cook Book
 Published by JC Penney
 160 pages, HB, $1.00

Complete Step-by-Step Cook Book
 by Better Homes & Gardens
 Published by Meredith in 1978
 384 pages, HB, $3.00

Congress Cook Book
 Published by D&L Slade Co. in 1899
 80 pages, PB, $60.00

Congressional Cook Book (The)
 Published by Congressional Club in 1933
 834 pages, HB, $60.00

Congressional Club Cookbook (The)
 Published by Congressional Club in 1982
 10th Edition
 744 pages, HB, $50.00

Congressional Club Cookbook (The)
 Published by Congressional Club in 1993
 12th Edition
 950 pages, HB, $50.00

Conservation Recipes
 Published by Wilbur's Cocoa c. 1900
 16 pages, PB, $40.00

Control Master Appliances Recipe Book
    Published by National Presto Industries in 1957
    104 pages, PB, $6.00

Cook Book For One
    by Pegeen and Swan O'Neil
    Published by Pegeen and Sean O'Neil in 1976
    143 pages, SHB, $5.00

Cook Book of Fabulous Foods for People You Love (The)
    by Carolyn Coggins
    Published by Pyramid Books R459 in 1959
    314 pages, PB, $3.00

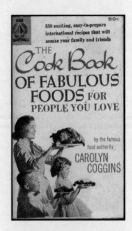

Cook Book of Fabulous Foods for People You Love (The)

Cookbook of the Month: Meat
    Published by Family Kitchen Institute in 1960
    96 pages, PB, $3.00

Cookbook of the Seven Seas
    by Dagmar Freuchen
    Published by M. Evans & Co. in 1968
    256 pages, HB w/dj, $6.00

Cook Book of the United States Navy (The)
    Published by US Government Printing Office in 1945
    456 pages, HB, $25.00

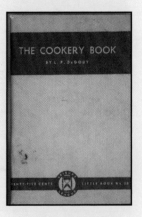

Cookery Book (The)
    by Louis DeGouy
    Published by Leisure League of America in 1936
    108 pages, PB, $6.00

Cookery Book (The)

Cookie Book
    by Irena Chalmers
    Published by Potpourri Press in 1977
    47 pages, PB, $3.00

Cookie Collection (McCall's Collection M1)
    by McCall's
    Published in 1965
    64 pages, PB, $3.00

Cookie-Craft
    Published by Kraft in 1946
    PAM, $3.00

Cookies Galore
    Published by General Foods in 1956
    39 pages, PB, $3.00

Cookie Book

Cookie-Craft

Cookies Galore

Cooking Hints and Tested Recipes

Cooking for the Crowd
    by Mary Blake
    Published by Carnation Co. in 1963
    23 pages, PB, $3.00

Cooking Hints and Tested Recipes
    by Winfred S. Carter
    Published by Procter & Gamble in 1937
    32 pages, PB, $12.00

Cooking in the Spotlight
    by Siegfried and Roy
    Published in 2000
    1,000 copies were printed, immediately after Roy Horn's injury.
    Some copies sold for as much as $500.00.
    160 pages, HB, $125.00

Cooking, Menus, Service
    by Ida Bailey Allen
    Published by Garden City Publishing in 1924
    977 pages, HB, $12.00

Cooking, Menus, Service
    by Ida Bailey Allen
    Published by Doubleday in 1935
    2nd Edition with 16 added pages
    977 + 16 pages, HB, $50.00

Cooking Out-of-Doors
    Published by Girl Scouts of America in 1960
    212 pages, SPB, $12.00

Cooking the Modern Way
    Published by Planters Edible Oil Co. in 1948
    39 pages, PB, $5.00

Cooking With a Food Processor
    Published by General Electric in 1978
    PB, $1.00

Cooking With a Foreign Accent
    by Sunset
    Published by Lane Book Co. in 1962
    5th printing
    155 pages, SHB, $3.00

Cooking With Astrology
    by Sydney Omarr & Mike Roy
    Published by World Publishing in 1970
    250 pages, HB w/dj, $5.00

Cooking With Cold
> Published by Kelvinator in 1933
> 55 pages, PB, $3.00

Cooking With Condensed Soups
> by Anne Marshall
> Published by Campbell Co., c. 1950
> 48 pages, PB, $1.00

Cooking With Curry
> by Florence Brobeck
> Published by M. Barrows & Co. in 1952
> 1st printing
> 192 pages, HB w/dj, $6.00

Cooking With Friends
> by Amy Lyles Wilson
> Published by Rutledge Hill Press in 1995
> Based on the NBC television series, *Friends*.
> 134 pages, HB w/dj, $15.00

Cooking With Herbs and Spices
> Published by Better Homes & Gardens in 1967
> 24 pages, PB, $3.00

Cooking With Love and Paprika
> by Joseph Pasternak
> Published by Bernard Geis Associates in 1966
> 374 pages, HB w/dj, $5.00

Cooking With Mickey Around Our World
> Published by Walt Disney Co. in 1986
> 292 pages, SPB, $15.00

Cooking With Soup
> Published by Campbell Co. in 1968
> 200 pages, SHB, $4.00

Cooking With Wine
> by Cora, Rose, & Bob Brown
> Published by Castle Books in 1960
> 462 pages, HB w/dj, $5.00

Cook's Handbook (The)
> by Mary Blake
> Published by Carnation Co. in 1951
> 95 pages, SPB, $3.00

Cook's Own Book (The)
> by Mrs. N. K. M. Lee
> Published by Alex T. Loyd & Co. in 1887
> 337 pages, HB, $175.00

Cooking Out-of-Doors

Cooking With Condensed Soups

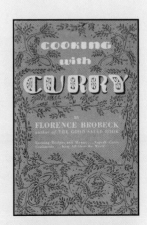

Cooking With Curry

Cooking With Soup

Cook With Soup

Cook's Handbook (The)

Cook's Quiz (A)
   by Antoinette & Francois Pope
   Published by MacMillan Co. in 1952
   188 pages, HB w/dj, $15.00

Cook With Soup
   Published by HJ Heinz Co. in 1977
   31 pages, PB, $1.00

Cosmo Cookery
   Published by Cosmopolitan Books in 1971
   245 pages, HB w/dj, $12.00

Cosmopolitan Cook and Recipe Book
   Published by Dingens Bros. in 1882
   405 pages, HB, $150.00

Country Cookbook
   Published by Bob Evans Farms, c. 1955
   32 pages, PB, $3.00

Crabtree & Evelyn Cook Book
   by Elizabeth Kent
   Published by Stewart, Taboni, and Chang in 1989
   256 pages, HB w/dj, $5.00

Craig Claiborne's Favorites
   by Craig Claiborne
   Published by Times Books in 1975
   371 pages, HB w/dj, $6.00

Craig Claiborne's Favorites, Series II
   by Craig Claiborne
   Published by Times Books in 1976
   442 pages, HB w/dj, $6.00

Craig Claiborne's Kitchen Primer
   by Craig Claiborne
   Published by Alfred A. Knopf in 1969
   258 pages, HB w/dj, $6.00

Creamette Cookbook
   Published by Creamette, c. 1980
   PB, $1.00

Creative Cookery
   by Martha Logan
   Published by Swift & Co., c. 1960
   31 pages, PB, $3.00

Creative Cooking Course (The)
    by Charlotte Turgeon
    Published by Weathervane Books in 1975
    HB w/dj, $10.00

Creative Cooking Made Easy
    the Golden Fluffo Cookbook
    Published by Procter & Gamble in 1956
    108 pages, SPB, $5.00

Creative Food Processor Recipes
    by Ann Greer
    Published in 1982
    SPB, $1.00

Crepe Cookery
    by Mable Hoffman
    Published by HP Books in 1976
    176 pages, PB, $3.00

Crisco Recipes for the Jewish Housewife
    Published by Procter & Gamble in 1935
    154 pages, PB, $50.00

Crockery Cooker Cook Book
    by Better Homes & Gardens
    Published by Meredith in 1976
    96 pages, HB, $3.00

Crown Home Canning Book
    Published by Crown Cork & Seal Co. in 1936
    72 pages, PB, $6.00

Culinary Gems: A Collection of Choice Recipes
    by Emily E. Squire
    Published by J.D. Cadle & Co. in 1884
    147 pages, HB, $100.00

Cutco Cookbook
    by Margaret Mitchell
    Published by Aluminum Cooking Utensil Co. in 1956
    white cover
    128 pages, HB, $2.00

Cutco Cookbook
    by Cutco
    Published by Aluminum Cooking Utensil Co. in 1980
    brown cover
    128 pages, HB, $2.00

Cook's Quiz (A)

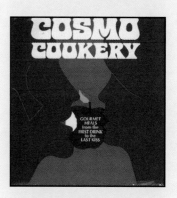
Cosmo Cookery

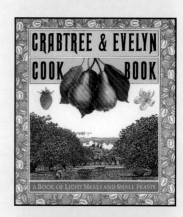
Crabtree & Evelyn Cook Book

Creative Cooking Made Easy

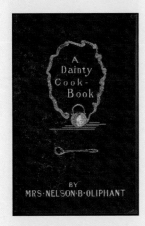

Dainty Cook-Book (A)

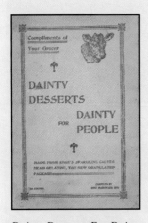

Dainty Desserts For Dainty People

Deep South Cookbook

Dainties
    by Sarah T. Rorer
    Published by Arnold & Co. in 1904
    HB, $36.00

Dainty Cook-Book (A)
    by Mrs. Nelson B. Oliphant
    Published by The Abbey Press in 1901
    175 pages, HB, $50.00

Dainty Desserts
    by Ida Bailey Allen
    Published by Buzza Company, c. 1920
    57 pages, PB, $100.00

Dainty Desserts For Dainty People
    Published by Knox Gelatine, c. 1898
    7th Edition
    32 pages, PB, $20.00

Dainty Home Lunches
    Published by C. Schmidt & Sons in 1913
    12 pages, PB, $18.00

Dark Shadows Cookbook
    by Jody Cameron Malis
    Published by Ace Books in 1970
    Based on the television series.
    PB, $50.00

Date With a Dish: A Cook Book of American Negro Recipes
    by Freda de Knight
    Published by Hermitage Press in 1948
    426 pages, HB w/dj, $120.00

Davis Master Pattern Baking Formulas
    by Davis Baking Powder
    Published by RB Davis Co. in 1940
    2nd Edition
    80 pages, PB, $15.00

Davis' O.K. Cook Book
    by Davis Baking Powder
    Published by R.B. Davis Co. in 1904
    64 pages, PB, $24.00

Deep South Cookbook
    by Southern Living
    Published by Favorite Recipes Press in 1972
    192 pages, HB, $6.00

Delicious Dairy Dishes
by Meta Given & Ruth Cooper
Publisher not listed
62 pages, PB, $12.00

Delicious Desserts
Published by Dr. Price's Vanilla Extract in 1917
PB, $30.00

Delicious Recipes
by Nestle's
Published by Lamont, Corliss, & Co. in 1939
12 pages, PB, $3.00

Delicious, Nourishing Dishes
Published by National Biscuit Co. in 1950
24 pages, PB, $3.00

Delightful Cooking
Published by Corn Products, c. 1930
63 pages, PB, $6.00

Deluxe Osterizer Recipes
Published by John Oster Mfg. Co. in 1955
96 pages, PB, $3.00

Democrats' Cook Book (The)
Published by Islip (NY) Democratic Committee in 1976
Signed by Jimmy Carter.
SPB, $60.00

Dessert Cook Book
by Better Homes & Gardens
Published by Meredith in 1960
160 pages, HB, $3.00

Dessert Discoveries M7
by McCall's
Published in 1965
64 pages, PB, $3.00

Dessert Magic
Published by General Foods in 1944
6th printing
26 pages, PB, $3.00

Desserts and Salads
by Gesine Lemcke
Published by Gesine Lemcke in 1892
296 pages, HB, $75.00

Delicious Recipes

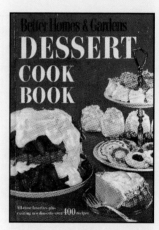

Dessert Cook Book

Dishes Men Like

Desserts of the World

Do-Ahead Party Book, M10

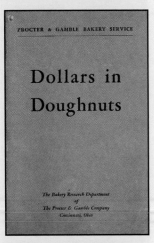

Dollars in Doughnuts

Desserts Cookbook
    by Southern Living
    Published by Favorite Recipes Press in 1971
    192 pages, HB, $6.00

Desserts From Southern Kitchens
    Published by Southern Kitchens in 1967
    HB, $3.00

Desserts of the World
    by Jell-O
    Published by Genesee in 1909
    24 pages, PB, $40.00

Desserts Salads Candies and Frozen Dishes
    Published by Charles B. Knox Co. in 1933
    PB, $20.00

Dinner Year-Book (The)
    by Marion Harland
    Published by Scribner's in 1878
    720 pages, HB, $175.00

Dishes Men Like
    Published by Lea & Perrins, Inc. in 1952
    62 pages, PB, $10.00

Do-Ahead Party Book, M10
    by McCall's
    Published in 1965
    64 pages, PB, $3.00

Dollars in Doughnuts
    Published by Procter & Gamble in 1933
    81 pages, PB, $12.00

Dolphin Dishes
    by Submarine Cook Book Committee
    Published in 1961
    286 pages, SPB, $6.00

Dora's Cook Book
    by Dora Fairfield
    Published by Hunter, Ross in 1888
    311 pages, HB, $75.00

Dormeyer Electric-Mix Treasures
    Published by Dormeyer Corporation in 1949
    32 pages, PB, $2.00

Double Action for Double Sure Success
 Published by Calumet Baking Powder in 1948
 PAM, $3.00

Doubleday Cookbook Vol. 1
 by Jean Anderson & Elaine Hanna
 Published by Doubleday in 1975
 780 pages, HB w/dj, $5.00

Doubleday Cookbook Vol. 2
 by Jean Anderson & Elaine Hanna
 Published by Doubleday in 1975
 774 pages, HB w/dj, $5.00

Down on the Farm Cook Book
 by Helen Worth
 Published in 1943
 322 pages, HB w/dj, $25.00

Downright Delicious Sun-Maid Raisin Recipes
 by Sun-Maid
 Published by HJ Heinz Co., c. 1940
 32 pages, PB, $3.00

Dr. Chase's Recipes
 by A. W. Chase
 Published by A. W. Chase in 1866
 384 pages, HB, $30.00

Dr. Chase's Recipes
 by A. W. Chase
 Published by A. W. Chase in 1867
 383 pages, HB, $30.00

Dr. King's Guide to Health
 Published by H. E. Bucklen & Co. in 1903
 32 pages, PB, $30.00

Dr. Price Cook Book (The New)
 Published by Royal Baking Powder Co. in 1921
 51 pages, PB, $15.00

Dr. Price Cook Book (The)
 Published by Royal Baking Powder Co. in 1929
 PB, $15.00

Duncan Hines Dessert Book (The)
 by Duncan Hines
 Published by Cardinal C-188 in 1955
 361 pages, PB, $3.00

Dormeyer Electric-Mix Treasures

Downright Delicious Sun-Maid Raisin Recipes

Duncan Hines Dessert Book (The)

Easy Ways to Delicious Meals

Economy Cook Book — A Book of Practical Recipes for the Housewife

Electric Refrigerator Recipes and Menus

Eagle Brand Magic Recipes
Published by Borden Co. in 1946
25 pages, PB, $2.00

Eagle Brand 70 Magic Recipes
Published by Borden Co. in 1961
24 pages, PB, $2.00

Easy Hospitality
by Marni Wood
Published by Coca-Cola Co. in 1951
48 pages, PB, $5.00

Easy Recipes of California Winemakers
Published by Wine Advisory Board in 1970
128 pages, SHB, $3.00

Easy Ways to Delicious Meals
by Carolyn Campbell
Published by Campbell Co., c. 1960
204 pages, SHB, $2.00

Eat It
by Dana Crumb, Shery Cohen and R. Crumb
Published by Bellerophon Books in 1972
R. Crumb was an important artist of underground comix.
64 pages, PB, $100.00

Eat It
by Dana Crumb, Shery Cohen and R. Crumb
Published by Bellerophon Books in 1974
64 pages, PB, $50.00

Ebony Cookbook (The), A Date With a Dish
by Freda DeKnight
Published by Johnson Publishing in 1962
390 pages, HB, $40.00

Economical Cook Book
by Sara T. Paul
Published by John C. Winston Company in 1905
338 pages, HB, $45.00

Economy Administration Cook Book
by Susie Root Rhodes
Published by Syndicate Pub. Co. in 1913
306 pages, HB, $35.00

Economy Cook Book — A Book of Practical Recipes for the Housewife
Published by Consolidated Book Pub. in 1932
244 pages, HB, $12.00

Electric Blender Recipes
>by Mabel Stegner
>Published by Gramercy Publishing in 1952
>226 pages, HB w/dj, $3.00

Electric Refrigerator Recipes
>by Alice Bradley
>Published by General Electric in 1927
>136 pages, HB, $15.00

Electric Refrigerator Recipes and Menus
>Published by General Electric in 1929
>144 pages, HB, $12.00

Elements of the Theory and Practice of Cookery
>Published by MacMillan Co. in 1908
>340 pages, HB, $45.00

Elsie's Cook Book
>by Harry Botsford (Elsie the Cow)
>Published by Bond Wheelwright Co. in 1952
>374 pages, HB w/dj, $50.00

Elsie's Cook Book
>by Harry Botsford (Elsie the Cow)
>Published by Bond Wheelwright Co. in 1952
>374 pages, PB, $40.00

Encyclopedia of Cookery
>Published by William H. Wise Co. in 1948
>1,269 pages, HB, $30.00

Encyclopedia of Cooking
>by Mary Margaret McBride
>Published by Homemaker's Research Institute in 1959
>1,536 pages, RB, $90.00

Encyclopedia of Creative Cooking
>by Jane Solmson
>Published by Weathervane Books in 1980
>797 pages, HB, $12.00

Enjoy Good Eating Every Day
>by Aunt Jenny
>Published by Lever Brothers Co. in 1949
>48 pages, PB, $3.00

Electric Blender Recipes

Epicurean (The) – 1920

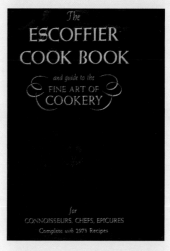

Escoffier Cook Book – 1941

Esquire Cook Book (The)

Every Woman's Home Cook Book

Everyday and Sunday Food For 2 or 4 or 6

Epicurean (The)
> by Charles Ranhofer
> Published by Charles Ranhofer in 1894
> Ranhofer served as chef at Delmonico's and is credited for having invented Eggs Benedict, Lobster Newburg, Baked Alaska, and other famous dishes.
> 1,182 pages, HB, $500.00

Epicurean (The)
> by Charles Ranhofer
> Published by John Willy in 1920
> 1,183 pages, HB, $300.00

Epicurean (The)
> by Charles Ranhofer
> Published by Hotel Monthly Press in 1920
> 1,183 pages, HB, $75.00

Epicurean (The)
> by Charles Ranhofer
> Published by Dover Pubs. in 1971
> Facsimile of the 1894 edition
> 1,182 pages, HB w/dj, $60.00

Escoffier Cookbook (The)
> by Auguste Escoffier
> Published by Crown Publishing in 1941
> 923 pages, HB w/dj, $50.00 (Book Club Edition: $20.00)

Escoffier Cook Book (The)
> by Auguste Escoffier
> Published by Crown Publishing in 1969
> 922 pages, HB w/dj, $25.00

Esquire Cook Book (The)
> Published by Crown Publishing in 1955
> 322 pages, HB w/dj, $10.00

Everyday and Sunday Food For 2 or 4 or 6
> Published by Pet Milk Co. in 1938
> 32 pages, PB, $3.00

Everyday Foods
> by Jessie W. Harris & Elisabeth Lacey Speer
> Published by Houghton Mifflin in 1944
> 583 pages, HB, $6.00

Every Woman's Home Cook Book
> Published by Hamming Publishing in 1913
> 224 pages, HB, $20.00

Fabulous Fry-Pan Favorites
    by Patricia Phillips
    Published by National Presto Industries in 1984
    160 pages, HB, $2.00

Fall and Winter Menus & Recipes for 2 or 4 or 6
    Published by Pet Milk Co. in 1935
    31 pages, PB, $6.00

Family and Householder's Guide
    by E.G. Storke
    Published by Auburn Publishing in 1859
    288 pages, HB, $250.00

Family Circle Dessert and Fruit Cookbook (The)
    Published by Family Circle in 1954
    144 pages, HB, $4.00

Family Cookbook
    by Cory SerVaas and Charlotte Turgeon
    Published by the Saturday Evening Post Society in 1981
    95 pages, PB, $6.00

Family Food Supply (The)
    Published by Metropolitan Life Insurance in 1943
    24 pages, PB, $6.00

Family Harvest (A)
    by Jane Moss Snow
    Published by Bobbs-Merrill in 1976
    221 pages, HB w/dj, $6.00

Family Receipts
    by Mrs. J.L. Nichols
    Published by J.L. Nichols Co. in 1905
    458 pages, HB, $65.00

Family-Style Cookbook M8
    by McCall's
    Published in 1965
    64 pages, PB, $3.00

Famous Economy Food Ideas
    by Dairy Products Institute
    Published by Olsen Publishing in 1939
    32 pages, PB, $6.00

Famous Mystery Chef Cook Book — The Never Fail Cook Book
    by the Mystery Chef
    Published by Theo. Gaus' Sons, c. 1953
    190 pages, HB, $5.00

Family Circle Dessert and Fruit Cookbook (The)

Family Cookbook

Family Food Supply (The)

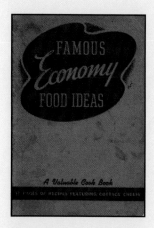

Famous Economy Food Ideas

Farm Journal's Complete
Pie Cookbook

Farmers' Almanac Cook
Book (The)

Farberware Gallery of Broiler & Rotisserie Masterpieces
Published by SW Farber in 1966
23 pages, PB, $1.00

Farmers' Almanac Cook Book (The)
Published by the Bond Wheelwright Co. in 1969
A reissue of *Elsie's Cook Book*
390 pages, HB w/dj, $6.00

Farm Journal's Complete Pie Cookbook
by Nell Nichols
Published by Doubleday in 1965
308 pages, HB w/dj, $20.00

Farm Journal's Country Cookbook
by Nell Nichols
Published by Doubleday in 1959
420 pages, HB, $25.00

Farm Journal's Freezing & Canning Cookbook
by Nell Nichols
Published by Doubleday in 1963
352 pages, HB w/dj, $10.00

Farm Journal's Homemade Ice Cream & Cake
by Elise Manning
Published by Doubleday in 1972
224 pages, HB w/dj, $10.00

Fast Gourmet Cook Book
by Poppy Cannon
Published by Fleet Publishing in 1964
285 pages, HB w/dj, $15.00

Favorite Breads from Rose Lane Farm
by Ada Lou Roberts
Published by Hearthside Press in 1960
128 pages, HB w/dj, $6.00

Favorite Recipes from Southern Kitchens — Desserts
Published by Progressive Farmer Co. in 1967
384 pages, HB, $6.00

Favorite Recipes of American Home Economics Teachers — Desserts
Published by Favorite Recipes Press in 1963
382 pages, SPB, $6.00

Favorite Recipes of American Home Economics Teachers — Meats
Published by Favorite Recipes Press in 1962
382 pages, SPB, $6.00

Favorite Ways With Chicken
  by Better Homes & Gardens
  Published by Meredith in 1967
  90 pages, HB, $3.00

Feeding the Lions
  by Frank Case
  Published by Greystone Press in 1942
  254 pages, HB w/dj, $50.00

Festive Christmas Foods
  Published by Brown & Bigalow in 1958
  16 pages, PB, $1.00

Fire-King Casserole Recipes
  Published by Anchor-Hocking Glass in 1944
  This booklet was available through the radio program, "Meet Corliss
    Archer," which was sponsored by Anchor-Hocking.
  30 pages, PB, $75.00

Fireside Cook Book (The)
  by James Beard
  Published by Simon & Schuster in 1949
  322 pages, HB w/dj, $20.00

First Principles of Household Management and Cookery
  by Maria Parloa
  Published by Houghton, Osgood Co. in 1879
  This was the first book with "household management" in the title.
  133 pages, HB, $125.00

Fish and Poultry Cook Book
  Published by Family Circle in 1955
  144 pages, HB, $3.00

Fish-n-Fowl Cookbook M13
  by McCall's
  Published in 1965
  64 pages, PB, $3.00

Fit For a King
  by Merle Armitage
  Published by Duell, Sloane, and Pierce in 1939
  256 pages, HB, $30.00

Flavor Touches
  Published by Kraft in 1944
  PAM, $3.00

Fleischmann's Recipes
  Published by Fleischmann's Yeast Co. in 1915
  47 pages, PB, $36.00

Favorite Breads from Rose Lane Farm

Festive Christmas Foods

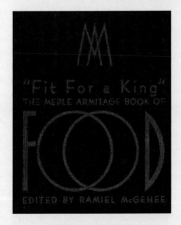

Fit For a King

Fleischmann Treasury of Yeast Baking (The)

Food and Feeding

Fondue Magic

Fleischmann's Recipes
Published by Fleischmann's Yeast Co. in 1920
45 pages, PB, $30.00

Fleischmann Treasury of Yeast Baking (The)
Published by Standard Brands, Inc. in 1962
51 pages, PB, $3.00

Food and Feeding
by Sir Henry Thompson
Published by Frederick Warne & Co. in 1880
2nd Edition, 1st printing
148 pages, HB, $100.00

Food Favorites
Published by Kraft in 1951
32 pages, SPB, $3.00

Food for Fifty
by Sina Faye Fowler & Bessie Brooks West
Published by John Wiley & Sons in 1941
383 pages, HB, $20.00

Food for Fitness for 2 or 4 or 6
Published by Sego Milk Products in 1942
29 pages, PB, $6.00

Food for the Body; For the Soul
Published by Moody Press in 1943
128 pages, SPB, $6.00

Fondue Magic
by Anita Prichard
Published by Heathside Press in 1969
192 pages, HB, $4.00

Ford Treasury of Favorite Recipes from Famous Eating Places
by Nancy Kennedy
Published by Simon & Schuster in 1950
252 pages, HB w/dj, $6.00

Foundation of All Reform (The)
by Otto Carque
Published by Kosmos Publishing in 1904
68 pages, HB, $30.00

Francatelli's Modern Cook
by Charles Elme Francatelli
Published by T. B. Peterson and Brother in 1876
Francatelli was Queen Victoria's chief cook.
The first edition of this book was issued in 1846. In it, Francatelli
  introduced "Indian Curry Sauce" to the general public.
585 pages, HB, $125.00

Freezer Cookery
    by Mary Berry
    Published by Octopus Books in 1977
    93 pages, HB w/dj, $3.00

From the Tropics to Your Table
    by Camille Den Dooven
    Published by Fruit Dispatch Co. in 1926
    30 pages, PB, $30.00

Garland Cookbook (The)
    by Garland School, Boston
    Published by Chester R. Heck, Inc. in 1946
    176 pages, HB w/dj, $12.00

Gayelord Hauser Cook Book (The)
    by Gayelord Hauser
    Published by Coward-McCann in 1946
    312 pages, HB w/dj, $5.00

Gem Chopper Cook Book
    Published by Sargent & Co. in 1902
    90 pages, PB, $10.00

General Foods Cook Book
    Published by General Foods in 1937
    5th printing
    370 pages, HB, $10.00

General Foods Kitchens Cookbook
    by General Foods Kitchens
    Published by Random House in 1959
    370 pages, HB, $8.00

Gold Cook Book (The)
    by Louis DeGouy
    Published in 1947
    1,098 pages, HB, $15.00

Golden Age Cook-Book
    by Henrietta Latham Dwight
    Published by Alliance Publishing in 1898
    178 pages, HB, $45.00

Golden Gate Cook Book
    Published by J. A. Folger & Co. in 1891
    128 pages, PB, $90.00

Golden Rule Cook Book
    by Ida Bailey Allen
    Published by Citizens' Wholesale Supply Co. in 1921
    141 pages, PB, $20.00

Foundation of All Reform (The)

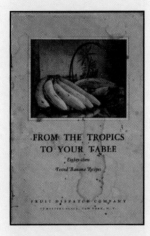

From the Tropics to Your Table

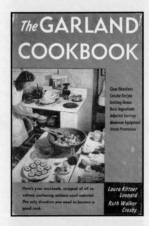

Garland Cookbook (The)

Gayelord Hauser Cook Book (The)

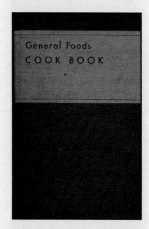

General Foods Cook Book

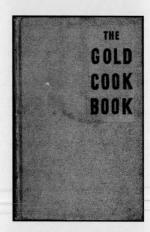

Gold Cook Book (The)

Gone With the Wind Cook Book
Published by Pebeco Tooth Paste in 1939
38 pages, PB, $60.00

Good Cook's Cookbook (The)
Published by Bonanza Books in 1970
511 pages, HB w/dj, $6.00

Good Food on a Budget
by Better Homes & Gardens
Published by Meredith in 1971
96 pages, HB, $3.00

Good Housekeeper's Cook Book
by Emma Paddock Tedford
Published by Cupples & Leon Co. in 1908
254 pages, HB, $40.00

Good Housekeeping 10PM Cook Book "18"
Published by Consolidated Book Pub. in 1958
68 pages, PB, $3.00

These 20 cookbooks can also be found in an optional blue and gold binder, valued separately at $5.00 in NM condition.

Good Housekeeping Appetizer Book "1"
Published by Consolidated Book Pub. in 1958
68 pages, PB, $3.00

Good Housekeeping Around the World "19"
Published by Consolidated Book Pub. in 1958
68 pages, PB, $3.00

Good Housekeeping Cake Book "3"
Published by Consolidated Book Pub. in 1958
68 pages, PB, $3.00

Good Housekeeping Casserole Book "5"
Published by Consolidated Book Pub. in 1958
68 pages, PB, $3.00

Good Housekeeping Cook Book
Published by *Good Housekeeping* in 1933
254 pages, HB, $20.00

Good Housekeeping Cook Book
Published by *Good Housekeeping* in 1942
946 pages, HB w/dj, $40.00 (+$50.00 for dj)

Good Housekeeping Cook Book
Published by *Good Housekeeping* in 1944
946 pages, HB, $40.00

Good Housekeeping Cook Book
> by Dorothy Marsh
> Published by *Good Housekeeping* in 1949
> 1014 pages, HB w/dj, $30.00

Good Housekeeping Cook Book
> Published by *Good Housekeeping* in 1955
> 760 pages, HB w/dj, $30.00 (+$40.00 for dj)

Good Housekeeping Cookbook
> by Dorothy Marsh
> Published by *Good Housekeeping* in 1962
> 760 pages, HB, $30.00

Good Housekeeping's Christmas Cook Book "B"

Good Housekeeping Cookbook
> by Dorothy Marsh
> Published by *Good Housekeeping* in 1963
> 805 pages, HB, $25.00

Good Housekeeping Cookbook
> by Dorothy Marsh
> Published by Harcourt, Brace, World in 1963
> 805 pages, HB, $25.00

Good Housekeeping Cookbook
> by Zoe Coulson
> Published by Hearst in 1973
> 811 pages, HB w/dj, $15.00

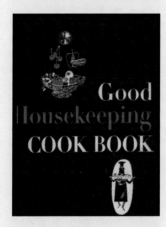

Good Housekeeping Cookbook – 1962

Good Housekeeping Everyday Cook Book
> Published by *Good Housekeeping* in 1903
> This was the magazine's first general cookbook.
> 320 pages, HB, $60.00

Good Housekeeping Hamburger and Hot Dog Book "8"
> Published by Consolidated Book Pub. in 1958
> 68 pages, PB, $3.00

Good Housekeeping Illustrated Cookbook
> by John Carter
> Published by Hearst in 1989
> 528 pages, HB, $12.00

Good Housekeeping Salads "6"
> Published by Consolidated Book Pub. in 1958
> 68 pages, PB, $3.00

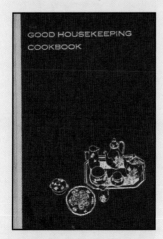

Good Housekeeping Cookbook – 1963

Good Housekeeping's Book of Cookies "2"
> Published by Consolidated Book Pub. in 1958
> 68 pages, PB, $3.00

Good Housekeeping's Book of Cookies "2"

Good Housekeeping's Fish and Shellfish Book "15"

Good Housekeeping's Ice Creams & Cool Drinks "17"

Good Housekeeping's Party Pie Book "7"

Good Housekeeping's Christmas Cook Book "B"
Published by Consolidated Book Pub. in 1958
68 pages, PB, $3.00

Good Housekeeping's Fish and Shellfish Book "15"
Published by Consolidated Book Pub. in 1958
68 pages, PB, $3.00

Good Housekeeping's Ice Creams & Cool Drinks "17"
Published by Consolidated Book Pub. in 1958
68 pages, PB, $3.00

Good Housekeeping's Party Pie Book "7"
Published by Consolidated Book Pub. in 1958
68 pages, PB, $3.00

Good Housekeeping's Quick 'N' Easy Cook Book "4"
Published by Consolidated Book Pub. in 1958
68 pages, PB, $3.00

Good Housekeeping Vegetables "10"
Published by Consolidated Book Pub. in 1958
68 pages, PB, $3.00

Good Meals and How to Prepare Them
by Katherine Fisher
Published by *Good Housekeeping* in 1927
256 pages, HB, $20.00

Good -n- Easy Cookbook
by Carnation
Published by Benjamin Co. in 1970
122 pages, HB, $3.00

Good Pies & How to Make Them (#5)
by Crisco
Published by Procter & Gamble in 1930
29 pages, PB, $12.00

Gorham Chafing Dish Book (The)
by Gorham Mfg. Co.
Published by Livermore & Knight in 1899
84 pages, PB, $30.00

Graham Kerr Cookbook (The)
by The Galloping Gourmet
Published by Doubleday in 1969
284 pages, HB, $6.00

Grandma's Old Fashioned Molasses Recipes
Published by Boston Molasses Co. in 1936
32 pages, PB, $8.00

Grandma's Recipes for Mother and Daughter
Published by Boston Molasses Co. in 1950
33 pages, PB, $6.00

Great Ground-Beef Recipes
by Grace White
Published by *Family Circle* in 1966
168 pages, PB, $3.00

Grennan Cake Cook Book of Holiday and Party Recipes
Published by Grennan Bakeries in 1928
22 pages, PB, $20.00

Griffith's Spice and Herb Handbook
Published by Griffith Laboratories in 1958
19 pages, PB, $3.00

Ground Beef Cookbook
Published by Favorite Recipes Press in 1967
124 pages, PB, $4.00

Ground Meat Cookbook
by Naomi Arbit and June Turner
Published by Ideals Publishing in 1981
64 pages, PB, $2.00

Guide for Nut Cookery
by Almeda Lambert
Published by Joseph Lambert & Co. in 1899
452 pages, HB, $275.00

Guide to Royal Success in Baking (A)
by Royal Baking Powder
Published by Standard Brands, Inc. in 1941
22 pages, PB, $5.00

Gunther Hostess Book (The)
Published by Gunther's Beer, c. 1950
64 pages, PB, $6.00

Handbook of Holiday Cuisine
by Margaret Happel & Elsa Harrington
Published by Downe Publishing in 1970
197 pages, HB w/dj, $6.00

Happy Eatings Make Christmas Greetings
Published by Borden Co. in 1956
PAM, $3.00

Good Housekeeping's Quick 'N' Easy Cook Book "4"

Gorham Chafing Dish Book (The)

Graham Kerr Cookbook (The)

Grandma's Old Fashioned Molasses Recipes

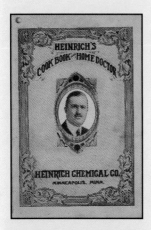

Heinrich's Cook Book and
Home Doctor

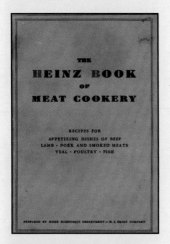

Heinz Book of Meat Cookery
(The) – 1932

Heinz Book of Meat Cookery –
1934

Happy Holidays Recipe Book
    by Hallmark Cards
    Published in 1965
    20 pages, PB, $3.00

Heinrich's Cook Book and Home Doctor
    Published by Heinrich Chemical Co., c. 1910
    64 pages, PB, $30.00

Heinz Book of Meat Cookery (The)
    Published by HJ Heinz Co. in 1932
    56 pages, PB, $12.00

Heinz Book of Meat Cookery (The)
    Published by HJ Heinz Co. in 1934
    108 pages, PB, $6.00

Helen Corbitt Cooks for Looks
    by Helen Corbitt
    Published by Houghton Mifflin in 1967
    115 pages, HB w/dj, $8.00

Hellmann's Menu Planner
    Vol VIII, No. 1 - looks like sheet music
    Published by Best Foods in 1941
    8 pages, PB, $3.00

Helps for the Hostess
    Published by Campbell Co., c. 1910
    64 pages, PB, $15.00

Herb and Spice Cook Book (An)
    by Craig Claiborne
    Published by Harper & Row in 1963
    334 pages, HB, $6.00

Herpitological Cookbook (A)
    by Ernest A. Liner
    Published by Ernest A. Liner in 1978
    60 pages, PB, $65.00

Hershey's Recipes
    Published by Hershey Chocolate Corporation in 1940
    32 pages, PB, $12.00

Higher Taste (The)
    Published by Bhaktivedanta Book Trust in 1984
    146 pages, PB, $3.00

"High-Ratio" Triple-Treat Way (The)
    by Sweetex
    Published by Procter & Gamble in 1941
    53 pages, PB, $6.00

Holiday Candy Book (The)
    by Virginia Pasley
    Published by Little, Brown, & Co. in 1952
    123 pages, HB w/dj, $10.00

Holiday Cook Book
    by Vee Guthrie
    Published by Peter Pauper Press in 1950
    62 pages, HB w/dj, $5.00

Holiday Recipes
    by Barbara Lane
    Published by Knudsen Creamery Co. in 1965
    19 pages, PB, $3.00

Holiday Recipes for 2 or 4 or 6
    by Mary Lee Taylor
    Published by Pet Milk Co. in 1951
    15 pages, PB, $3.00

Home-Baked Breads, M16
    by McCall's
    Published in 1965
    64 pages, PB, $3.00

Home Canners Text Book
    Published by Boston Woven Hose & Rubber Co. in 1940
    64 pages, PB, $3.00

Home Canning Guide
    by Westinghouse
    Published by Home Economics Institute in 1944
    47 pages, PB, $1.00

Home Comfort Cook Book
    Published by Wrought Iron Range Co. in 1938
    134 pages, SHB, $40.00

Home Cook Book (Household Library, The)
    Published by P. F. Collier & Son in 1905
    406 pages, HB, $150.00

Home Helps: A Pure Food Cook Book
    by Mary Lincoln, et al.
    Published by N.K. Fairbank Co. in 1910
    80 pages, HB, $100.00

Helen Corbitt Cooks for Looks

Hellmann's Menu Planner

Helps for the Hostess

Hershey's Recipes

Higher Taste (The)

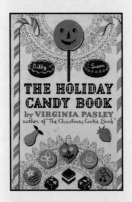

Holiday Candy Book (The)

Holiday Recipes

Holiday Recipes for 2 or 4 or 6

Homemade Bread
Published by Baltimore Gas & Electric Co. in 1953
29 pages, PB, $3.00

Homemade Desserts
Published by Baltimore Gas & Electric Co. in 1953
74 pages, PB, $5.00

Home Menu Cook Book (The)
by Myrtle Calkins
Published in 1934
253 pages, HB, $15.00

Honey in the Home
Published by Florida Agricultural Extension Service in 1957
44 pages, PB, $1.00

Hood's Cook Book Number One
Published by C. I. Hood & Co. in 1877
31 pages, PB, $30.00

Hood's High Street Cook Book
Published by C. I. Hood & Co. in 1888
32 pages, PB, $30.00

Horsford Almanac and Cook Book (The)
Published by Rumford Chemical Works in 1885
36 pages, PB, $30.00

Hot Weather Dishes
by Sarah T. Rorer
Published by Arnold & Co. in 1888
104 pages, HB, $50.00

Household Discoveries and Mrs. Curtis's Cook Book
by Isabel Gordon Curtis
Published by Success Co. in 1903
1,020 pages, HB, $50.00

Household Discoveries and Mrs. Curtis's Cook Book
by Isabel Gordon Curtis
Published by Success Co. in 1909
1,021 pages, HB, $30.00

Housekeeper's Handy Book
Published by LW Walter Co. in 1915
576 pages, PB, $15.00

Housewife's Almanac (The)
by Kellogg's
Published in 1938
36 pages, PB, $5.00

Housewife's Library (Many Volumes in One)
Published by Edgewood Publishing in 1885
644 pages, HB, $125.00

How America Eats
by Clementine Paddleford
Published by Scribner's in 1960
479 pages, HB, $50.00

How Things Have Changed Since Mother Was a Girl
Published by Swanson's Baking in 1916
24 pages, PB, $20.00

How to Cook a Husband and Other Things
by Puritan Millers
Published by Wells-Abbott-Nieman in 1905
Halloween-inspired cover
32 pages, PB, $125.00

How to Cook Better Meals Easier
Published by Westinghouse Electric & Manufacturing Co. in 1940
134 pages, SPB, $3.00

How to Cook With California Wines
Published by California Wine Advisory Board, c. 1965
16 pages, PB, $1.00

How to Cook Your Catch
by Rube Allyn
Published by Great Outdoors Publishing in 1963
80 pages, PB, $3.00

How to Enjoy Better Living with Your Crosley Home and Farm Freezer
Published by Crosley Shelvador in 1951
30 pages, PB, $3.00

How to Garnish
by Harvey Rosen
Published by International Culinary Consultants in 1983
96 pages, HB, $6.00

How to Get the Most out of Your Sunbeam Mixmaster
Published by Sunbeam Corporation, c. 1940
orange cover
42 pages, PB, $3.00

How to Get the Most out of Your Sunbeam Mixmaster
Published by Sunbeam Corporation in 1950
red cover
44 pages, PB, $3.00

Home Menu Cook Book (The)

Hood's High Street Cook Book

Horsford Almanac and Cook Book (The)

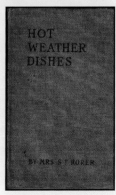

Hot Weather Dishes

How to Cook Better Meals Easier

How to Save Eggs by Using Dr. Price's Cream Baking Powder

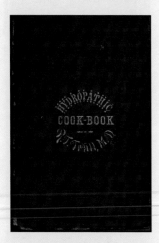

Hydropathic Cook-Book

How to Reduce and Stay Reduced
　　Published by Charles B. Knox Co. in 1955
　　34 pages, PB, $3.00

How to Save Eggs by Using Dr. Price's Cream Baking Powder
　　by Dr. Price's Baking Powder
　　Published by Royal Baking Powder Co. in 1917
　　22 pages, PB, $12.00

Hydropathic Cook-Book
　　by R. T. Trall
　　Published by Fowler & Wells in 1854
　　226 pages, HB, $350.00

Hygenic Cookery
　　by Susanna W. Dodds, MD
　　Published by Fowler & Wells in 1888
　　602 pages, HB, $150.00

Ice Creams: Frozen Without Stirring
　　Leaflet #49
　　Published by USDA in 1930
　　8 pages, PB, $12.00

Idle Hour Cook Book
　　Published by Chambers Gas Range Co. in 1927
　　40 pages, PB, $25.00

Idle Hour Cook Book
　　Published by Chambers Gas Range Co. in 1939
　　40 pages, PB, $25.00

Igleheart's Cake Secrets
　　by Swan's Down
　　Published by Igleheart Bros. in 1915
　　36 pages, PB, $35.00

I Hate to Cook Book (The)
　　by Peg Bracken
　　Published by Crest Books, d777 in 1965
　　144 pages, PB, $6.00

Illustrated Encyclopedia of American Cooking
　　Published by Favorite Recipes Press
　　Prospectus
　　HB, $1.00

I'm Getting Scarce
　　Published by Baker's Coconut, c. 1943
　　PAM, $3.00

Index and Holder for McCall's Cook Book Collection
    by McCall's
    Published in 1965
    Index is a PB, $3.00

In the Kitchen
    by Elizabeth S. Miller
    Published by Lee & Shepard in 1875
    568 pages, HB, $50.00

Invitation to Cooking
    Published by *Chicago Daily News* in 1955
    302 pages, HB, $12.00

It's a Picnic!
    by Nancy Fair McIntyre
    Published by Viking Press in 1969
    150 pages, HB w/dj, $6.00

It's Fun to Cook
    by Lucy Mary Maltby
    Published by John C. Winston Co. in 1938
    399 pages, HB w/dj, $15.00

It's So Good to Bake and Fry With Swift'ning
    by Martha Logan
    Published by Swift & Co. in 1955
    20 pages, PB, $2.00

James Beard Cookbook (The)
    by James Beard
    Published by Dutton in 1961
    Book Club Edition
    456 pages, HB w/dj, $6.00

James Beard Cookbook (The)
    by James Beard
    Published by Dell X1 in 1959
    544 pages, PB, $6.00

James Beard's Barbecue Cookbook
    by James Beard
    Published by Maco Publishing in 1967
    128 pages, PB, $3.00

James Beard's Menus for Entertaining
    by James Beard
    Published by Delacorte Press in 1965
    398 pages, HB w/dj, $6.00

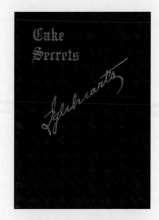

Igleheart's Cake Secrets

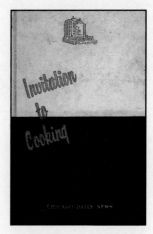

Invitation to Cooking

It's Fun to Cook

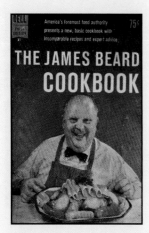

James Beard Cookbook (The)

Jell-O and The Kewpies

Jewel Cook Book (The)

Jell-O and The Kewpies
    by Jell-O; Artwork by Rose O'Neill
    Published by Genesee Foods in 1915
    18 pages, PB, $75.00

Jell-O Booklet, Train Tracks
    Published by Jell-O Co. in 1925
    18 pages, PB, $15.00

Jell-O Book of Menus
    Published by Genesee Foods in 1918
    24 pages, PB, $50.00

Jell-O Brings Dozens of Answers
    Published by P [ostum Cereal] Co. in 1928
    22 pages, PB, $15.00

Jell-O Pudding Idea Book
    Published by General Foods in 1968
    44 pages, PB, $3.00

Jell-O, America's Most Famous Dessert
    Published by Genesee Foods in 1902
    4 pages, PAM, $50.00

Jewel Cook Book (The)
    Published by Jewel Tea Co., c. 1950s
    Ad for Autumn Leaf Dinnerware by Hall China
    62 pages, PB, $50.00

Jewish Cook Book (The)
    by Florence Kreisler Greenbaum
    Published by Bloch Publishing in 1918
    419 pages, HB, $40.00

Jiffy Cooking
    by Better Homes & Gardens
    Published by Meredith in 1967
    90 pages, HB, $3.00

Johnny Appleseed Culinary Collection (The)
    Published by Alliance of Ft. Wayne (IN) Museum of Art in 1980
    111 pages, SHB, $6.00

Jolly Times Cook Book
    by Marjorie Noble Osborn
    Published by Rand McNally in 1934
    64 pages, HB, $15.00

Joy of Chocolate (The)
>by Judith Olney
>Published by Barron's in 1982
>182 pages, HB w/dj, $6.00

Joy of Cooking (The)
>by Irma S. Rombauer
>Published by A. C. Clayton in 1931
>The first edition of the legendary work; 3,000 copies were printed.
>Dust jackets exist for the early editions; they are all hard to find.
>396 pages, HB, $1,500.00+

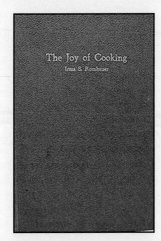

Joy of Cooking (The) – 1931

Joy of Cooking (The)
>by Irma S. Rombauer & Marion Becker
>Published by Bobbs-Merrill Co. in 1936
>This was the first "important" cookbook to list ingredients in order of
>use, followed by a list of chronological instructions.
>yellow cover
>628 pages, HB, $150.00

Joy of Cooking (The)
>by Irma S. Rombauer & Marion Becker
>Published by Bobbs-Merrill Co. in 1938
>blue cover
>628 pages, HB, $120.00
>Printings from 1939 to 1942 were reprints of the '36 edition and sell
>>for $30.00 to $50.00 each.

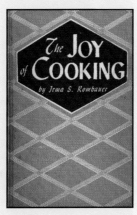

*Joy of Cooking (The) –
1946*

Joy of Cooking (The)
>by Irma S. Rombauer & Marion Becker
>Published by Bobbs-Merrill Co. in 1943
>884 pages, HB, $75.00

Joy of Cooking (The)
>by Irma S. Rombauer & Marion Becker
>Published by Bobbs-Merrill Co. in 1946
>Same as the 1943 edition, but the wartime info was replaced with
>material from Rombauer's Streamlined Cooking.
>884 pages, HB, $50.00

Joy of Cooking (The)
>by Irma S. Rombauer & Marion Becker
>Published by Bobbs-Merrill Co. in 1951
>1,013 pages, HB, $40.00
>The 1951 edition was reprinted in 1952 and again in 1953, with
>corrections and enhancements to the index.

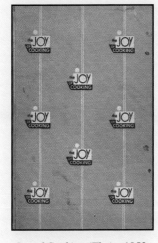

Joy of Cooking (The) – 1953

Joy of Cooking (The)
>by Irma S. Rombauer & Marion Becker
>Published by Bobbs-Merrill Co. in 1962
>Full of errors, this edition was not authorized by Marion Becker.
>849 pages, HB, $30.00

Karo Kookery

Kelvinator Book of Recipes (The)

Kitchen Tested Recipes

Marion Becker made corrections for the 1963 and 1964 reprints of the 1962 edition. These copies sell for $20.00 to $30.00. The book underwent further major revisions in 1975 and in 1997. Ethan Becker, Marion's son, is now an editor.

Joys of Jell-O
Published by General Foods
4th Edition, 1st printing
95 pages, PB, $3.00

Joys of Jell-O
Published by General Foods
6th Edition
95 pages, PB, $3.00

Joys of Jell-O Brand Gelatin
Published by General Foods in 1981
128 pages, SHB, $3.00

Joys of Jewish Cooking
by Stephen & Ethel Longstreet
Published by Weathervane Books in 1978
360 pages, HB w/dj, $6.00

Junior Jewish Cook Book
by Aunt Fanny
Published by KTAV Publishing House in 1956
64 pages, HB, $15.00

Karo Kookery
Published by Corn Products in 1942
32 pages, PB, $3.00

Kate Smith's Breakfast Book
by Kate Smith
Published by General Foods in 1941
45 pages, PB, $60.00

KC Cook's Book
Published by KC Baking Powder in 1930
33 pages, PB, $6.00

Keep It Short & Simple Cookbook (The)
by Ruth H. Brent
Published by Holt, Rinehart, & Winston in 1972
180 pages, HB, $3.00

Kelvinator Book of Recipes (The)
Published by Kelvinator, c. 1930s
32 pages, PB, $5.00

Kitchen Craft
> Published by Kitchen Craft Co. in 1935
> 32 pages, PB, $3.00

Kitchen Fun
> by Louise Price Bell
> Published by Harter of Cleveland in 1932
> 28 pages, HB, $60.00

Kitchen Tested Recipes
> by Sunbeam Mixmaster
> Published by Chicago Flexible Shaft Co. in 1933
> 40 pages, PB, $12.00

Knox Gelatine Desserts Salads Candies and Frozen Dishes
> Published by Charles B. Knox Co. in 1933
> 71 pages, PB, $8.00

Knox Gelatine Desserts Salads Candies and Frozen Dishes – 1933

Knox Gelatine Desserts Salads Candies and Frozen Dishes
> Published by Charles B. Knox Co. in 1941
> 55 pages, PB, $6.00

Knox On-Camera Recipes
> by Knox Gelatine
> Published by Knox Gelatine in 1963
> 48 pages, PB, $2.00

Kraft Miniature Marshmallows
> Published by Kraft, c. 1945
> 12 pages, PB, $3.00

Ladies' Home Journal Cookbook
> by Carol Truax
> Published by Doubleday in 1963
> 728 pages, HB, $6.00

Larkin Housewives' Cook Book

Larkin Housewives' Cook Book
> Published by Larkin Co. in 1923
> HB, $25.00

Latest Cake Secrets (The)
> Published by General Foods in 1939
> 4th printing
> 64 pages, PB, $6.00

Laurel's Kitchen
> by Laurel Robertson, et al.
> Published by Nilgin Press in 1981
> 508 pages, HB w/dj, $9.00

Latest Cake Secrets (The)

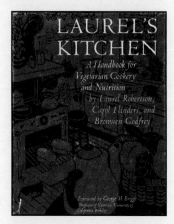

Laurel's Kitchen

Les Diners de Gala

Let's Cook it Right

LBJ Barbecue Cook Book
    by Walter Jettson & Arthur Whitman
    Published by Simon & Schuster in 1965
    HB, $20.00

LBJ Barbecue Cook Book
    by Walter Jettson & Arthur Whitman
    Published by Pocket Books
    77 pages, PB, $5.00

Learn to Bake...You'll Love It!
    Published by General Foods in 1947
    2nd printing
    80 pages, PB, $3.00

Learn to Bake...You'll Love It!
    Published by General Foods in 1947
    6th printing
    80 pages, PB, $3.00

Lee's Priceless Recipes
    by Dr. N. T. Oliver
    Published by Laird & Lee in 1895
    368 pages, HB, $60.00

Les Diners de Gala
    by Salvador Dali
    Published by "Felicie, Inc." in 1973
    321 pages, HB w/dj, $175.00

Let's Cook Fish
    Published by U. S. Dept. of Commerce in 1976
    54 pages, PB, $3.00

Let's Cook it Right
    by Adelle Davis
    Published by Harcourt, Brace & Co. in 1947
    626 pages, HB, $3.00

Let's Cook it Right
    by Adelle Davis
    Published by Harcourt, Brace & Co. in 1957
    Has 1947 copyright but lists book from 1954.
    626 pages, HB, $3.00

Let's Eat Right to Keep Fit
    by Adelle Davis
    Published by Harcourt, Brace & Co. in 1954
    1961 copy
    322 pages, HB, $3.00

Liberace Cooks
    by Carol Truax
    Published by Doubleday in 1970
    225 pages, HB w/dj, $60.00

Lifespice Salt-Free Cookbook
    by Ruth and Hilary Baum
    Published in 1985
    PB, $4.00

Little Book of Excellent Recipes (The)
    by the Mystery Chef
    Published by RB Davis Co. in 1934
    102 pages, PB, $6.00

Little Mother's Cook Book
    by Lon Amick
    Published by Pixie Press in 1952
    30 pages, HB w/box, $25.00

Look! Tasty, Appetizing Recipes with the Modern Meal Maker
    Published by John Oster Mfg. Co. in 1953
    64 pages, PB, $3.00

Low Cost Cookbook
    by *Southern Living*
    Published by Favorite Recipes Press in 1972
    192 pages, HB, $5.00

Low Fat, Low Cholesterol Diet (The)
    by E. Virginia Dobbin, et. al.
    Published by Doubleday in 1951
    362 pages, HB w/dj, $6.00

Lowney's Cook Book
    by Maria Willett Howard
    Published by Walter M. Lowney Co. in 1908
    421 pages, HB, $90.00

Lowney's Cook Book
    by Maria Willett Howard
    Published by Walter M. Lowney Co. in 1912
    421 pages, HB, $50.00

Lunches and Brunches (Creative Cooking Library, C7)
    by Better Homes & Gardens
    Published by Meredith in 1963
    62 pages, HB, $3.00

Magical Desserts With Whip 'n Chill
    Published by General Foods in 1966
    44 pages, PB, $1.00

Look! Tasty, Appetizing Recipes with the Modern Meal Maker

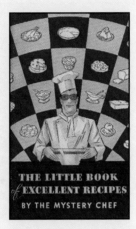

Little Book of Excellent Recipes (The)

Lunches and Brunches (Creative Cooking Library, C7)

Make It Now – Bake It Later!

Mary Dunbar's Favorite Recipes

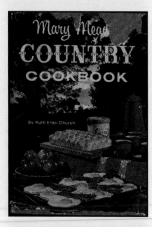

May Meade's Country Cookbook

Magic Chef Cooking
   by Dorothy Shank
   Published by American Stove Co. in 1935
   12th printing
   204 pages, HB, $6.00

Makamix Recipes
   Published by Jel Sert Co. c. 1930s
   PAM, $2.00

Make It Now – Bake It Later!
   by Barbara Goodfellow
   Published by Trident Press in 1965
   111 pages, SHB, $6.00

Make It With Candy
   Published by Graff Publications in 1966
   31 pages, PB, $2.00

Make It With Salt
   by Louise Driggs
   Published by Leslie Salt Co., c. 1950
   20 pages, PB, $3.00

Making and Using Cottage Cheese in the Home
   by Farmers' Bulletin #1451
   Published by USDA in 1927
   12 pages, PB, $6.00

Manual for Army Cooks
   Published by U. S. War Department in 1916
   300 pages, HB, $100.00

Martha Washington Cook Book
   by Marie Kimball
   Published by Coward-McCann in 1940
   212 pages, HB, $35.00

Mary Dunbar's Favorite Recipes
   by Mary Dunbar
   Published by Jewel Tea Co. in 1936
   80 pages, PB, $6.00

Marye Dahnke's Salad Book
   by Marye Dahnke
   Published by Cardinal C-129 in 1954
   307 pages, PB, $3.00

Mary Frances Cook Book
   by Jayne Fryer
   Published by John C. Winston Co. in 1912
   175 pages, HB, $60.00

Mary Poppins Cook Book
    by C&H Frosting Sugar
    Published by Walt Disney Co. in 1963
    25 pages, PB, $40.00

May Meade's Country Cookbook
    by Ruth Ellen Church
    Published by Rand McNally & Co. in 1964
    376 pages, HB w/dj, $8.00

May Meade's Magic Recipes for the Electric Blender
    by Ruth Church
    Published by Bobbs-Merrill in 1956
    256 pages, HB, $6.00

Maytag Dutch Oven Gas Range Instruction and Cook Book
    Published by Maytag Company in 1949
    120 pages, PB, $3.00

Mazola Salad Bowl
    Published by Corn Products in 1939
    32 pages, PB, $5.00

McCall's Cook Book
    Published by Random House in 1963
    786 pages, HB, $10.00

MCP Recipe Book
    Published by Mutual Citrus Products in 1940
    48 pages, PB, $3.00

Meals in Minutes (Creative Cooking Library, C6)
    by Better Homes & Gardens
    Published by Meredith in 1963
    62 pages, HB, $3.00

Meals: Tested, Tasted, and Approved
    Published by Good Housekeeping in 1930
    256 pages, HB, $5.00

Meals With a Foreign Flair (Creative Cooking Library, C5)
    by Better Homes & Gardens
    Published by Meredith in 1963
    62 pages, HB, $3.00

Mealtime Magic Desserts, Vol. 2
    by Margaret Mitchell
    Published by Aluminum Cooking Utensil Co. in 1951
    127 pages, HB, $3.00

Marye Dahnke's Salad Book

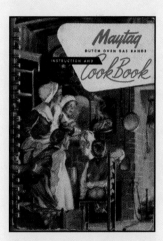

Maytag Dutch Oven Gas Range Instruction and Cook Book

Meals With a Foreign Flair (Creative Cooking Library, C5)

Meals: Tested, Tasted, and Approved

Meat Makes the Meal

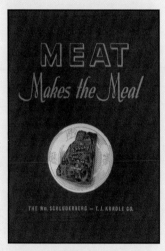

Merita Sandwich Book

Meat Cookery
Published by Baltimore Gas & Electric Co. in 1953
72 pages, PB, $3.00

Meat Makes the Meal
Published by Schludenberg-Kardle Co. in 1953
36 pages, PB, $3.00

Meat Recipes for the 1960s
Published by National Live Stock and Meat Board in 1959
40 pages, PB, $3.00

Meier and Frank's Cook Book
by Mabel Clarke
Published by Meier and Frank in 1932
HB, $100.00

Menu Magic for Camps
Published by General Foods, c. 1970
42 pages, PB, $3.00

Merita Sandwich Book
by Bruce Dunbar
Published by American Bakeries in 1948
24 pages, PB, $3.00

Metropolitan Cook Book
Published by Metro. Life Insurance in 1924
64 pages, PB, $12.00

Metropolitan Cook Book
Published by Metro. Life Insurance in 1933
64 pages, PB, $6.00

Metropolitan Cook Book
Published by Metro. Life Insurance in 1957
56 pages, PB, $3.00

Metropolitan Cook Book
Published by Metro. Life Insurance in 1953
56 pages, PB, $3.00

Metropolitan Cook Book
Published by Metro. Life Insurance in 1964
64 pages, PB, $2.00

Michael Field's Cooking School
by Michael Field
Published by M. Barrows & Co. in 1965
369 pages, HB w/dj, $6.00

Microwave Miracles
    Published by Sears in 1979
    160 pages, PB, $1.00

Microwaving Fruits & Vegetables
    by Barbara Methven and Sara Jean Thoms
    Published by Publication Arts in 1981
    160 pages, HB w/dj, $2.00

Milk Made Candies
    Published by Evaporated Milk Association in 1951
    15 pages, PB, $3.00

Minute Man Cook Book
    by Wayne Whipple
    Published by Minute Tapioca in 1909
    34 pages, PB, $20.00

Miracles with Minute Tapioca
    Published by General Foods in 1948
    22 pages, PB, $3.00

Miss Beecher's Housekeeper and Healthkeeper
    by Catherine Beecher
    Published by Harper & Brothers in 1873
    482 pages, HB, $150.00

Miss Fluffy's Rice Cook Book
    Published by Rice Council, c. 1960
    32 pages, PB, $3.00

Miss Leslie's New Receipts for Cooking
    by Eliza Leslie
    Published by TB Peterson in 1854
    520 pages, HB, $250.00

Miss Minerva's Cook Book
    by Emma Speed Sampson
    Published by Baily & Lee Co. in 1931
    Collected because of its African-American connection.
    280 pages, HB, $300.00

Miss Parloa's Kitchen Companion (21st Ed.)
    by Maria Parloa
    Published by Dana Estes & Co. in 1887
    966 pages, HB, $50.00

Miss Parloa's New Cook Book and Marketing Guide
    by Maria Parloa
    Published by Dana Estes & Co. in 1908
    430 pages, HB, $60.00

Microwaving Fruits & Vegetables

Milk Made Candies

Miss Fluffy's Rice Cook Book

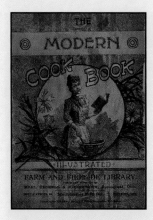

Modern Cook Book (The)

Modern Encyclopedia of Cooking, 2 vols.

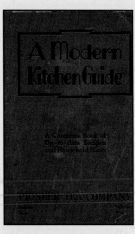

Modern Kitchen Guide (A)

Model Cook Book (The)
    by Frances Willey
    Published by S. I. Bell & Co. in 1890
    598 pages, HB, $120.00

Model Cook Book (The)
    by Frances Willey
    Published by R. B. Jones in 1903
    528 pages, HB, $60.00

Modern Cook Book (The)
    by Mrs. T. J. Kirkpatrick
    Published by Mast, Crowell, & Kirkpatrick in 1890
    320 pages, PB, $100.00

Modern Cooking
    by Mary A. Wilson
    Published by Students Educational Publishing Co. in 1920
    409 pages, HB, $25.00

Modern Encyclopedia of Cooking, 2 vols.
    by Meta Given
    Published by JG Ferguson & Associates in 1951
    6th printing
    1,699 pages, HB, $50.00

Modern Family Cook Book (The)
    by Meta Given
    Published by JG Ferguson & Associates in 1958
    Revised Edition
    632 pages, HB, $12.00

Modern Guide to Home Canning
    Published by National Pressure Cooker in 1946
    93 pages, PB, $3.00

Modern Guide to Pressure Canning & Cooking
    Published by National Presto Industries in 1955
    111 pages, PB, $5.00

Modern Home Cook Book
    by Grace E Denison
    Published by Southern Publishers in 1938
    534 pages, HB, $30.00

Modern Kitchen Guide (A)
    by Pioneer Tea Co.
    Published by Bunting Publications in 1940
    255 pages, SPB, $12.00

Modern Meal Maker
> by Martha Meade
> Published by Sperry Flour in 1935
> 745 pages, SHB, $15.00

Modern Method of Preparing Delightful Foods
> by Ida Bailey Allen
> Published by Corn Products in 1927
> 108 pages, HB, $6.00

Modern Priscilla Cook Book
> Published by Modern Priscilla in 1924
> 352 pages, HB, $60.00

Monarch Malleable Book of Cookery
> Published by Monarch Iron Range Co. in 1925
> 120 pages, PB, $45.00

More Downright Delicious Sun-Maid Raisin Recipes
> Published by Sun-Maid in 1949
> 24 pages, PB, $3.00

Mother Maybelle's Cook Book
> by June Carter Cash
> Published by Wynwood Press in 1989
> 192 pages, HB, $100.00

Mr. & Mrs. Roto-Broil Cook Book
> by Sarah Alexander
> Published by Roto-Broil Corporation in 1956
> 255 pages, PB, $6.00

Mr. Peanut's Guide to Nutrition
> Published by Standard Brands, Inc. in 1970
> 32 pages, PB, $1.00

Mrs. Bliss' Practical Cook Book
> by Mrs. Bliss
> Published by Lippencott, Grambo, and Co. in 1850
> 273 pages, HB, $175.00

Mrs. Gillette's Cook Book
> by F. L. Gillette
> Published by Werner Co. in 1899
> 605 pages, HB, $40.00

Mrs. Lincoln's Boston Cook Book
> by Mrs. D. A. Lincoln
> Published by Roberts Brothers in 1889
> 536 pages, HB, $125.00

Modern Meal Maker

Mr. & Mrs. Roto-Broil Cook Book

Mrs. Bliss' Practical Cook Book

Mrs. Lincoln's Boston Cook Book

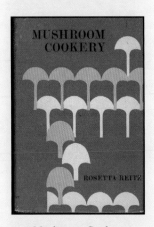

Mushroom Cookery

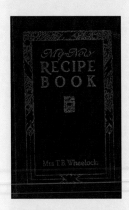

My New Recipe Book

Mrs. Owens' Cook Book
    by Mrs. Owens
    Published by Owens Publishing in 1883
    HB, $75.00

Mrs. Owens' New Cook Book and Complete Household Manual
    by Mrs. Owens
    Published by Owens Publishing in 1897
    1,000+ pages, HB, $250.00

Mrs. Peterson's Simplified Cooking
    by Anna J. Peterson
    Published by The People Gas, Light & Coke Company in 1926
    255 pages, HB, $10.00

Mrs. Porter's New Southern Cookery Book
    by Mrs. M. E. Porter
    Published by John E. Potter Co. in 1871
    416 pages, HB, $300.00

Mrs. Putnam's Receipt Book
    by Elizabeth H. Putnam
    Published by Philip Sampson & Co. in 1858
    233 pages, HB, $75.00

Mrs. Rorer's Cook Book
    by Sarah T. Rorer
    Published by Arnold & Co. in 1886
    581 pages, HB, $120.00

Mrs. Rorer's Every Day Menu Book
    by Sarah T. Rorer
    Published by Arnold & Co. in 1905
    300 pages, HB, $50.00

Mrs. Rorer's New Cook Book
    by Sarah T. Rorer
    Published by Arnold & Co. in 1902
    724 pages, HB, $40.00

Mrs. Seely's Cook Book
    by Mrs. Seely
    Published by MacMillan Co. in 1902
    425 pages, HB, $75.00

Mrs. Shillaber's Cook Book
    by Lydia Shillabers
    Published in 1887
    265 pages, HB, $100.00

Mushroom Cookery
    by Rosetta Reitz
    Published by Gramercy Publishing in 1945
    206 pages, HB w/dj, $6.00

My Better Homes & Gardens Cook Book
    Published by Better Homes & Gardens in 1936
    14th printing
    RB, $20.00

My 40 Favorite Recipes
    by Mary Alden
    Published by Quaker Oats in 1959
    38 pages, PB, $3.00

My New Better Homes & Gardens Cook Book
    Published by Meredith Publishing in 1937
    RB, $15.00

My New Recipe Book
    by Mrs. T. B. Wheelock
    Published by Mrs. T. B. Wheelock in 1912
    310 pages, HB, $40.00

NAFC Members' Cookbook
    Published by North American Fishing Club in 1997
    208 pages, HB, $5.00

National Foods Cookbook
    by Beatrice Trum Hunter
    Published by Simon & Schuster in 1961
    296 pages, HB, $5.00

National Yeast Co.
    Published by National Yeast Co. in 1885
    44 pages, PB, $30.00

Nestle's Semi-Sweet Chocolate Kitchen Recipes
    Published by Nestle's in 1951
    32 pages, PB, $3.00

Nestle's Semi-Sweet Chocolate Kitchen Recipes
    Published by Nestle's in 1957
    64 pages, PB, $3.00

New American Cook Book (The)
    by Lily Wallace
    Published by American Publishers' Alliance in 1941
    931 pages, HB, $15.00

National Yeast Co.

Nestle's Semi-Sweet Chocolate Kitchen Recipes – 1951

Nestle's Semi-Sweet Chocolate Kitchen Recipes – 1957

New American Cook Book
(The)

New Art (The)

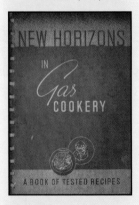

New Horizons in Gas
Cookery

New Presto Cooker
Recipe Book

New American Cook Book (The)
    by Lily Wallace
    Published by Books Inc. in 1948
    931 pages, HB, $12.00

New Angle to Simplify Cookie Production (A)
    Published by Procter & Gamble in 1944
    28 pages, PB, $6.00

New Art (The)
    Published by General Electric in 1933
    112 pages, PB, $8.00

New Art (The)
    Published by General Electric in 1936
    148 pages, SPB, $6.00

New Art (The)
    Published by General Electric in 1939
    48 pages, PB, $6.00

New Art of Simplified Cooking (The)
    Published by General Electric in 1940
    84 pages, PB, $20.00

New Casserole Cookery
    by Marian Tracy
    Published by Viking Press in 1952
    229 pages, HB w/dj, $6.00

New Cook's Cook Book (The)
    Published by Edison Electric in 1953
    52 pages, PB, $6.00

New Delicacies
    Published by Kraft in 1946
    PAM, $3.00

New Dinners for All Occasions
    by Elizabeth O. Miller
    Published by P. F. Volland Co., c. 1930
    60 pages, PB, $20.00

New England Cook Book (The)
    Published by Hezekiah Howe Co. in 1836
    115 pages, HB
    Rare in any condition, $600.00

New England Cook Book
    by Marion Harland, et al.
    Published by Chas. E. Brown Pub. in 1906
    286 pages, HB, $25.00

New England Economical Housekeeper
    by Mrs. E. A. Howland
    Published by E. A. Howland in 1847
    108 pages, HB, $150.00

Newest Recipes for Better Meals
    by Jane Ashley
    Published by Corn Products in 1952
    81 pages, PB, $3.00

New Favorite Cooking Receipts of the Shakers
    Published by AJ White in 1883
    36 pages, PB, $60.00

New Horizons in Gas Cookery
    by Home Service Dept.
    Published by Ohio Fuel & Gas Co. in 1939
    61 pages, SPB, $3.00

New Horsford's Bread and Pastry Cook (The)
    Published by Rumford Chemical Works, c. 1892
    48 pages, PB, $75.00

New Interest in Simple Menus
    Published by Sun-Maid Raisins c. 1940
    48 pages, PB, $5.00

New Jell-O Recipes
    Published by Jell-O Co. in 1926
    18 pages, PB, $15.00

New Joys of Jell-O
    Published by General Foods in 1979
    128 pages, HB, $3.00

Newman's Own Cookbook
    by Paul Newman, et al.
    Published by Simon & Schuster in 1998
    222 pages, HB w/dj, $8.00

Newman's Own 22 Favorite Recipes
    by Ursula Hotchner
    Published by Klein's Printing Co., c. 1990
    16 pages, PB, $3.00

New Presto Cooker Recipe Book
    Published by National Presto Industries in 1954
    64 pages, PB, $4.00

New Recipes for Durkee's Delicious Dishes

New Recipes for Good Eating

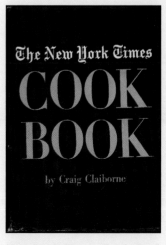

New York Times Cook Book (The)

Newest Recipes for Better Meals

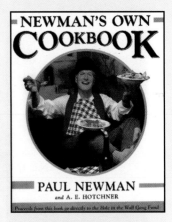

Newman's Own Cookbook

Night Before Cookbook (The)

New Recipes
> by Mary Lee Taylor
> Published by Pet Milk Co. in 1955
> 30 pages, PB, $3.00

New Recipes
> Published by Procter & Gamble in 1930
> 18 pages, PB, $12.00

New Recipes for Durkee's Delicious Dishes
> Published by ER Durkee & Co. in 1927
> 16 pages, PB, $12.00

New Recipes for Good Eating
> by Crisco
> Published by Procter & Gamble in 1951
> 112 pages, PB, $3.00

New Revised Universal Cook Book (The)
> Published by World Syndicate in 1930
> 752 pages, HB, $35.00

New Rumford Bread and Pastry Cook (The)
> Published by Rumford Chemical Works, c. 1894
> 48 pages, PB, $50.00

New Thrills of Freezing w/ a Frigidaire Food Freezer
> Published by Frigidaire in 1955
> 60 pages, SPB, $3.00

New York Times Cook Book (The)
> by Craig Claiborne
> Published by Harper & Row in 1961
> 717 pages, HB w/dj, $30.00

New York Times Heritage Cook Book
> by Jean Hewitt
> Published by Bonanza in 1952
> 804 pages, HB w/dj, $30.00

New York Times Heritage Cook Book
> by Jean Hewitt
> Published by Bonanza Books in 1980
> 804 pages, HB w/dj, $20.00

New York Times Menu Cook Book
> by Craig Claiborne
> Published by Harper & Row in 1966
> 727 pages, HB, $12.00

Night Before Cookbook (The)
　　by Paul & Leslie Rubenstein
　　Published by MacMillan Co. in 1967
　　210 pages, HB w/dj, $12.00

Nonfat Dry Milk Recipes
　　by Mary Lee Taylor
　　Published by Pet Milk Co. in 1953
　　30 pages, PB, $3.00

Norway Sardine Cookbook
　　by Ted Saucier
　　Published by Norwegian Canners Association
　　48 pages, PB, $3.00

Now's the Time for Jell-O (Matchbooks)
　　Published in 1953
　　Four designs exist, each with one recipe.
　　PAM, $8.00

Old Favorite Honey Recipes
　　Published by American Honey Institute in 1945
　　52 pages, PB, $5.00

Old Favorite Honey Recipes

Omelette Originals
　　by Irena Kirshman
　　Published by Potpourri Press in 1970
　　47 pages, PB, $3.00

Our Best Cooky Recipes
　　by Martha Logan
　　Published by Swift & Co. in 1962
　　24 pages, PB, $3.00

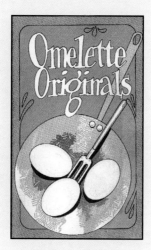

Omelette Originals

Our Home Cyclopedia
　　by Frank S. Burton
　　Published by Mercantile Publishing in 1889
　　400 pages, HB, $200.00

Pan-Pacific Cook Book
　　by L. L. McLaren
　　Published by Blair-Murdock Co. in 1915
　　170 pages, HB, $150.00

Parade Cookbook
　　by Parade Magazine
　　Published by Simon & Schuster in 1978
　　493 pages, HB, $3.00

Our Best Cooky Recipes

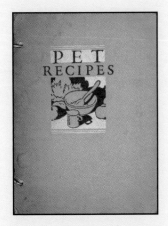

Pet Recipes

Picture Cook Book

Pocket Cook Book (The)

Party Sweets
    by Mary Blake
    Published by Carnation in 1957
    8 pages, PB, $3.00

Peanuts Lunch Bag Cook Book
    by June Dutton
    Published by Determined Productions in 1970
    91 pages, HB w/dj, $10.00

Peanuts Lunch Bag Cook Book
    by June Dutton
    Published by Scholastic Books in 1974
    91 pages, PB, $3.00

Perfect Hostess (The)
    by Maureen Daly
    Published by Pocket Books #751 in 1951
    289 pages, PB, $3.00

Peter Pan Peanut Butter Cook Book
    Published by Derby Foods in 1963
    26 pages, PB, $8.00

Pet Recipes
    Published by Pet Milk Co. in 1931
    84 pages, RB, $15.00

Picayune Creole Cook Book (The Original)
    11th Edition
    Published by Times-Picayune Pub. in 1947
    458 pages, HB, $50.00

Picnic and Patio Cook Book M18
    by McCall's
    Published in 1965
    64 pages, PB, $3.00

Picture Cook Book
    Published by Time, Inc. in 1958
    292 pages, SHB, $15.00

Picture Pies (Tested Recipes from Marie Gifford's Kitchen)
    Published by Armour in 1953
    32 pages, PB, $4.00

Plantation Recipe Book
    Published by Plantation Blackstrap Molasses, c. 1940
    12 pages, PB, $6.00

Pocket Cook Book (The)
   by Elizabeth Woody
   Published by Pocket Books #181 in 1942
   490 pages, PB, $30.00

Polly-O Recipe Book
   Published by Pollio Dairy Products in 1968
   72 pages, PB, $6.00

Polly-O Recipe Book

Polly, Put the Kettle On, We'll All Make Jell-O
   by Jell-O
   Published by Genesee in 1924
   Maxfield Parrish covers
   18 pages, PB, $50.00

Pooh Cook Book (The)
   by Virginia Ellison
   Published by EP Dutton & Co., in 1969
   120 pages, HB w/dj, $20.00

Practical Cook Book (The)
   by Mrs. Bliss
   Published by JB Lippencott Co. in 1856
   303 pages, HB, $250.00

Practical Cookery
   by Maria Parloa
   Published by New York Tribune in 1884
   32 pages, PB, $15.00

*Practically Cookless Cookbook,
M3*

Practically Cookless Cookbook, M3
   by McCall's
   Published in 1965
   64 pages, PB, $3.00

Praise for the Cook
   by Crisco
   Published by Procter & Gamble in 1959
   120 pages, SPB, $6.00

Praktisches Koch-Buch fur de Deutschen in Amerika
   by George Brumder
   Published by George Brumder in 1897
   648 pages, HB, $75.00

Premium Cook Book (The)
   by Marion Harland
   Published by American Technical Book Co. in 1894
   284 pages, HB, $40.00

Praise for the Cook

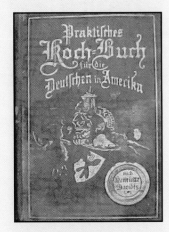

Praktisches Koch-Buch fur de Deutschen in Amerika

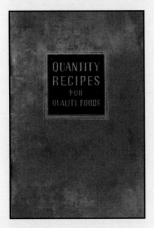

Quantity Recipes for Quality Foods

Quick 'n' Easy Riceland Rice Cook Book

Presidential Cook Book (The)
    by F. L. Gillette
    Published by Werner Co. in 1905
    Adapted from the *White House Cook Book*
    440 pages, HB, $45.00

President's Cook Book (The)
    by Poppy Cannon and Patricia Brooks
    Published by Funk & Wagnalls in 1968
    545 pages, HB, $12.00

Presto Cooker Fry Master
    Published by National Pressure Cooker, c. 1948
    95 pages, PB, $6.00

Presto Cooker (Model 40) Recipe Book
    Published by National Pressure Cooker in 1946
    128 pages, PB, $6.00

Presto Cooker (Model 40) Recipe Book
    Published by National Pressure Cooker in 1947
    128 pages, PB, $6.00

Presto Cooker (Model 60) Recipe Book
    Published by National Pressure Cooker in 1947
    128 pages, PB, $6.00

Presto Cooker Recipe Book (103, 104, 106)
    Published by National Presto Industries, c. 1950
    127 pages, PB, $5.00

Presto Pressure Cooker Recipe Book
    Published by National Presto Industries in 1961
    64 pages, PB, $3.00

Presto Pressure Cooker Recipe Book
    Published by National Presto Industries in 1966
    60 pages, PB, $3.00

Presto Pressure Cooker Recipe Book
    Published by National Presto Industries in 1968
    64 pages, PB, $2.00

Pyrex Prize Recipes
    by Corning Glass Works
    Published by Greystone Press in 1953
    128 pages, HB, $20.00

Quantity Cookery
    by Lenore Richards & Nola Treat
    Published by Little, Brown & Co. in 1925
    200 pages, HB, $8.00

Quantity Recipes for Quality Foods
Published by Evaporated Milk Association in 1944
blue cover
63 pages, PB, $12.00

Quantity Recipes for Quality Foods
Published by Evaporated Milk Association in 1948
brown cover
63 pages, PB, $8.00

Queen of Hearts Cook Book
Published by Peter Pauper Press in 1955
64 pages, HB w/dj, $5.00

Quick and Easy Gourmet Recipes
by Hyla O'Connor
Published by Vollrath Co. in 1968
128 pages, HB, $5.00

Quick and Easy Recipes
by Better Homes & Gardens
Published in 1972
PB, $1.00

Quicker Ways to Better Eating
Published by Wesson Oil in 1955
100 pages, PB, $3.00

Quick 'n' Easy Riceland Rice Cook Book
Published by Arkansas Rice Growers, c. 1950
32 pages, PB, $2.00

Ralston Mother Goose Recipe Book
Illustrated
Published by Ralston Purina Co. in 1919
16 pages, PB, $45.00

Ransom's Family Receipt Book
Published by D. Ransom, Son, & Co. in 1887
32 pages, PB, $15.00

Rare Old Receipts
by Jacqueline Harrison Smith
Published by John C. Winston Co. in 1906
30 pages, HB, $25.00

Rawleigh's 1916 Almanac
Published by WT Rawleigh Co. in 1916
98 pages, PB, $20.00

Quicker Ways to Better Eating

Ransom's Family Receipt Book

Rawleigh's 1916 Almanac

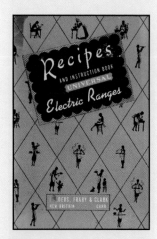

Recipes and Instruction Book

Recipes and Menus for Buffet Entertaining

Robertshaw Measured Heat Cook Book

Recipes
    by Sarah T. Rorer
    Published by Wesson Oil in 1913
    48 pages, PB, $15.00

Recipes and Instruction Book
    by Universal Electric Ranges
    Published by Frito Company in 1958
    8 pages, PB, $1.00

Recipes and Menus for Buffet Entertaining
    by Daisy Dean
    Published by TreeSweet Products, c. 1960
    3rd Edition
    24 pages, PB, $3.00

Recipes and Suggestions from TreeSweet
    Published by TreeSweet Products, c. 1960
    3rd Edition
    24 pages, PB, $3.00

Recipes for Cooking Forty Fathom Fish
    by Ritz-Carlton Chefs
    Published by Bay State Fishing Co. in 1927
    16 pages, PB, $25.00

Recipes for Good Eating
    by Crisco
    Published by Procter & Gamble in 1945
    64 pages, PB, $6.00

Recipes for Tasty Frozen Foods
    Published by Stewart-Warner Refrigerator in 1932
    23 pages, PB, $6.00

Recipes for Today
    Published by General Foods in 1943
    39 pages, PB, $3.00

Recipes of the Five Brothers (The), Volume I
    Published by Sandy Bottom Press in 1997
    42 pages, HB w/dj, $3.00

Recipes Prize Winning 4-H FHS Favorite Food Shows
    Published by Suburban Propane in 1963
    76 pages, PB, $6.00

Recipe Yearbook 1989
    by Bon Appetit
    Published by Knapp Press in 1989
    133 pages, HB, $3.00

Reddy Killowatt Baking Contest Cook Book
    Published by Empire District Electric in 1951
    143 pages, SPB, $60.00

Reddy Killowatt's Sportsman Cook Book
    Published in 1945
    12 pages, PB, $75.00

Reliable Recipes
    Published by Calumet Baking Powder in 1920
    32 pages, PB, $8.00

Robertshaw Measured Heat Cook Book
    Published by Robertshaw-Fulton in 1947
    87 pages, SPB, $6.00

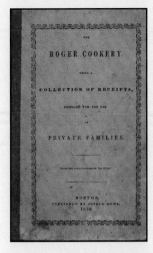

Roger Cookery (The)

Roger Cookery (The)
    Published by Joseph Dowe in 1838
    48 pages, HB, $300.00

'Round the Clock Recipes
    by Mary Alden
    Published by Quaker Oats in 1963
    47 pages, PB, $3.00

Round-the-World Cook Book
    by Ida Bailey Allen
    Published by Best Foods in 1934
    2nd printing
    96 pages, HB, $3.00

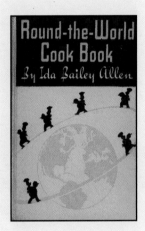

Round-the-World Cook Book

Roundup of Beef Cookery
    by American National Cowbelles
    Published by Bonanza Books in 1960
    198 pages, HB, $12.00

Royal Baker and Pastry Cook
    by Royal Baking Powder
    Published by Royal Baking Co. in 1906
    42 pages, PB w/dj, $15.00

Royal Baker and Pastry Cook
    by Royal Baking Powder
    Published by Royal Baking Co. in 1911
    43 pages, PB, $12.00

Royal Cook Book
    by Royal Baking Powder
    Published by Royal Baking Co. in 1925
    48 pages, PB, $6.00

Royal Baker and Pastry Cook – 1906

Royal Baker and Pastry Cook – 1911

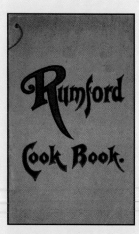

Rumford Complete Cook Book (The) – 1908

Rumford Cook Book – 1908

Royal Cook Book
> by Royal Baking Powder
> Published by Royal Baking Co. in 1929
> 49 pages, PB, $6.00

Royal Cook Book
> by Royal Baking Powder
> Published by Standard Brands, Inc. in 1932
> Similar cover to the 1929 edition, but with changes.
> 49 pages, PB, $5.00

Royal Cook Book
> by Royal Baking Powder
> Published by Standard Brands, Inc. in 1937
> 64 pages, PB, $3.00

Rumford Complete Cook Book (The)
> by Lily Haxworth Wallace
> Published by Rumford Chemical Works in 1908
> 236 pages, HB, $30.00

There were at least 44 editions of the *Rumford Complete Cook Book*; the 1908 edition is the first. The early "copyright editions," at which times the content was revised, are: 1908; 1918; and 1929.

Lily Wallace graduated from London's National Training School of Cookery. She was hired by Rumford and began to publish cooking and domestic booklets for them. In 1900, she came to America and began to teach and lecture throughout the United States. *The Rumford Complete Cook Book* was her first major work. During the 1920s she was hired to serve as the Director of Domestic Science for *Woman's World* magazine, where she released her second major work, the *Woman's World Cook Book*, in 1931. Her other works include the *New American Cook Book* (1941) and its companion, *The New American Etiquette* (1941).

Rumford Complete Cook Book (The)
> by Lily Haxworth Wallace
> Published by Rumford Chemical Works in 1918
> 241 pages, HB, $20.00

Rumford Complete Cook Book (The)
> by Lily Haxworth Wallace
> Published by Rumford Co. in 1931
> 234 pages, HB, $12.00

Rumford Complete Cook Book (The Revised)
> by Lily Haxworth Wallace
> Published by Rumford Co. in 1936
> 209 pages, HB, $10.00

Rumford Complete Cook Book (The Revised)
    by Lily Haxworth Wallace
    Published by Rumford Co. in 1950
    228 pages, HB, $6.00

Rumford Cook Book
    Published by Rumford Chemical Works in 1884
    48 pages, PB, $100.00

Rumford Cook Book
    Published by Rumford Chemical Works, c. 1905
    A little girl shouting is on the cover.
    48 pages, PB, $75.00

Rumford Cook Book
    by Fannie Farmer
    Published by Rumford in 1908
    48 pages, PB, $20.00

Rumford Fruit Cook Book
    Published by Rumford Chemical Works in 1927
    48 pages, PB, $20.00

Salads & Salad Dressings, M4
    by McCall's
    Published in 1965
    64 pages, PB, $3.00

Salads: Alluring and New
    by Alice Bradley
    Published by Gebhardt Chili Powder Co. in 1926
    12 pages, PB, $15.00

Salads: "Tossed" and Otherwise
    Published by Kraft in 1946
    PAM, $3.00

Salmon Recipe Book
    by Dorothy Fisher
    Published by Deming's Salmon
    32 pages, PB, $3.00

Salute to Cooking — Dinner in a Dish
    Published by Favorite Recipes Press in 1966
    380 pages, SPB, $6.00

Sandwich Fun
    by Imperial Margarine
    Published by Hearst Corporation in 1963
    31 pages, PB, $3.00

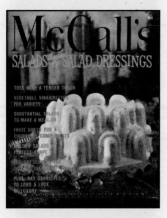

Salads & Salad Dressings, M4

Salads: Alluring and New

Salute to Cooking — Dinner in a Dish

Searchlight Recipe Book (The Household) – 1936

Searchlight Recipe Book – 1942

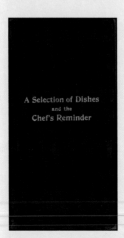

Selection of Dishes and the Chef's Reminder (A)

Savory Prize Recipe Book
    Published by Savory Roaster in 1922
    47 pages, PB, $45.00

Savory Stews
    by Mary Savage
    Published by Doubleday in 1969
    230 pages, HB w/dj, $5.00

Science in the Kitchen
    by Mrs. Ellen E. Kellogg
    Published by Modern Medicine Publishing in 1893
    573 pages, HB, $90.00

Seafood Cookery
    Published by Baltimore Gas & Electric Co. in 1953
    31 pages, PB, $3.00

Searchlight Recipe Book (The Household)
    by Ida Migliario, et al.
    Published by *Household Magazine* in 1936
    8th printing
    304 pages, HB, $45.00

Searchlight Recipe Book (The Household)
    by Ida Migliario, et al.
    Published by *Household Magazine* in 1937
    10th printing, newly revised
    320 pages, HB, $45.00

The Household Searchlight Recipe Book was a very popular thumb-indexed cookbook, put out by a magazine from Topeka, Kansas. Originally made in 1931, the first printing quickly sold out, giving way to about two dozen later printings. In 1942, the cover was completely redesigned, showing the title as *Searchlight Recipe Book*.

Searchlight Recipe Book (The Household)
    by Ida Migliario, et al.
    Published by *Household Magazine* in 1939
    12th printing
    320 pages, HB, $30.00

Searchlight Recipe Book (The Household)
    by Ida Migliario, et al.
    Published by *Household Magazine* in 1940
    13th printing
    320 pages, HB, $15.00

Searchlight Recipe Book
    by Ida Migliario, et al.
    Published by *Household Magazine* in 1942
    320 pages, HB, $12.00

Searchlight Recipe Book
by Ida Migliario, et al.
Published by *Household Magazine* in 1947
320 pages, HB, $10.00

Searchlight Recipe Book
by Ida Migliario, et al.
Published by *Household Magazine* in 1958
320 pages, HB, $8.00

Seasoning Makes the Difference
by Carol French
Published by RT French Co. in 1951
31 pages, PB, $4.00

Selection of Dishes and the Chef's Reminder (A)
by Charles Fellows
Published by Hotel Monthly in 1909
220 pages, PB, $75.00

Service Cook Book Number One (The)
by Ida Bailey Allen
Published by JW Clement Co. in 1933
RB, $6.00

Service Cook Book Number Two (The)
by Ida Bailey Allen
Published in 1935
SHB, $6.00

Settlement Cook Book (Way to a Man's Heart)
by Mrs. Simon Kander
Published by the Settlement Cook Book Co.
3rd Edition
470 pages, HB, $100.00

The original publication of *The Way to a Man's Heart* was a 200-page pamphlet largely designed for German-Jewish immigrants to the United States. Its author, Lizzie Black (Mrs. Simon) Kander, was the daughter of pioneer farmers and established the Milwaukee Jewish Mission. It was at this mission that Mrs. Kander began the cooking classes that evolved into her famous cookbook. *The Settlement Cook Book* became immensely popular, but its first ten printings can be quite elusive; printings from the 30s and early 40s are the most common.

Settlement Cook Book (Way to a Man's Heart)
by Mrs. Simon Kander
Published by Settlement Cook Book Co. in 1936
623 pages, HB, $25.00
22nd Edition; 1938, $20.00
24th Edition, 1941, $20.00
27th Edition, 1945, $25.00
29th Edition, 1949, $25.00

Service Cook Book Number One (The)

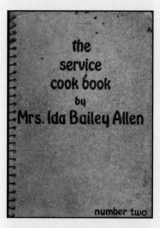

Service Cook Book Number Two (The)

Settlement Cook Book (The Way to a Man's Heart) (The) – 1936

Shaker Cook Book (The)

Sing a Song of Salads

Sleepy Eye Milling Co. Cook Book

Settlement Cook Book (Way to a Man's Heart)
> by Mrs. Simon Kander
> Published by Settlement Cook Book Co. in 1951
> 30th Edition, revised
> 624 pages, HB, $25.00

Settlement Cook Book (The New)
> by Mrs. Simon Kander
> Published by Simon & Schuster in 1954
> 757 pages, HB w/dj, $20.00

Settlement Cook Book
> by Mrs. Simon Kander
> Published by Simon & Schuster in 1965
> Revised Edition
> 535 pages, HB w/dj, $15.00

Settlement Cook Book
> by Mrs. Simon Kander
> Published by Simon & Schuster in 1976
> Revised Edition
> 737 pages, HB w/dj, $9.00

Shaker Cook Book (The)
> by Caroline B. Piercy
> Published by Crown Publishing in 1953
> 283 pages, HB w/dj, $8.00

Sharing Our Favorite Recipes
> Published by LDS Relief Society in 1959
> SPB, $5.00

Sharp Carousel Microwave Cook Book
> Published by Sharp Electronics in 1981
> HB, $1.00

Short Cut to Better Jams and Jellies
> Published by Certo (General Foods) in 1943
> 30 pages, PB, $5.00

Show-off Cook Book M14
> by McCall's
> Published in 1965
> 64 pages, PB, $3.00

Sing a Song of Salads
> Published by Kraft in 1945
> PAM, $3.00

Six Little Cooks
　　by Aunt Jane's Cooking Class
　　Published by A. C. McLurg in 1891
　　232 pages, HB, $60.00

Skillet Cook Book
　　by Wesson Oil
　　Published in 1958
　　64 pages, PB, $3.00

Sleepy Eye Milling Co. Cook Book
　　Published by Sleepy Eye Milling, c. 1899
　　Shaped like a loaf of bread and wears easily.
　　96 pages, PB, $100.00

Slenderella Cook Book (The)
　　by Myra Waldo
　　Published by GP Putnam's Sons in 1957
　　335 pages, HB w/dj, $6.00

Sloan's Handy Hints and Up-to-Date Cook Book
　　Published by Sloan's Liniment in 1901
　　48 pages, PB, $40.00

Slovak-American Cook Book (The)
　　Published by 1st Catholic Slovak Ladies Union in 1952
　　437 pages, HB, $35.00

Snack Jar Plan (The)
　　Published by National Peanut Council in 1946
　　16 pages, PB, $3.00

Snacks and Refreshments (Creative Cooking Library, C4)
　　by Better Homes & Gardens
　　Published by Meredith in 1963
　　62 pages, HB, $3.00

So-Good Meals (Creative Cooking Library, C3)
　　by Better Homes & Gardens
　　Published by Meredith in 1963
　　62 pages, HB, $3.00

Some Favorite Recipes of the Duchess of Windsor
　　by the Duchess of Windsor
　　Published by Scribner's in 1942
　　177 pages, HB w/dj, $100.00

Someone's in the Kitchen With Dinah
　　by Dinah Shore
　　Published by Doubleday in 1972
　　179 pages, HB w/dj, $10.00

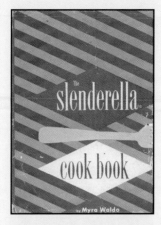

Slenderella Cook Book (The)

So-Good Meals (Creative Cooking Library, C3)

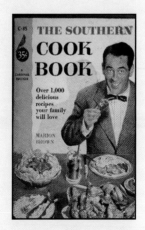

Southern Cook Book (The) – 1956

Spice Cook Book (The)

Spice Islands Cook Book (The) – 1961

Sunkist Recipes: Oranges – Lemons

Southern Cook Book (The)
  by Marion Brown
  Published by Cardinal C-85 in 1956
  414 pages, PB, $5.00

Southern Cookbook
  by Sallie F. Hill
  Published by Progressive Farmer Co. in 1961
  470 pages, HB w/dj, $6.00

Southern Cooking
  by Mrs. S.R. Dull
  Published by Ruralist Press in 1928
  384 pages, HB w/dj, $45.00

Southwestern Cookbook
  by Southern Living
  Published by Favorite Recipes Press in 1972
  192 pages, HB, $6.00

Spam: The Cookbook
  by Linda Eggers
  Published by Longstreet in 1998
  84 pages, PB, $3.00

Spice Cook Book (The)
  by Avanelle Day & Lillie Stuckey
  Published by Grosset & Dunlap in 1968
  623 pages, HB, $12.00

Spice Islands Cook Book (The)
  Published by Lane Book Co. in 1961
  208 pages, HB w/dj, $20.00

Spice Islands Recipe Folio
  Published by Spice Islands Co. in 1964
  RB, $20.00

Spice Islands Sampler
  by w/samples of 4 spices
  Published by Spice Islands Co. in 1964
  8 pages, PB, $3.00

Spin Cookery Blender Cook Book
  Published by John Oster Mfg. Co. in 1966
  96 pages, PB, $3.00

Square Meals...Speedy Meals...
  Published by Kraft in 1945
  PAM, $3.00

Staley's Selected Recipes and Menus
Published by A. E. Staley Mfg. Co., c. 1930s
64 pages, PB, $60.00

Standard Book of Recipes
by Alice A. Johnson
Published by W. E. Scull in 1901
HB, $35.00

Successful Baking for Flavor and Texture
Published by Arm & Hammer in 1935
32 pages, PB, $5.00

Successful Baking for Flavor and Texture
Published by Arm & Hammer in 1938
38 pages, PB, $5.00

Summer Cookbook (The)
by Lousene Rousseau Brunner
Published by Harper & Row in 1966
200 pages, HB w/dj, $6.00

Sunkist Lemons
by Sunkist
Published by California Fruit Growers Association in 1939
33 pages, PB, $12.00

Sunkist Recipes: Oranges – Lemons
by Alice Bradley
Published by California Fruit Growers Exchange in 1916
64 pages, PB, $20.00

Sun-Maid Raisins Selected Recipes
Published by California Raisin Co. in 1921
28 pages, PB, $20.00

Sunset Cook Book of Breads
Published by Lane Book Co. in 1963
127 pages, HB w/dj, $3.00

Sunset Menu Cook Book
Published by Lane Magazine & Book Co. in 1969
208 pages, HB w/dj, $3.00

Sunset Mexican Cook Book
Published by Lane Publishing in 1983
96 pages, PB, $3.00

Sunset Oriental Cook Book
Published by Lane Publishing in 1977
96 pages, PB, $3.00

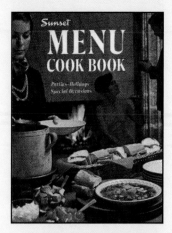

Sunset Menu Cook Book

Sunset Seafood Cook Book

Superb Recipes for Smooth-Melting Velveeta

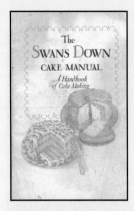

Swan's Down Cake Manual (The)

Sweet Treats

Table and Kitchen

Tempting Banana Recipes

Sunset Salad Book
Deluxe Edition
Published by Lane Publishing, c. 1960
90 pages, PB w/dj, $5.00

Sunset Salad Book
by Genevieve A. Callahan
Published by Lane Publishing in 1937
47 pages, PB, $3.00

Sunset Seafood Cook Book
Published by Lane Publishing in 1977
88 pages, PB, $3.00

Superb Recipes for Smooth-Melting Velveeta
Published by Kraft in 1946
PAM, $3.00

Swan's Down Cake Manual (The)
Published by General Foods in 1944
2nd Edition; 3rd printing
48 pages, PB, $3.00

Sweet Treats
Published by Carnation Co., c. 1950s
PAM, $1.00

Table and Kitchen
by Dr. Price's Baking Powder
Published by Royal Baking Powder Co. in 1916
57 pages, PB, $15.00

Tempting Banana Recipes
Published by United Fruit Co. in 1958
PAM, $3.00

Tempting Kosher Dishes
Published by Manischewitz Co. in 1930
156 pages, HB, $125.00

Tempting Nutritious Desserts
by Mary Mason
Published by Chr. Hanson's Laboratory in 1941
30 pages, PB, $6.00

Tested & Proven Recipes
Published by Mueller's in 1930
40 pages, PB, $3.00

Tested Recipes
Published by Guardian Service, c. 1940s
Girl in garden is on the cover.
49 pages, PB, $35.00

Tested Recipes
Published by Enterprise Aluminum in 1949
32 pages, PB, $30.00

Tested Recipes
Published by Guardian Service, c. 1950
Cover divided into blocks with food items.
72 pages, PB, $30.00

That Amazing Ingredient: Mayonnaise
by Alice Joy Miller et al.
Published by CPC International in 1979
125 pages, HB w/dj, $6.00

That Pinch of Salt
Published by General Foods in 1944
12 pages, PB, $3.00

Thoughts for Buffets
Published by Houghton Mifflin in 1958
425 pages, HB, $6.00

Thousand Ways to Please a Husband (A)
by Louise Bennett Weaver & Helen Cowles LeCron
Published by Britton Publishing in 1917
479 pages, HB, $90.00

Three Meals a Day
Published by Metro. Life Insurance in 1946
16 pages, PB, $12.00

Thrifty New Tips on a Grand Old Favorite
Published by HJ Heinz Co. in 1932
19 pages, PB, $12.00

Timeless Recipes with Minute Rice
Published by General Foods in 1965
81 pages, PB, $2.00

Time-Life Holiday Cook Book
Published by Time-Life Publications in 1976
HB w/dj, $3.00

Timely Meat Recipes
Published by National Live Stock and Meat Board in 1944
39 pages, PB, $3.00

Tempting Nutritious Desserts

Tested & Proven Recipes

That Pinch of Salt

Three Meals a Day

Timeless Recipes with
Minute Rice

Treasury of Great
Recipes (A)

Treasury of Outdoor Cooking

Universal Simplified
Gas Cookery

Today's Woman Buffet Cook Book
Published by Fawcett in 1954
144 pages, PB, $6.00

Today's Woman Cook Book (A)
Published by Fawcett in 1950
144 pages, PB, $6.00

Towns, Trails, and Special Times
A Marlboro Country Cookbook
Published by Phillip Morris in 1997
163 pages, HB, $25.00

Trail Cookery
for Girl Scouts of America
Published by Kellogg Co. in 1945
30 pages, PB, $15.00

Treasury of Great Recipes (A)
by Mary & Vincent Price
Published by Ampersand Press in 1965
456 pages, HB, $60.00

Treasury of Outdoor Cooking
by James Beard
Published by Gallery Press in 1960
282 pages, HB w/dj, $15.00

Try the New Jell-O
Published by General Foods in 1932
24 pages, PB, $6.00

Twentieth Century Home Cook Book
by Mrs. Francis Carruthers
Published by Thompson, Thomas, & Co. in 1906
491 pages, HB, $40.00

Universal Simplified Gas Cookery
Published by Cribben & Sexton Co., c. 1940
53 pages, PB, $12.00

Unusual Old World and American Recipes
Published by Nordic Ware, c. 1965
38 pages, PB, $6.00

US Navy Cook-Book
Published by Division of Naval Militia Affairs in 1908
62 pages, PB, $20.00

Velda Recipes
Published by Velda Dairy, c. 1965
48 pages, PB, $3.00

Walt Disney's Mickey Mouse Cookbook
Published by Walt Disney Productions in 1975
93 pages, HB, $15.00

Walton Family COOK BOOK
by Sylvia Resnick
Published by Bantam Books in 1975
148 pages, PB, $50.00

War Cook Book for American Women
Published by U. S. Food Administration in 1918
32 pages, PB, $20.00

Wartime-Ration Recipes For Delicious Meals For 2 and 4 and 6
Published by Sego Milk Products in 1943
28 pages, PB, $6.00

Wartime-Ration Recipes For Delicious Meals For 2 and 4 and 6

Watergate Cookbook (The)
by N. Y. Alplaus
Published by Emporium Publications in 1973
92 pages, PB, $12.00

Watkins Almanac, Home Doctor, and Cook Book
Published by JR Watkins Co. in 1917
64 pages, PB, $30.00

Watkins Almanac, Home Doctor, and Cook Book
Published by JR Watkins Co. in 1922
96 pages, PB, $25.00

Watkins Cook Book
Published by JR Watkins Co. in 1938
288 pages, SHB, $20.00

Watergate Cookbook (The)

Watkins Hearthside Cook Book
Published by JR Watkins Co. in 1952
256 pages, SHB w/dj, $35.00

Ways With Wine
by Morrison Wood
Published by Paul Masson Vineyards in 1968
30 pages, PB, $2.00

Way to a Railroad Man's Heart Cookbook (The)
by Jeanette DeVore
Published by The Railroad Trainman, c. 1930
48 pages, PB, $30.00

Wear-Ever MicroRave
Published by Wear-Ever Aluminum in 1979
19 pages, PB, $1.00

Watkins Almanac, Home Doctor, and Cook Book – 1917

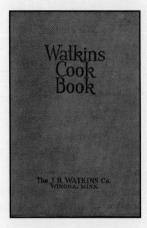

Watkins Cook Book

Watkins Hearthside Cook Book

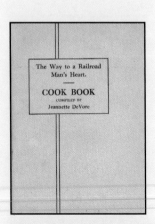

*Way to a Railroad Man's
Heart Cookbook (The)*

Wear-Ever New Method Cooking Instruction Book
Published by Aluminum Cooking Utensil Co. in 1940
11th Edition
63 pages, PB, $30.00

Wear-Ever New Method of Cooking (The)
Published by Aluminum Cooking Utensil Co. in 1928
47 pages, PB, $50.00

Westinghouse Refrigerator Book
by Julia Kiene
Published by Westinghouse, c. 1940
40 pages, PB, $3.00

What Makes Jelly "Jell"?
Published by General Foods in 1945
23 pages, PB, $3.00

What's Cooking on the B&O?
Published by B&O Railroad, c. 1955
32 pages, PB, $40.00

What Shall I Cook Today?
Published by Lever Brothers Co., c. 1940
48 pages, PB, $3.00

What Shall I Serve (Family Recipes for Jewish Housewives)
Published by in Rumford Chemical Co. in 1931
32 pages, PB, $60.00

What Shall the Next Meal Be?
by Martha Meade
Published by Sperry Flour in 1928
48 pages, PB, $12.00

Where There's Fire, There's Smoke
Published by Fla. Dept of Natural Resources in 1970s
PAM, $1.00

White House Chef Cookbook
by Rene Verdon
Published by Doubleday in 1967
287 pages, HB, $10.00

White House Cook Book (The)
by F. L. Gillette
Published by L. P. Miller & Co. in 1887
Silver cover. No copies have sold recently, so the value is an estimate.
This book was first published in 1887 as *The American Cook Book*.
It quickly became a classic. Copies of most editions are seldom
found in higher grades; the covers tended to come loose.
521 pages, HB, $200.00

White House Cook Book (The)
> by F. L. Gillette
> Published by L. P. Miller & Co. in 1889
> silver cover
> 521 pages, HB, $150.00

White House Cook Book (The)
> by F. L. Gillette and Hugo Ziemann
> Published by R. S. Peale & Co. in 1889
> The book received a new publisher and cover design in 1889. Hugo
> Ziemann was brought in to work on the book.
> 570 pages, HB, $125.00

What Shall the Next Meal Be?

White House Cook Book (The)
> by F. L. Gillette and Hugo Ziemann
> Published by the Werner Co. in 1890
> 570 pages, HB, $125.00

White House Cook Book (The)
> by F. L. Gillette and Hugo Ziemann
> Published by the Werner Co. in 1891; reprint of the 1890 edition
> 570 pages, HB, $100.00

White House Cook Book (The)
> by F. L. Gillette and Hugo Ziemann
> Published by the Werner Co. in 1893; reprint of the 1890 edition
> 570 pages, HB, $100.00

White House Cook Book (The) –
1889

White House Cook Book
> by F. L. Gillette and Hugo Ziemann
> Published by Werner Co. in 1894
> 568 pages, HB, $125.00
> The 1894 edition was reprinted in 1898.

Das Weisse-Haus Kochbuch
> by F. L. Gillette & Hugo Ziemann
> Translated into German.
> Published by Louis Lange Publishing in 1899
> 651 pages, HB, $60.00

White House Cook Book (The)
> by FL Gillette and Hugo Ziemann
> Published by Saalfield Publishing in 1899
> The book received another new publisher and cover design in 1899.
> 590 pages, HB, $100.00
> The 1899 edition was reprinted in every year from 1900 through
> 1907 (at least), with a photo being added of Edith Carew Roosevelt
> after her husband, Theodore, became president.

White House Cook Book (The) –
1894

White House Cook Book (The) –
1902

White House Cook Book (The) –
1929

Wholesome   Baking
Powder (The)

White House Cook Book (The)
> by F. L. Gillette and Hugo Ziemann
> Published by Saalfield Publishing in 1909
> 619 pages, HB, $75.00
> The above edition was reprinted in 1911, 1912, and 1913.

White House Cook Book (The)
> by F. L. Gillette and Hugo Ziemann
> Published by Saalfield Publishing in 1914
> 619 pages, HB, $60.00

White House Cook Book (The)
> by F. L. Gillette and Hugo Ziemann
> Published by Saalfield Publishing in 1915
> With first lady photos up through Helen Axon Wilson.
> 619 pages, HB, $60.00
> The above edition was reprinted in 1916 and 1919 (at least).

White House Cook Book (The)
> by F. L. Gillette and Hugo Ziemann
> Published by Saalfield Publishing in 1920
> 609 pages, HB, $60.00
> The above edition was reprinted in 1923.

White House Cook Book (The)
> by F. L. Gillette and Hugo Ziemann
> Published by Saalfield Publishing in 1924
> Revised by Mary E. Dague with recipes "for large and small families;" contains photos up through Grace Coolidge.
> 605 pages, HB, $60.00
> The above edition was reprinted in 1925, 1926, and 1929 — each valued the same as the above. Fanny Gillette died in 1926. There is also a 1937 edition with a picture of Eleanor Roosevelt. That one contains the same recipes as the 1924 edition and appears to be the most recent edition of the original series.

> The White House Cook Book was updated and revised beginning in the 1960s and remains in print today. Some of the reprints claiming to be of the original 1887 edition are actually of the 1915 edition, and none of the modern reprints is actually of either the 1887 edition (as claimed) or even of the 1889 edition.

White Lily Flour Cook Book
> Published by J. Allen Smith & Co. in 1931
> 65 pages, PB, $30.00

White's Cook Book and Kitchen Guide for the Busy Woman
> by Mabel Claire
> Published by Greenberg Publisher in 1932
> This book also exists with other companies (instead of "White's") in the title.
> 416 pages, HB, $8.00

Wholesome Baking Powder (The)
Published by Rumford Chemical Works, c. 1907
8 pages, PB, $20.00

Why Evaporated Milk Makes Food Better
Published by the Evaporated Milk Association in 1934
48 pages, PB, $5.00

Wilcolator Cook Book (The)
by Form 118
Published by Wilcolator, c. 1920s
32 pages, PB, $12.00

Wolf & Dessauer Tried and Proved OK Recipe Book
Published by Wolf & Dessauer in 1914
447 pages, HB, $60.00

Woman's Day Collector's Cook Book
by Geraldine Rhoads
Published by Simon & Schuster in 1973
519 pages, HB w/dj, $6.00

Woman's Day Encyclopedia of Cookery, 12 vols.
Published by Woman's Day in 1966
HB, $25.00 (set)

Woman's Favorite Cook Book
by Annie R. Gregory
Published by Monarch Book Co. in 1902
575 pages, HB, $60.00

Woman's Home Companion Cook Book
Published by P. F. Collier & Son in 1942
951 pages, HB, $100.00

Woman's Home Companion Cook Book
Published by P. F. Collier & Son in 1946
951 pages, HB, $80.00

Woman's Home Companion Cook Book
Published by P. F. Collier & Son in 1947
951 pages, HB, $60.00

Woman's Home Companion Cook Book
Published by P. F. Collier & Son in 1953
987 pages, HB, $60.00
The above volume was reprinted in 1955.

Woman's World Calendar Cook Book
by Ida Bailey Allen
Published by *Woman's World Magazine* in 1922
96 pages, PB, $35.00

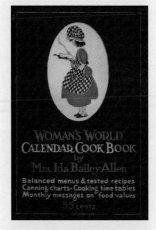

Woman's World Calendar Cook Book

Wonderful Ways With Soups

World Famous Chefs' Cook Book

World's Modern Cook Book (The)

World-Wide Cooking, M12

Young Housekeeper's Friend

Woman's World Cook Book
by Lily Haxworth Wallace
Published by Reilly & Lee in 1931
468 pages, HB, $25.00

Wonderful Ways With Soups
Published by Campbell Co. in 1958
64 pages, PB, $3.00

World Famous Chefs' Cook Book
by Ford Naylor
Published by Otto Naylor Corporation in 1941
637 pages, HB, $50.00

World's Modern Cook Book (The)
by Mabel Claire
Published by World Syndicate Publishing in 1932
416 pages, HB, $12.00

World-Wide Cooking, M12
by McCall's
Published in 1965
64 pages, PB, $3.00

Young Folks' Cook Book (The)
by Harriet and Lawrence Lustig
Published by Citadel Press in 1946
27 pages, PB w/dj, $50.00

Young Housekeeper's Friend
by Mrs. Mary Hooker Cornelius
Published by Brown, Taggard, and Chase, c. 1859
200 pages, HB, $200.00

This is the first deluxe hardback edition of Mrs. Cornelius's book, which was originally published in a less costly edition by Tappan, Whittemore & Mason in 1845.

Young Wife's Own Cook Book
by Mrs. Jane Warren
Published by Grand Union Tea Company, c. 1890
124 pages, HB, $40.00

Your Favourite Recipes
Published by Robin Hood Flour in 1960s
31 pages, PB, $3.00

Your Frigidaire Recipes
Published by Frigidaire in 1935
48 pages, PB, $8.00

Brides' Cook Book (The)
 Published by Merchants of San Francisco in 1915
 138 pages, PB, $30.00

Cook Book
 Published by Upland Woman's Club in 1933
 108 pages, PB, $25.00

Dorchester Woman's Club Cook Book
 Published by Dorchester Woman's Club in 1897
 146 pages, HB, $40.00

Elena's Favorite Foods California Style
 by Elena Zelayeta
 Published by Prentice-Hall in 1967
 310 pages, HB, $3.00

Franklin's Kitchen Secrets
 by Franklin Parents Club
 Published by Bev-Ron Publishing in 1951
 "mammy" cover
 50 pages, SPB, $12.00

Home Helps
 by Ladies Aid Society
 Published by 1st Baptist Church of Santa Ana, c. 1910
 48 pages, PB, $50.00

Look What's Cooking In and Near San Francisco
 by Katherine Kerry
 Published by James A. Pike in 1953
 136 pages, HB w/dj, $15.00

Oakland Ladies Aid Cook Book
 Published by Ladies' Aid Society in 1902
 156 pages, PB, $175.00

Ontario Cook Book
 Published by Ladies' Aid Society in 1898
 HB, $150.00

San Francisco Firehouse Favorites
 by Tony Calvello, et al.
 Published by Bonanza Books in 1965
 192 pages, HB, $12.00

Sharing Our Favorite Recipes
 Published by Richmond Ward LDS in 1959
 121 pages, SPB, $3.00

Hon-Dah a La Fiesta Cook Book

Franklin's Kitchen Secrets

Look What's Cooking In and Near San Francisco

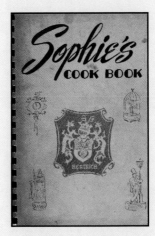

Sophie's Cook Book

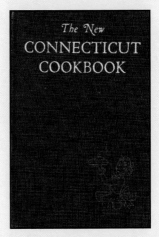

New Connecticut Cook Book (The)

Cross Creek Cookery

Sophie's Cook Book
> by Sophie Gwerder
> Published by Sophie Gwerder in 1951
> 64 pages, SPB, $5.00

Area: Colorado

Central City Celebrity Cook Book
> by Marjorie Barrett
> Published by Monitor Pubs (CO) in 1967
> 149 pages, SPB, $25.00

How We Cook in Colorado
> by Ladies of 1st Baptist Church
> Published by Denver Printing & Pub. in 1907
> 123 pages, HB, $200.00

Sigma Kappa Cook Book
> Published by Iota Chapter, Denver in 1924
> 197 pages, HB, $200.00

Three Hundred Choice Recipes
> by Ladies of 1st Baptist Church
> Published by E. L. Wepf in 1895
> 112 pages, HB, $150.00

Area: Connecticut

Granby Cook Book
> Published by Ladies' Aid Society in 1929
> 55 pages, PB, $15.00

New Connecticut Cook Book (The)
> by Women's Club of Westford
> Published by Harper & Brothers in 1947
> 338 pages, HB, $10.00

Something Special Recipes
> by St. Laurent's School Parents
> Published by St. Laurent's School Parents Guild in 1976
> 178 pages, SPB, $3.00

What's Cooking in New England?
> Published by University of CT in 1959
> 19 pages, PB, $5.00

Area: Florida

Additions School Volunteers CB
> by Gene Burns
> Published by Orange County in 1977
> 96 pages, SPB, $5.00

Cross Creek Cookery
by Marjorie Kinnan Rawlings
Published by Charles Scribner's Sons in 1942
230 pages, HB, $35.00

Favorite Recipes
by Alachua County Extension Homemakers
Published by Cookbook Publishers, Inc., in 1979
130 pages, SPB, $3.00

Florida Cook Book
Published by Gainesville Women's Club in 1963
168 pages, SPB, $6.00

Florida Cooking from the Halifax Area
by Woman's Society of Christian Service
Published by Bev-Ron Publishing in 1966
46 pages, SPB, $4.00

Florida Fish Recipes
Published by Florida Fisheries in 1966
16 pages, PB, $2.00

Florida Mullet Recipes
Published by Florida Dept. of Natural Resources, c. 1975
PAM, $1.00

Florida's Favorite Recipes for Citrus Fruits
Published by Agricultural Extension Service in 1954
48 pages, PB, $5.00

Florida's Favorite Seafoods
Published by Board of Conservation in 1960
PB, $3.00

Florida Tropical Cook Book
Published by 1st Presbyterian Church of Miami in 1912
224 pages, HB, $200.00

Food Favorites of St. Augustine
by Joan Adams Wickham
Published by CF Hamblen Inc. in 1988
187 pages, SPB, $3.00

Gasparilla Cookbook
Published by Junior League of Tampa in 1961
326 pages, HB w/dj, $6.00

Key West Cook Book
Published by Key West Women's Club in 1949
304 pages, SPB, $12.00

Florida Cook Book

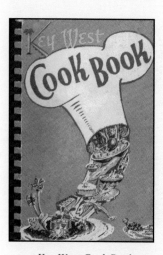

Key West Cook Book

Palm Beach Cook Book (The)

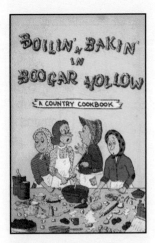

Boilin' n Bakin' in Boogar Hollow

Savannah Cook Book (The) – 1961

Hawaii's Favorite Maxi Meals for Mini Money

Let Us Break Bread Together
> by Lake Placid Woman's Club
> Published by Circulation Service in 1978
> 120 pages, SPB, $3.00

Louise's Florida Cook Book
> by Louise Lamme
> Published by Star Press in 1968
> 47 pages, PB, $3.00

Mormon Recipes from Florida
> Published by Ferris Printing in 1968
> 208 pages, SPB, $6.00

Palm Beach Cook Book (The)
> Published by The Garden Club of Palm Beach in 1968
> 62 pages, SPB, $5.00

Area: Georgia

Boilin' n Bakin' in Boogar Hollow
> by Nick Powers
> Published by Country Originals in 1971
> 40 pages, PB, $3.00

Cook Book
> Published by DAR of West Point in 1926
> 22 pages, PB, $30.00

Nora Mill Granary Cookbook 2
> by Janet M. Fain
> Published by Balok Printing, c. 1980s
> 69 pages, SPB, $3.00

Savannah Cook Book (The)
> by Harriet Ross Colquitt
> Published by Farrar & Rinchart in 1933
> 186 pages, HB, $35.00

Savannah Cook Book (The)
> by Harriet Ross Colquitt
> Published by Colonial Publishers in 1961
> 186 pages, SHB, $25.00

Savannah Cook Book (The)
> by Harriet Ross Colquitt
> Published by Colonial Publishers in 1963
> 186 pages, SHB, $20.00

Area: Hawaii

Hawaii's Favorite Maxi Meals for Mini Money
    by Muriel Kamada Miura
    Published by Associated Printers in 1975
    144 pages, SPB, $4.00

Hoihoi ke Aloha i kauhale
    by Barbara Brendilnger-Gray
    Published by Food Consultants of Hawaii in 1971
    28 pages, PB, $2.00

Wiki Wiki Kau Kau
    by Tutu Kay
    Published by Watkins & Sturgis in 1954
    77 pages, PB, $6.00

Wiki Wiki Kau Kau

Wiki Wiki Kau Kau (The New)
    by Tutu Kay
    Published by Mid-Pacific Press in 1964
    97 pages, SPB, $3.00

Area: Idaho

Good Eats
    by Idaho Rebekahs
    Published by Caxton Printers in 1929
    169 pages, HB, $25.00

Recipes from the All-American City
    Published by PEO Sisterhood, Coeur d'Alene in 1993
    118 pages, SPB, $10.00

Best Receipts

Area: Illinois

Bethany Union Cook Book
    by Woman's Society
    Published by Bethany Union Church in 1912
    225 pages, HB, $45.00

Cook Book
    Published by Woman's Missionary Society 1st Baptist Church,
        Jacksonville, in 1951
    145 pages, SPB, $12.00

Culinary Capers
    Published by Evanston Infant Welfare Juniors in 1941
    527 recipes, SPB, $6.00

Culinary Collection
    by Linda Boxer
    Published by Library Staff Assn. in 1974
    SPB, $3.00

Cook Book 1963

Good Eats

Recipes from the All-American City

Cook Book

Mary Meade Recipes...Cooky Recipes
Published by *Chicago Tribune*, c. 1950
52 pages, PB, $4.00

Area: Indiana

Augustana Eatery
by Maxiene Rogers
Published by Augustana Circle in 1986
37 pages, PB, $3.00

Wood Brook Cook Book
Published by Wood Brook Elementary PTO in 1971
204 pages, SPB, $3.00

Area: Iowa

Best Receipts
by Kate Powers
Published by Kate Powers in 1900
132 pages, PB, $50.00

Cook Book 1963
Published by School Sisters of St. Francis in 1963
195 pages, SPB, $8.00

Rockwell City Cook Book
Published in 1923
3rd Edition
132 pages, PB, $30.00

Templeton's Treasure of Personal Recipes
Published by Catholic Daughters of America in 1952
SPB, $50.00

Tested Recipes
by Ladies of Methodist Episcopal Church, Grelley
Published by Delaware County News in 1911
186 pages, HB, $40.00

Area: Kansas

Almena Plaindealer's Cook Book
Published by Almena Plaindealer in 1911
45 pages, PB, $45.00

Famous Green Parrot Recipes
by Nena May Dowd
Published by Nena May Dowd in 1964
304 pages, HB, $20.00

Fort Leavenworth Cook Book
   by Officers' Wives
   Published by American Printing in 1966
   232 pages, SPB, $6.00

Area: Kentucky

Cabbage Patch Famous Kentucky Recipes
   by the Cabbage Patch Circle
   Published by Gateway Press in 1956
   216 pages, SPB, $3.00

Favorite Recipes
   by S. S. Simon & Jude Catholic Church
   Published by Circulation Service in 1976
   126 pages, SPB, $3.00

Kentucky Cookery Book
   by Mrs. Peter A. White
   Published by Morrill, Higgins, & Co. in 1892
   315 pages, HB, $55.00

Kentucky Home Cook Book
   Published by Maysville Ladies of the Methodist Episcopal Church
      South in 1899
   HB, $300.00

Area: Louisiana

Cajun Cuisine
   Published by Bajou Publishing in 1985
   222 pages, HB, $5.00

Celebrity Cookbook
   Published by Lincoln Savings & Loan in 1967
   93 pages, PB, $10.00

Mme. Bégué's Recipes of Old New Orleans Creole Cookery
   Published by Harmanson in 1937
   64 pages, PB, $30.00

New Orleans Creole Recipes
   by Mary Moore Bremer
   Published by General Publishing in 1932
   SPB, $50.00

New Orleans Creole Recipes
   by Mary Moore Bremer
   Published by Dorothea Forshee in 1944
   90 pages, SPB, $45.00

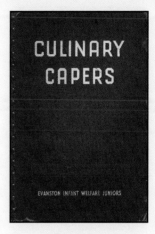

Culinary Capers

Famous Green Parrot Recipes

Fort Leavenworth Cook Book

Cabbage Patch Famous Kentucky Recipes

Favorite Recipes

*New Orleans Creole Recipes –
1957*

New Orleans Creole Recipes
> by Mary Moore Bremer
> Published by Dorothea Thompson in 1957
> 86 pages, SPB, $20.00

Recipes and Reminiscences of New Orleans, v. 2
> Published by Parents Club of Ursuline Academy in 1983
> 389 pages, SPB, $20.00

Recipes From Antoine's Kitchen
> by *This Week Magazine*
> Published in 1948
> 21 pages, PB, $6.00

Area: Maine

Cooking Down East: Favorite Maine Recipes
> by Majorie Standish
> Published by Gannett Publishing in 1969
> 256 pages, HB, $15.00

Lake Kezar Cookbook
> by Fay Burg
> Published by JAR Publishers in 1981
> 304 pages, HB w/dj, $75.00

Our Community Family Recipes
> by Orff's Corner Community Church
> Published by Fundcraft Publishing, c. 1985
> 104 pages, SPB, $3.00

Sanford Cook Book
> Published by North Congregational Ladies' Aid Society in 1904
> 227 pages, HB, $20.00

State of Maine Potato Cook Book
> Published by Maine Potato Committee in 1950s
> 30 pages, PB, $3.00

Uses & Preparation of Maine Sardines
> Published by Maine Sardine Industry in 1952
> 31 pages, PB, $3.00

Area: Maryland

Cook's Tour Of The Eastern Shore Of Maryland (A)
> by Junior Auxiliary of the Memorial Hospital
> Published by "Farrar, Straus, & Co." in 1949
> 360 pages, PB, w/dj, $20.00

Area: Massachusetts

Cooking With Faith
Published by Sen Fu Club, Boston, in 1971
112 pages, SPB, $6.00

Flavor of New England
Published by Foxboro Company in 1974
30 pages, PB, $3.00

Good Things for the Table
by Springfield's Housekeepers
Published by Clark W. Bryan Co. in 1877
39 pages, PB w/dj, $175.00

Island Cook Book
Published by Methodist Episcopal Church, Oak Bluffs, in 1924
191 pages, PB, $45.00

Road to Good Food (The)
by Franklin Co. Public Hospital
Published by New England Blue Print Paper Co. in 1936
278 pages, SPB, $15.00

Area: Michigan

Blue Book of Cooking
Published by Michigan Alumnae Club of Ann Arbor in 1938
204 pages, SHB, $6.00

Area: Minnesota

Let's Cook with Gail
by Gail Palmby
Published by the Farmer in 1954
96 pages, SPB, $6.00

Madelia Cook Book
Published by Young People's Society in 1905
127 pages, PB, $20.00

Ramsey Co. 4-H'ers Make the Best Better Recipes
Published by Ramsey Co. Extension in 1973
237 pages, SPB, $4.00

Area: Missouri

Cook Book
by Woman's Association
Published by 2nd Presbyterian Church, St. Louis, in 1927
256 pages, HB, $12.00

Cooking With Faith

Road to Good Food (The)

State of Maine Potato Cook Book

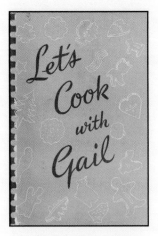

Let's Cook with Gail

Ramsey Co. 4-H'ers Make
The Best Better Recipes

Ma's Cookin' – 1969

Lucile Cook Book (The)
 by A. G. Morehouse
 Published in St. Louis, MO, or New Haven, CT, in 1892
 280 pages, HB, $150.00

Ma's Cookin'
 Published by Ozark Maid Candies in 1969
 56 pages, PB, $8.00

Ma's Cookin'
 Published by Ozark Maid Candies in 1975
 56 pages, PB, $8.00

Suburban Cookie Book
 Published by Malta Bend Union Extension Club, c. 1940
 SPB, $30.00

Area: Montana

First Ladies' Cookbook
 by Mrs. Tim Babcock
 Published by Montana Territorial Centennial Commission in 1963
 286 pages, SPB, $5.00

Area: Nebraska

Choice Recipes
 by Ladies of the Congregational Church
 Published by Cong. Church, Red Cloud, c. 1880
 15 pages, HB, $150.00

Dodge County Cook Book
 Published by Extension Club in 1949
 175 pages, PB, $40.00

Favorite Recipes of the Nebraska Czechs
 Published by Nebraska Czechs of Wilber in 1976
 224 pages, SPB, $6.00

Area: Nevada

Country Cookin'
 by Future Homemakers of Lund
 Published by Walter's Publishing in 1985
 143 pages, SPB, $1.00

Great Basin College Cook Book
 Published by Fundcraft Publishing in 1997
 Contains several recipes by the author of this book.
 225 pages, SPB, $5.00

Kit Carson's "Chuck Wagon"
    by the Carson-Tahoe Hospital Woman's Auxiliary
    Published by Cookbook Publishers, Inc. in 1976
    183 pages, SPB, $3.00

Nevada Cook Book
    by Woman's Art & Industrial Association
    Published by Appeal Steam Print in 1887
    168 pages, PB, $150.00

Tested Recipes
    Published by Ely LDS Relief Society in 1937
    109 pages, SPB, $20.00

Treasure of Personal Recipes
    Published by Our Lady of the Snows Inst. in 1952
    SPB, $3.00

Area: New Hampshire

Whitefield Bicentennial Cook Book
    Published by Whitefield, NH in 1974
    SPB, $20.00

Area: New Jersey

Favorite Recipes
    Published by Members & Friends of Montclair in 1974
    SPB, $15.00

Palisades Cook Book (The)
    Published by Tenafly Pres. Church in 1910
    265 pages, HB, $60.00

Pequannock Township Sampler
    Published by Arts and Crafts Committee in 1976
    150 pages, SHB, $45.00

Gun Club Cook Book (The)
    by Charles Browne
    Published by Princeton Gun Club in 1931
    HB, $45.00

Area: New Mexico

Rex's Rancid Recipes
    by Rex Munger
    Published by Radio Station KOB, c. 1960s
    91 pages, SPB, $5.00

First Ladies' Cookbook

Favorite Recipes of the Nebraska Czechs

Rex's Rancid Recipes

 105

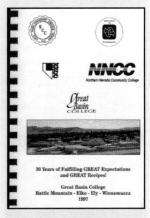

Great Basin College Cook Book

Kit Carson's "Chuck Wagon"

Tested Recipes

Area: New York

Bedford Cook Book (The)
Published by Bedford Garden Club in 1958
299 pages, SPB, $6.00

Choice Recipes
by Ladies of the Presbyterian Society
Published by Naples News Print in 1899
97 pages, PB, $15.00

New York Evening Telegram Cook Book
Published by NY Evening Telegram in 1908
254 pages, PB, $125.00

Area: North Carolina

Gate City Cook Book
Published by Greensboro Ladies' Aid Society in 1902
98 pages, PB, $20.00

Maroon and Gold Cook Book
Published by Mitchell Alumni Assn. in 1937
62 pages, PB, $60.00

Taste of the Town
Published by Charity League, Lexington, in 1977
380 pages, SPB, $20.00

Area: North Dakota

Auxillary Cook Book
Published by Rolette American Legion Auxiliary, c. 1920
86 pages, PB, $20.00

Area: Ohio

Cook Book
Published by Wilmington OH Mothers' Club in 1922
HB, $45.00

Cooking for Ohio Families
Published by Agricultural Extension Service, OSU in 1953
152 pages, PB, $6.00

Massillon Cook Book
Published by St. Timothy's Parish in 1928
216 pages, HB, $15.00

Seasoned With Love
Published by State Rd. Comm. Church of the Nazarene in 1978
102 pages, SPB, $3.00

Area: Oklahoma

Cook Book 1946
Published by West Methodist Church, Guthrie in 1946
115 pages, PB, $15.00

How We Cook in Oklahoma
Published by Clinton First Christian Church in 1909
187 pages, PB, $100.00

Yukon's Best Cook Book
Published by Yukon Mill & Grain in 1939
30 pages, PB, $25.00

Area: Oregon

Let's Eat Out
by Barbara Angell
Published by Barbara Angell in 1957
64 pages, SHB, $45.00

Oregon State Fair Cookbook
by Mary Kay Callaghan
Published by Oregon State Fair Expo Center in 1983
453 pages, SPB, $3.00

Area: Pennsylvania

Bethlehem Cook Book
Published by Ladies of Bethlehem, c. 1900
76 pages, HB, $100.00

Favorite Recipes
Published by Episcopal Church Women, c. 1970s
54 pages, PB, $1.00

Glen Rock Cook Book
by Ladies of The Friendly Helpers Bible Class
Published by Trinity Reformed Sunday School in 1934
136 pages, PB, $50.00

Pennsylvania Dutch Cooking
Published by Yorkraft in 1960
48 pages, PB, $3.00

Philadelphia Homestyle Cookbook
by Wimmer Brothers
Published by Norwood-Fontbonne Academy in 1984
286 pages, SPB, $3.00

Three Rivers Cookbook
Published by Child Health Association of Sewickley in 1973
250 pages, SPB, $3.00

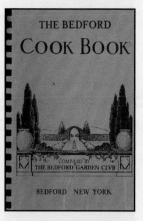
Bedford Cook Book (The)

Cooking for Ohio Families

Seasoned With Love

Cook Book 1946

Oregon State Fair Cookbook

Philadelphia Homestyle Cookbook

York Hospital Benefit Cook Book
Published by York Hospital in 1880
PB, $100.00

Area: Rhode Island

Je Me Souviens La Cuisine de La Grandmère
Published by American French Genealogical Society, c. 1950s
243 pages, SPB, $5.00

Newport Cookbook
by Ceil Dyer
Published by Weathervane Books in 1972
240 pages, HB w/dj, $5.00

Rhode Island's Hostess Cook Book
Published by RI Assn for the Blind, c. 1940
172 pages, HB, $10.00

Area: South Carolina

Beaufort Cook Book
by Dee Hryharrow & Isabel M. Hoogenboom
Published by Beaufort Book Shop in 1965
135 pages, SPB, $20.00

Charleston Receipts
Published by Junior League of Charleston in 1975
340 pages, SPB, $10.00

Potluck from Pawley's
Published by Crab Hall Publications in 1974
93 pages, SPB, $4.00

Area: South Dakota

500 Dakota Recipes
by Mrs. L. A. Cook
Published by SD Federated Women's Clubs in 1961
158 pages, SPB, $6.00

Your Neighbor Lady Book
Published by WNAX radio in 1960
67 pages, PB, $6.00

Area: Tennessee

Hillbilly Cookin' 2
by Sam M. Carson
Published by C & F Sales in 1972
63 pages, PB, $6.00

Reelfoot (Lake) Cook Book
Published by Matron's Bible Class in 1950
65 pages, PB, $25.00

Cookin' With the Wildcats
Published by Fundcraft Publishing, c. 1987
SPB, $1.00

Area: Texas

Hostess Delights
Published by Home Interiors and Gifts, Inc., in 1977
242 pages, SPB, $2.00

PTA Secrets
Published by Round Rock PTA in 1924
25 pages, PB, $50.00

Savory Sampler
Published by Ladies Auxiliary, Camp Piniel in 1978
219 pages, SPB, $3.00

Wesley Bible Class Cook Book
Published by Jasper First Methodist Church, c. 1940
32 pages, PB, $35.00

Area: Utah

DUP Cook Book
Published by Daughters of UT Pioneers in 1989
101 pages, RB, $3.00

Favorite Recipes
Published by St. Mark's Hospital Charity Association, c. 1950s
48 pages, SPB, $3.00

Home Tested Recipes
Published by Lark Ward Relief Society, c. 1940s
76 pages, SPB, $5.00

Mormon Cookin'
Published by Baxter Lane Co. in 1976
64 pages, PB, $3.00

Pioneer Cook Book (The)
by Kate B. Carter
Published by Daughters of Utah Pioneers in 1963
48 pages, PB, $6.00

Area: Vermont

Mrs. Appleyard's Family Kitchen
by Louise Andrews Kent
Published by Vermont Life and Houghton Mifflin in 1977
373 pages, HB, $5.00

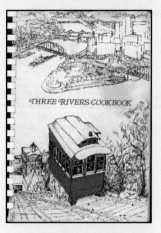

Three Rivers Cookbook

*Je Me Souviens La Cuisine
de La Grandmère*

Potluck from Pawley's

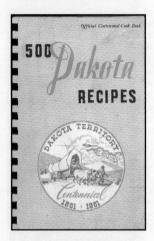

500 Dakota Recipes

Your Neighbor Lady Book

Hillbilly Cookin' 2

Out of Vermont Kitchens
> Published by St. Paul's Church in 1964
> 360 pages, SPB, $10.00

Vermont Maple Recipes
> by Mary Pearl
> Published by Lane Press in 1952
> 86 pages, SPB, $5.00

Vermont Recipes
> Published by Maltex Company in 1950s
> PAM, $1.00

Yankee Hill Country Cooking
> by Beatrice Vaughan
> Published by Stephen Greene Press in 1963
> 202 pages, HB w/dj, $6.00

Area: Virginia

Old Falls Church Cook Book
> Published by Old Falls Church in 1928
> 80 pages, PB, $30.00

Area: Washington

Best in Cooking in Renton (The)
> Published by LDS Relief Society in 1967
> 56 pages, SPB, $3.00

Washington Women's Cook Book
> Published by Washington Equal Suffrage Assn. in 1909
> 256 pages, HB, $250.00

Area: West Virginia

Booster's Guide In Cooking
> Published by Buffalo HS Booster Club in 1928
> 32 pages, PB, $6.00

Area: Wisconsin

Choice Recipes: A Collection
> Published by Williams Bay Ladies' Aid Society in 1910
> 88 pages, PB, $12.00

Federation Cook Book (The)
> Published by Whitewater Women's Club in 1940
> 260 pages, SPB, $35.00

Julia and Helen's Cook Book
> by Mrs. A. A. Washburn
> Published by Dairyman-Gazette Co. in 1935
> 175 pages, PB, $20.00

Service Club Cook Book (The)
    Published by Waukesha Service Club in 1934
    144 pages, PB, $35.00

The Waupaca Cook Book
    Published by Women's Club of Waupaca in 1910
    185 pages, PB, $30.00

Trinity XX Cookbook
    Published by Trinity Methodist Church, Milwaukee, c. 1940
    223 pages, HB, $6.00

Area: Wyoming

Cooking in Wyoming
    Published by Bighorn Book Co. in 1965
    32 pages, HB, $6.00

Area: International

101 Recipes of World-Wide Fame
    by Simon Roggo
    Published by Remington Arms Co. in 1938
    31 pages, PB, $5.00

Cheeses of the World
    by U. S. Department of Agriculture
    Published by Dover Publications in 1972
    151 pages, PB, $3.00

Cookbook of the United Nations (The)
    by Barbara Kraus
    Published by United Nations Assn. of the USA in 1965
    1st printing
    146 pages, SPB, $4.00

International Cook Book
    by Beta Sigma Phi
    Published by Walter W. Ross & Co. in 1956
    269 pages, SPB, $5.00

International Cook Book (The)
    by Margaret Heywood
    Published by Merchandisers Inc. in 1929
    2nd printing
    383 pages, HB, $15.00

Round the World Cook Book
    by Myra Waldo
    Published by Bantam, A1427, in 1956
    227 pages, PB, $3.00

Hostess Delights

Savory Sampler

Favorite Recipes

111

Home Tested Recipes

Vermont Maple Recipes

*Yankee Hill Country
Cooking*

*Best in Cooking in
Renton (The)*

Woman's Day International Collector's Cook Book
Published by Woman's Day/Fawcett in 1967
192 pages, PB, $3.00

Wonderful World of Cooking
by William Kaufmann
Published by Dell in 1967
4 vols., boxed
285 to 288 pages each, PB, $10.00

Area: Africa

West African Cook Book (A)
by Ellen Gibson Wilson
Published by M. Evans and Co in 1971
267 pages, HB w/dj, $15.00

Area: Armenia

Dinner at Omar Khayyam's
by George Mardikian
Published by Viking Press in 1944
HB w/dj, $20.00

Area: Aruba

Aruba Home Cooking
Published by Seroe Colorado Community Church in 1973
SPB, $50.00

Area: Austria

Simple Viennese Cookery
Published by Peter Pauper Press in 1960
62 pages, HB w/dj, $3.00

Viennese Cookery
by Rosl Philpot
Published by Hodder and Stoughton in 1965
246 pages, HB w/dj, $5.00

Area: Bermuda

Bermuda's Best Recipes
Published in 1939
3rd Printing
199 pages, HB, $100.00

Bermuda's Best Recipes
Published in 1948
4th Printing
230 pages, PB, $75.00

Area: Brazil

Best of Brazilian Food (The): From My Mother's Kitchen
    by Diva Oliveria da Silva
    Published in 1983
    Autographed
    105 pages, SPB, $6.00

Area: Canada

Centennial Cook-Book
    by Save the Children Fund
    Published by Tri-Graphics in 1967
    2nd printing
    180 pages, SHB, $12.00

Area: China

100 Most Honorable Chinese Recipes
    by Yu Wen Mei and Charlotte Adams
    Published by Avenel Books in 1963
    140 pages, HB w/dj, $6.00

American Oriental Foods
    by Chun King
    Published by Book Production Industries in 1961
    36 pages, PB, $1.00

Chinese Cooking
    by Irena Chalmers
    Published by Potpourri Press in 1973
    47 pages, PB, $3.00

Chinese Home Cooking
    by Julia Chih Cheng
    Published by Kodansha International in 1981
    136 pages, PB, $3.00

Chinese Village Cookbook (Cantonese)
    by Rhoda Yee
    Published by Taylor & Ng in 1975
    1st Edition
    92 pages, PB, $8.00

Chop Suey
    by Mei-Mei Ling
    Published by South Sea Sales in 1953
    34 pages, PB, $3.00

Culinary Road to China
    by Grace H. Young
    Published by Chung Tai Publishing in 1965
    149 pages, SPB, $6.00

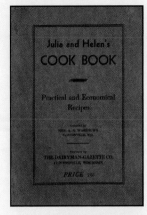

Julia and Helen's Cook Book

Booster's Guide In Cooking

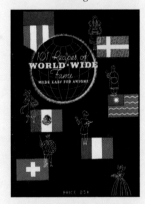

101 Recipes of World-Wide Fame

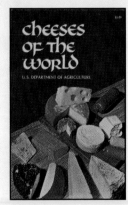

Cheeses of the World

Cookbook of the United
Nations (The)

Simple Viennese Cookery

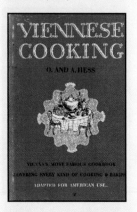

Viennese Cookery

Best of Brazilian Food (The):
From My Mother's Kitchen

Encyclopedia of Chinese Cooking (An)
    by Chang, Chang, Kutscher, K.
    Published by Crown Publishing in 1970
    234 pages, HB w/dj, $12.00

Fine Art of Chinese Cooking
    by Dr. Lee Su Jan
    Published by Gramercy Publishing in 1962
    7th printing
    78 pages, HB w/dj, $6.00

Mandarin Chop Suey Cook Book
    Published by Pacific Trading Co. in 1928
    2nd Edition
    78 pages, PB, $30.00

New Chinese Recipes
    by Fred Wing
    Published by Edemuth Co. in 1948
    7th printing
    100 pages, SPB, $3.00

Quick & Easy Chinese Cooking
    by Constance D. Chang
    Published by Shufunotomo Co. in 1969
    32 pages, SPB, $3.00

Area: Cuba

What's Really Cooking in Gitmo!
    Published by Teagle & Little, Inc. in 1964
    180 pages, SHB, $15.00

Area: Czechoslovakia

Czech National Cook Book
    by M. L. Jandacek
    Published by M. L. Jandacek in 1961
    2nd Edition
    416 pages, HB, $45.00

Area: Denmark

Danish Food Cook Book
    by Ruth L. Pedersen
    Published in 1960
    64 pages, PB, $3.00

Wonderful, Wonderful Danish Cooking
    by Ingeborg Dahl Jensen
    Published by Simon & Schuster in 1965
    335 pages, HB, $15.00

Area: Egypt

Egyptian Cook Book
Published by St. Mark's Episcopal Mission, Carmi, in 1898
186 pages, HB, $45.00

Area: France

Classic French Cuisine (The)
by Joseph Donon
Published by Alfred A. Knopf in 1959
324 pages, HB w/dj, $20.00

Cooking in a Castle
by William I. Kaufman
Published by Holt, Rinehart, and Winston in 1965
224 pages, HB w/dj, $15.00

Everyday French Cooking for the American Home
by Henri-Paul Pellaprat
Published by World Publishing in 1968
1,171 pages, HB w/dj, $6.00

French Chef Cookbook (The)
by Julia Child
Published by Alfred A. Knopf in 1968
424 pages, HB w/dj, $20.00

French Cook Book (The)
Published by Jas. Hewson Co., c. 1900
96 pages, PB, $10.00

French Pocket Cookbook (The)
by Ginette Mathiot
Published by Pocket Books in 1965
319 pages, PB, $3.00

Mastering the Art of French Cooking
by Julia Child, Louisette Bertholle, and Simone Beck
Published by Alfred A. Knopf in 1961
1st printing
HB w/dj, $30.00

Mastering the Art of French Cooking
by Child, Bertholle, and Beck
Published by Alfred A. Knopf in 1966
13th printing
HB w/dj, $12.00

Mastering the Art of French Cooking, volume 2
by Julia Child and Simone Beck
Published by Alfred A. Knopf in 1970
622 pages, HB w/dj, $15.00

Centennial Cook-Book

Culinary Road to China

Mandarin Chop Suey Cook Book

What's Really Cooking in Gitmo!

Danish Food Cook Book

Wonderful, Wonderful Danish Cooking

Classic French Cuisine (The)

Cooking in a Castle

Simple French Cookery
　　by Edna Beilenson
　　Published by Peter Pauper Press in 1958
　　60 pages, HB w/dj, $5.00

Area: Germany

German Cook Book (The)
　　by Mimi Sheraton
　　Published in 1965
　　HB w/dj, $15.00

Area: Greece

Complete Greek Cook Book (The)
　　by Theresa Karas Yianilos
　　Published by Funk and Wagnalls in 1970
　　254 pages, HB, $6.00

Home Book of Greek Cookery
　　by Joyce M. Stubbs
　　Published by Faber and Faber in 1963
　　159 pages, PB, $5.00

Area: Guam

LePBlon Fina'Tinas Para Guam (Guam Cookbook)
　　by Y Inetnon Famalaon
　　Published in 1974
　　54 pages, PB, $25.00

Area: Guatemala

False Tongues and Sunday Bread
　　by Guatemalan & Mayan
　　Published by M. Evans & Co. in 1985
　　408 pages, HB w/dj, $30.00

Area: Hungary

Cuisine of Hungary (The)
　　by George Lang
　　Published by Bonanza Books in 1971
　　495 pages, HB w/dj, $6.00

Rare Hungarian Cookery (The)
　　by Filomena Bunevacz
　　Published by Bun Publishing in 1972
　　RB, $6.00

Area: Iran

In a Persian Kitchen
　　by Maideh Mazda
　　Published by Charles E. Tuttle Co. in 1960
　　175 pages, HB w/dj, $12.00

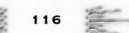

Area: Iraq

Recipes from Baghdad
> by May Beattie; Indian Red Cross
> Published by Govt. Press, Baghdad, in 1946
> HB w/dj, $75.00

Area: Israel

Israeli Cook Book
> by Molly Lyons Bar-David
> Published by Crown Publishers in 1964
> 422 pages, HB, $6.00

Area: Italy

Art of Italian Cooking
> by Maria LoPinto
> Published by Doubleday in 1955
> 222 pages, HB, $20.00

Cooking From an Italian Garden
> by Paola Scaravelli
> Published by Harcourt, Brace, Jovanovich in 1984
> small edition
> 354 pages, PB, $6.00

Cook's Tour of Rome (A)
> by Doris Muscatine
> Published by Scribner's in 1964
> 369 pages, HB w/dj, $6.00

Ferrara's Little Italian Cook Book
> by Alfred Lepore
> Published by Berkeley Medallion in 1968
> 159 pages, PB, $3.00

Instant Italian Cuisine
> by Esther Riva Solomon
> Published by Pocket Books in 1969
> 255 pages, PB, $3.00

Italian Cook Book (The)
> by Maria Luisa Taglienti
> Published by Random House in 1955
> 309 pages, HB w/dj, $6.00

Italian Cook Book
> by Maria Gentile
> Published by Italian Book Co. in 1919
> 160 pages, HB w/dj, $25.00

French Pocket Cookbook (The)

Mastering the Art of French Cooking – 1961

German Cook Book (The)

Complete Greek Cook Book (The)

 117

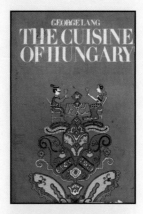

Cuisine of Hungary (The)

Rare Hungarian
Cookery (The)

Italian Cook Book (The)

Talisman Italian Cook
Book (The)

Italian Recipes, Vol. II
    by Ruth Conrad Bateman
    Published by Phillip Weil in 1966
    38 pages, PB, $3.00

Leone's Italian Cook Book
    by Gene Leone
    Published by Harper and Row in 1967
    244 pages, HB w/dj, $15.00

Southern Italian Cookbook (The)
    by Colette Black
    Published by Collier in 1967
    188 pages, PB, $5.00

Talisman Italian Cook Book (The)
    by Ada Boni
    Published by Crown Publishers in 1970
    268 pages, HB, $6.00

Your Amaretto di Saronno Gourmet Secrets
    Published by Amaretto di Saronno in 1978
    24 pages, PB, $1.00

Area: Japan

Cooking of Japan
    by Rafael Steinberg
    Published by Time-Life in 1969
    208 pages, HB, $3.00

Tempura and Sukiyaki
    by Japanese Cooking Companions
    Published by Japan Publications Trading Co. in 1969
    10th printing
    56 pages, PB, $6.00

Area: Korea

Korean Recipes
    by Harriett Morris
    Published in 1945
    96 pages, SPB, $40.00

Area: Lebanon

Lebanese Cook Book
    by Dawn Anthony
    Published by Chartwell Books in 1978
    109 pages, HB, $12.00

Area: Mexico

Favorite Mexican Cookin'
    Published by Baxter Lane Co. in 1972
    64 pages, PB, $3.00

Mexican Cooking
    by Irena Chalmers
    Published by Potpourri Press in 1977
    47 pages, PB, $3.00

Mexican Cooking
    by Isabella Lopez
    Published by K-Mart in 1981
    64 pages, SHB, $12.00

Mexico Through My Kitchen Window
    by Maria de Carbia & Imelda Calderon
    Published by Maria de Carbia in 1938
    215 pages, HB, $25.00

Southwest Cookery
    by Richard Wormser
    Published by Doubleday in 1969
    176 pages, HB w/dj, $6.00

Area: North America

North American Cook Book
    by Nellie Lyle Pattinson
    Published by Ladies Home Journal Book Club in 1954
    529 pages, HB, $6.00

Area: Orient

Pearl S. Buck's Oriental Cookbook
    by Pearl S. Buck
    Published by Simon & Schuster in 1972
    256 pages, HB w/dj, $6.00

Recipes From the East
    by Irma Walker Ross
    Published by Charles E. Tuttle Co. in 1955
    90 pages, SPB, $12.00

Area: Philippines

Philippine Cookbook (The)
    by Reynaldo Alejandro
    Published by Perigee in 1985
    256 pages, PB, $10.00

Recipes of the Philippines
    by Enriqueta David-Perez
    Published by Facilities Printing in 1972
    170 pages, PB, $12.00

Tempura and Sukiyaki

Lebanese Cookbook

Favorite   Mexican Cookin'

Mexican Cooking – 1981

Recipes From the East

Taste of Portugal (A)

Eating the Russian Way

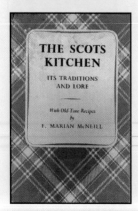

Scots Kitchen (The)

Area: Poland

Polish Cookery
   by Marja Ochorowicz-Monatowa
   Published by Crown Publishers in 1958
   314 pages, HB, $25.00

Area: Portugal

Taste of Portugal (A)
   by Shirley Sarvis
   Published by Scribner's in 1967
   1st printing
   192 pages, HB w/dj, $8.00

Portuguese Food
   by Carol Wright
   Published by JM Dent & Sons in 1969
   214 pages, HB, $6.00

Area: Puerto Rico

Puerto Rican Cook Book
   by Eliza B. K. Doolie
   Published by Dietz Press in 1950
   175 pages, HB, $25.00

Area: Romania

Romanian Cook Book (The)
   by Anisoara Stan
   Published by Carol Publishing Group in 1969
   229 pages, PB, $25.00

Area: Russia

Cooking the Russian Way
   by Musia Soper
   Published in 1961
   242 pages, HB, $15.00

Dining and Wining in Old Russia
   by Nina Nikolaevna Selivanova
   Published in 1933
   154 pages, HB, $75.00

Eating the Russian Way
   by Beryl Gould-Marks
   Published by Holt, Rinehart & Winston in 1964
   128 pages, HB w/dj, $6.00

Area: Scotland

Scots Kitchen (The)
  by F. Marian McNeill
  Published by Blackie in 1959
  259 pages, PB, $6.00

Area: Spain

Spanish Cookbook
  by Barbara Norman
  Published by Bantam in 1967
  197 pages, PB, $3.00

Area: Sweden

Swedish Recipes Old and New
  Published by American Daughters of Sweden, c. 1950
  180 pages, SPB, $15.00

Area: Syria

Art of Syrian Cookery (The)
  by Helen Corey
  Published by Doubleday in 1964
  186 pages, HB w/dj, $15.00

Area: Thailand

Everyday Siamese Dishes
  by Sibhan Sonakul
  Published by Prachandra Press in 1963
  3rd printing, 2,000 copies
  81 pages, PB, $15.00

Area: Turkey

Famous Turkish Cookery (The)
  by Edith E. Sencil
  Published by Galeri Minyatür in the 1960s
  160 pages, PB, $15.00

Area: U. S. Virgin Islands

Good Hope School Mixing Spoon II (The)
  Published by Good Hope School in 1984
  232 pages, SPB, $3.00

Art of Syrian Cookery (The)

Everyday Siamese Dishes

Famous Turkish Cookery (The)

Good Hope School Mixing Spoon II (The)

The Delineator magazine from 1878

1901 *Souvenir of The Butterick Exhibit from Pan-American Exposition*

Last Butterick issue of *Delineator* – 1937

The cookbooks listed in this section were made by the Culinary Arts Institute or related companies. The CAI of Chicago was one of the largest producers of cookbooks in the United States, beginning humbly with Leonard Davidow's Culinary Arts Press. Since Davidow purchased the right to issue material previously published by Butterick Publishing (and the Delineator Institute), books by Butterick/ Delineator are also listed in this section.

Cookbooks, booklets, and pamphlets listed in this section and in those that follow will be listed in a narrative format that follows chronologically. Certain abbreviations will occasionally appear:

HB — hardback — stiff covers, pages usually bound via stitching

SHB — spiral hardback — stiff covers, pages bound with a metal spiral or plastic comb

PB — paperback — soft covers, pages bound by stitching or stapling

SPB — spiral paperback — soft covers, pages bound with a metal spiral or plastic comb

RB — ring binder

WB — wood back — a paperback book housed in an additional cover of real or simulated wood

PAM — pamphlet — a single sheet, which may be folded; no staples

The Scarcity Index, referred to in the listings by the initials SI, is described in more detail in the introduction (see page 7).

The value given is for a copy in Near Mint condition. For values in lower grades, consult the section in this book on grading (see page 6).

The four divisions comprising this section cover material as follows:
Butterick-Delineator cookbooks, 1890 – 1937
Culinary Arts Press cookbooks, 1934 – 1939
Culinary Arts Institute cookbooks, 1940 – 1949
Culinary Arts Institute cookbooks, 1950 – 1980s

This chapter proposes to begin the history of the Culinary Arts Institute, based in Chicago, which has published many useful cookbooks throughout the years and which at one time was the leading publisher of cooking literature. The CAI story really begins with Butterick Publishing, for before Leonard S. Davidow published his first cookbook, the *Pennsylvania Dutch Cook Book*, in 1934, there were several influential books which came to be used by CAP/CAI as the company expanded. Therefore, we must begin in the middle of the nineteenth century.

The Butterick (Publishing) Company opened in New York in 1864 after Ellen Butterick suggested the invention of the sewing pattern (in Spring 1963) to her husband Ebenezer, who began marketing them publicly in 1866. Butterick quickly became the leading marketing agent for items directed towards women. To this day, the name Butterick is still associated with sewing patterns. *The Delineator*, begun in 1873, was originally a fashion magazine intended to market these patterns. It was not Butterick's first magazine, for "in 1868, the *Metropolitan Monthly* was issued. And, in 1875, the *Quarterly and Monthly* were merged and became Delineator." (Delineator, 9/36, p. 66) The company continued to expand after Ebenezer Butterick's death on March 31, 1903. Famous author Theodore Dreiser was an editor for *The Delineator* in 1907. Recipes began to appear, and a desire arose for Butterick to publish a cookbook, or two, or three. *The Pattern Cook Book*, published in 1890, appears to have been Butterick's first attempt at producing a hardback book directed at the cooking public. The grand success of their sewing patterns is reflected in the title. No editor or individual author is listed. This 624-page book is most difficult to locate. It was part of the *Metropolitan Culture Series*, which included books on manners, social life, housekeeping, beauty, and "physical culture." Each of the books cost one dollar originally.
SI = 8, $100.00

Soon after, Butterick issued the 72-page paperback book, *The Perfect Art of Canning and Preserving*. The book was part of the *Metropolitan Pamphlet Series*, which was issued quarterly.
SI = 7, $100.00+

In 1892, Butterick published the 76-page softbound book, *The Correct Art of Candy Making (at Home)*. Not only does the book describe how to make many different kinds of candy, but also a number of different candy containers are depicted. This, too, was part of the *Metropolitan Pamphlet Series*, which was issued quarterly. The cover states that the volume came out in March 1892; copies from 1894 display the copyright as being from 1894. Every book in the series cost 15 cents, including those that did not deal with cooking. The booklet was reissued in 1902 with a different cover.

1892 – 1894 edition: SI = 8, $100.00+

Pattern Cook Book (The)

Correct Art of Candy Making at Home (The)

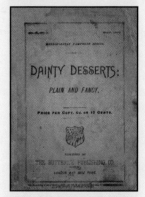

Dainty Desserts

Extracts and Beverages

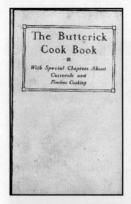

Butterick Cook Book (The)

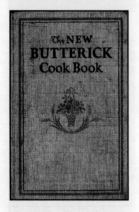

*Butterick Cook Book
(The New)*

*Butterick Book of
Recipes and Household
Helps (The)*

Cooking for Two

1899 edition: SI = 7, $60.00
1902 edition: $40.00

In mid-1892, another book in the series, *Dainty Desserts*, came out. This one deals with puddings, custards, pies, creams, frozen desserts, and much more. Original cost: 15¢.
SI = 8, $100.00+

Yet another book in the series, from September of 1892, was called *Extracts and Beverages*. The 36-page booklet indicates how to prepare syrups, beverages, and "various toilette accessories" to boot.
SI = 8, $100.00+

Volume V, No. 1 and Volume VI, No. 2 of the *Metropolitan Handy Series* were Butterick's *Correct Cookery*, issued first in March of 1899 and again in May of 1900. *Correct Cookery* contains material from the *Pattern Cook Book*. It would be improper, though, to call this a revision of the *Pattern Cook Book*, since so much material is new or different. More correctly we say that the *Pattern Cook Book* was a source for this 204-page book. Original cost: 25¢. Drawing of a chef on the front cover.
SI = 7, $100.00+

1911:

The original *Butterick Cook Book*, edited by Helena Judson, does not appear similar to the Culinary Arts Press material. However, its subsequent edition, *The New Butterick Cook Book*, originally printed in 1924, contained much the same format as the Culinary Arts Institute collection that would be taken from it. The revision was undertaken by Flora Rose and Martha Van Rensselaer, chairs of the Cornell University school of home economics, with the assistance of 13 members of the department. Cornell's home economics school had developed largely under the tutelage of Van Rensselaer and Rose, who headed the project together for 25 years. By 1920, the school of home economics was ready to become the first college of home economics in the New York system, but there were significant obstacles in the state legislature. An alliance between Cornell and Butterick/Delineator proved to be most beneficial for both parties. Van Rensselaer also became the home-making editor of *The Delineator* magazine, and in 1923, the National League of Women Voters selected her as one of the 12 most distinguished women in the United States. Butterick's 1925 publication *The Story of a Pantry Shelf* reports that over 60 colleges adopted the *1924 New Butterick Cook Book* as a textbook for home economics. Van Rensselaer died in 1932; Cornell University has a building named on her behalf, a structure that was in the process of construction at the time of her death. Flora Rose retired in 1940.

1911 edition, SI = 6, $30.00
1924 edition, SI = 4, $25.00 (+$10.00 for dj)

1927:

The Butterick Book of Recipes and Household Helps (1927, 255 pages) is not mentioned in any CAP/CAI publication as having any bearing on their literature, but much of its material appears in the *Delineator Cook Book*, first published the following year, a book which is mentioned by way of copyright information in the *American Woman's Cook Book*. SI = 4, $30.00

1927 on:

Throughout this period, the Delineator Institute was publishing original cookbooklets. These cost 10¢ – 25¢ each and were available directly from the Delineator Home Institute, where Elizabeth Bennett was service director. At least through 1927, these booklets were tested at the home economics department of Cornell University. Every one of the booklets now appears to be scarce. The Delineator booklets were collected into the various hardback books and were eventually copied (virtually verbatim) into CAI's *American Woman's Cook Book*.

Delineator Service Booklets known to relate to cooking include:

\# 5. *Dieting to Gain or Lose*
#11. *Cooking for Two*
#13. *Holiday Menus and Recipes*
#14. *Cooking for Crowds*
#15. *Food Values and Calories* or *What to Eat*
#16. *The Complete Canner*
#23. *Birthday Parties*
#24. *Bride's Recipe Shower*
#25. *Three Parties*
#26. *Party Sandwiches*
#33. *Refrigerators*
#35. *Picnics and Porch Meals*
#40. *Modern Cooking by Temperature*
#41. *Salads for All Occasions*
#43. *Beverages for Parties*
#47. *How to Give a Bridge Party*
#48. *Yearbook of Delineator Recipes*
#49. *Second Yearbook Delineator Recipes*
#50. *Third Year Book Delineator Recipes*
#59. *37 Ways to Cook Chicken*
#60. *How to Entertain Six and Eight*
#63. *Hors D'Oeuvres and Canapes*
#64. *Afternoon Tea*
#75. *Fourth Year Book Delineator Recipes*
#76. *Fifth Year Book Delineator Recipes*

Many of the booklets cost 10¢ each, but numbers 5, 11, 16, 23, 25, and 48 were larger, each costing 25¢. Item #14 cost 20¢ originally. Prices changed as time passed, however. A box that contained ten booklets was sold for 25¢; these boxes are scarce today.

Each of the booklets has a Scarcity Index of 5 – 8, $12.00 each.

The Complete Canner

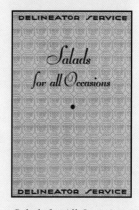

Party Sandwiches

Salads for All Occasions

Beverages for Parties

How to Give a Bridge Party

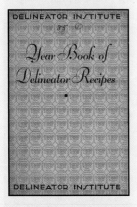

Year Book of Delineator Recipes

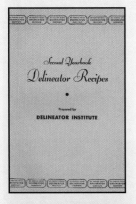

Second Yearbook Delineator Recipes

Third Year Book Delineator Recipes

1928:

In the Service Booklet numbering system, which is found in the Delineator and which does not appear to be chronological, the *Delineator Cook Book* is numbered 34.

The original edition of *The Delineator Cook Book* dates to 1928. It was reprinted in 1934. Officially, it is a revision of the *New Butterick Cook Book*, having been revised under the direction of Mildred Maddocks Bentley, the director of the Delineator Institute. It has 788 pages. The 1934 edition, apparently the most recent, was also a source for the CAI material. In fact, the *American Woman's Cook Book* (1939) states "from the *Delineator Cook Book*" and "edited by the Delineator Institute" on the interior copyright page. Original price: $2.65; (later) discounted price, $2.50.

1928 edition, SI = 4, $25.00
1934 edition, SI = 6, $30.00

1929:

The Delineator Cook Book was supplemented the following year.

The 1929 (222 pages) edition of *New Delineator Recipes* exists in four different cover configurations: red print; light green print; dark green print; or black print. Regardless of the colors, the first printings seem to be the copies with fancy scrolling around the titles on the title pages. Information on the cover of the 1930 edition shows that it "includes ten recipes by Ann Batchelder" (224 pages).
Copies in lower grades are generally not collected.

1929 edition (any color scheme), SI = 3, $12.00
1929 edition ("salesman's sample" copy), SI = 9, $40.00
1930 edition (green cover), SI = 2, $10.00

1932:

The ten Batchelder recipes and other material were collected into *Cookery For Today*, a 164-page, hardback volume. This was published by the Delineator Institute, Butterick Publishing Co. The book was bound in purple cloth with nice decorative graphics on the front board. SI = 4, $25.00

From 1930 through at least 1934, Ann Batchelder developed recipes for the Delineator that were published in the magazine.

Batchelder's other publications, not through Butterick, include:

Ann Batchelder's Own Cookbook, published by Barrows originally in 1941, apparently reissued as *Ann Batchelder's Cookbook* in 1957, also by M. Barrows & Company.

Batchelder was the one-time food editor of the *Ladies' Home Journal*, and so, with the Delineator association, her name was somewhat important.

Also supplementing the *Delineator Cook Book*, notice the five "Yearbooks" listed as part of the service booklet series. These were: *Year Book of Delineator Recipes* (11/29, later "First Yearbook"; 56 pages); Second Yearbook (11/30; 48 pages), Third Year Book (11/31; 48 pages), Fourth Year Book (2/33; 48 pages), and Fifth Year Book (2/34; 40 pages). The timing of the booklets marked the years following the release of the *Delineator Cook Book* in 1928. From 1930 on, they consisted of the recipes developed that year for Delineator by Ann Batchelder. Since these booklets occupy a special place as supplements to the hardback book which became the basis for a major CAI publication, it is worthwhile to mention them separately. Each of the five booklets seldom comes up; therefore, they are more difficult to evaluate. Three printings are known for the first Yearbook, while two printings are known for the second.

Elizabeth Bennett left Delineator in the spring of 1930. She was soon replaced as service editor by Dorothy Higgins, who held the post at least into 1933.

As the Great Depression continued its extended run, Butterick Publishing began to devote much less time to its flagship magazine, *Delineator*, instead focusing on clothing patterns — Butterick's mainstay. The *Delineator* merged with *Pictorial Review* in May of 1937, meaning that Butterick was no longer publishing one of their flagship magazines. While the last Butterick issue of the magazine contains no indicators of change, the first combined issue contains statements by the editors of *Pictorial Review* and by Butterick announcing the change. The editors stated, "With this May 1937 issue *Pictorial Review* adds to its own distinguished name the name of the longest-lived among all women's publications in America: *Delineator*." For their part, Butterick's full-page ad indicates the reason why they sold not only the magazine but probably the service booklets as well: "The Butterick Company ... will concentrate upon the further expansion of its pattern business." The Delineator materials were then sold to a growing cookbook publisher: Culinary Arts Press.

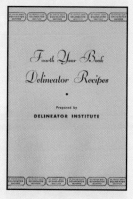

Fourth Year Book Delineator Recipes

Fifth Year Book Delineator Recipes

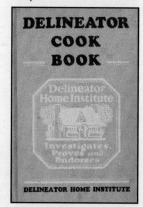

Delineator Cook Book – 1928

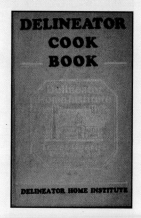

Delineator Cook Book – 1934

*New Delineator Recipes –
1929 A*

*New Delineator Recipes –
1929 B*

*New Delineator Recipes –
1929 C*

*New Delineator Recipes –
1929 D*

Checklist

Title	Edition	Value in Mint Condition
Butterick Book of Recipes and Household Helps	1927	$30.00
The Butterick Cook Book	1911	$30.00
Butterick's Correct Cookery	1899 – 1900	$100.00
Cookery for Today	1932	$25.00
Correct Art of Candy Making	1892 – 1894	$100.00
Correct Art of Candy Making	1899	$60.00
Correct Art of Candy Making	1902	$40.00
Dainty Desserts	1892	$100.00
Delineator Cook Book	1928	$25.00
Delineator Cook Book	1934	$30.00
Extracts and Beverages	1892	$100.00
New Butterick Cook Book (w/dj)	1924	$25.00 $35.00
New Delineator Recipes (salesman's sample)	1929	$40.00
New Delineator Recipes	1929	$12.00
New Delineator Recipes	1930	$10.00
The Pattern Cook Book	1890	$10.00
Perfect Art of Canning & Preserving	1892	$50.00
Typical Delineator Service booklet	1927 – 1934	$12.00

Leonard S. Davidow was an enterprising man who worked for the Cuneo Press. His office operated out of Reading, Pennsylvania, in the 1930s. Not coincidentally, Cuneo had been contracted to publish several books on behalf of the Delineator Institute. As the Great Depression rolled on, Davidow conceived of an idea for publishing quality cook booklets at the reasonably low price of 15¢ each. All of this, and the genesis of one of the most important cookbook publishers, Culinary Arts Press, began with a single book, privately issued, in 1934.

Pennsylvania Dutch Cook Book – 1934

1934:

The first printing of the *Pennsylvania Dutch Cook Book* was privately published by Leonard S. Davidow: a humble beginning. The true first edition is distinguishable only by its dust jacket, since copies printed in 1935 have the same contents but different dust jackets; all of them claim to be from 1934. The dust jacket for the first printing does not mention Culinary Arts Press, indicating only to send to Davidow's address in Reading for more copies of the cookbook. Some copies have "15¢" added to the front cover. From this meager beginning quickly sprang the fastest-growing publishing company associated with cookery. The name "Culinary Arts Press" was soon chosen, and the first work published under that name (then in Reading, Pennsylvania) was an issue of the *Pennsylvania Dutch Cook Book.*

There is one major problem with many CAP/CAI publications: the publication date listed inside sometimes has no bearing on the actual date of printing. I will describe the early copies in detail. As I mentioned, the first printing dust jacket mentions only the *Pennsylvania Dutch Cookbook* (see photo). The information in the book itself says (c) 1934 Leonard S. Davidow. The address is given as 14 No. 6th Street in Reading, PA (an address they stopped using in 1936), but the address in the dust jacket is shown as Post Office Box 250 in Reading.

Pennsylvania Dutch Cook Book – 1940s

The second printing, from 1935, has the same contents, but the dust jacket mentions ordering this book and the *Southern Cook Book* from Culinary Arts Press. The address in the dust jacket is the same as in the first edition. On the back flap of the dust jacket there is an order form for prints of the "Dutch Schnitzelbank Song" — the prints came in two sizes and could be ordered from Culinary Arts Press.

The following printings of the *Pennsylvania Dutch Cook Book* have been observed:

First printing, SI = 7, $40.00+, w/dj

Second printing, same contents and similar dust jacket, but dust jacket lists later book (1935).
SI = 6, $35.00

Pennsylvania Dutch Cook Book – 1937

Southern Cook Book – 1935

Southern Cook Book – 1936

Southern Cook Book – 1937

Third printing, CAP logo and 15¢ price added in black; girl's dress in red, and "Cook Book" appears below girl — as in earlier printings (1935 – 1936).
SI = 5, $35.00

Fourth printing, 15¢ price in black; "COOK BOOK" appears above girl; girl's dress is green (1936).
SI = 5, $35.00

Fifth printing, oval cover with 15¢ price on dust jacket (1937).
SI = 4, $30.00

Other 1937 printing with map of Pennsylvania, SI = 7, $30.00

Common "oval" printing, SI = 2, $5.00 – 10.00

There are many later copies of this book with different covers. The ones actually dating to the 1930s originally had dust jackets. The most common of the reissues of this booklet have dates like "1936" inside and feature a single-colored background with the central figure in a large oval on the front cover. These copies were actually issued throughout the 1940s, as evidenced by their listing the later CAI booklets on the back cover. With Claire Davidow's name instead of Leonard's, the book was in print at least as late as the mid-1970s. Later printings have little collector value but contain some good recipes!

1935:

With 1935, CAP began publishing cookbooks in earnest, eventually releasing them bi-monthly. The second booklet published by CAP was the *Southern Cook Book* from 1935. Also known as *Fine Old Dixie Recipes*, the booklet was compiled and edited by Lillie S. Lusting, S. Claire Sondheim, and Sarah Renset — with decorations by H. Charles Kellum.

The true first printing was available only for a short time in 1935. Shown on the previous page is the dust jacket depicting a family; the cover itself has the same picture. The price inside is 15¢, and the only books shown as available are this book and the *Pennsylvania Dutch Cook Book*. The address shown inside is POB 250 in Reading.

The second printing features an entirely different cover and a 15¢ price. This reissue was part of the bi-monthly series and was probably issued in May – June 1936, even though the copyright still says "1935." The stereotyped black family has been replaced by a white woman serving a turkey.

Later, the "mammy" returns with a mixing bowl. In the 1940s, a mammy appears on the cover in an oval surrounded by a tan background. Like the *Pennsylvania Dutch Cook Book*, these reissues are dated much earlier inside than their actual dates of publication.

First printing, SI = 5, $35.00 – 40.00

Second printing, white woman, banner at top, c. 1936
SI = 5, $35.00

Third printing, white woman, price in black, c. 1936
SI = 5, $25.00

Common "oval" printing with 15¢ price on front cover,
c. 1937 – 1938
SI = 3, $15.00 – 20.00

Common "oval" printing with 25¢ price on front cover, c. 1939
SI = 3, $15.00

More common 1940s "oval" printing without 15¢ price
SI = 2, $10.00

Other later printings, $5.00 each

Due to the collectible nature of African-American memorabilia, prices vary widely on all editions of this book.

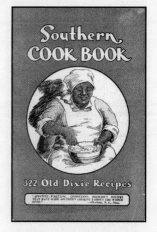

Southern Cook Book –
1940s

1936:

The *Chinese Cookbook*, by M. Sing Au, was the third in the Culinary Arts Press series of books. I have seen a copy like mine where a Chinese "cash" coin was tied to the hole in the top of the Cookbook by a silken ribbon. The first edition is uncommon. Mr. Au's written introduction dates January 1936, and the booklet does not bear a 15¢ price tag on the cover, so this first edition came out before the booklets, which collectively, were considered to be a series. At any rate, Warren G. Troutman provided the illustrations, and the address listed inside is POB 915 in Reading, PA.

The second printing, also from 1936, has a black and red dust jacket. At that time, the book became part of the growing series of CAP books. The 15¢ tag was removed c. 1940. The book continued to be reissued and was more popular in reissue than its 1930s printings.

First printing, yellow cover
SI = 5, $35.00

Second printing, 15¢, red and black colors on brown paper dust jacket, 1936
SI = 5, $30.00

Third printing, 15¢, blue cover, dust jacket, c. 1937
SI = 3, $20.00 – 25.00

Fourth printing, blue cover, no 15¢ price on front cover, 1940s
SI = 3, $15.00 – 20.00

Later printings, SI = 2, $5.00 each (but good recipes)

Southern Cook Book – 1960s

Chinese Cookbook – 1936

Chinese Cookbook (The) –
1937

New England Cook Book –
1936

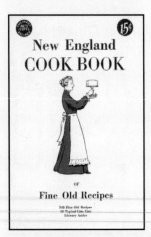

New England Cook Book –
1937

By the middle of 1936, CAP was really "cooking" (pun intended). Their fourth book, the *New England Cook Book* may have been published first in July – August 1936 as part of the series. Also called *Fine Old Yankee Recipes*, the book was edited by Kay Morrow, assisted by Pauline Dubin, with decorations by Florence Bowe and others. This one is also subtitled *Characteristic Dishes and a Salty Charm*.

Like its predecessors, this book continued to be reissued throughout the years. Another 1930s printing looks much the same but without the 15¢ price banner on the cover. The 1940s "oval cover" reissue, which is common, is usually dated 1936 inside. *The New England Cook Book* became part of a series of CAI booklets in 1954, where it remained at least through the 1960s.

First printing, 15¢ price, white cover, ribbon across top; top information in blue, 1936
SI = 6, $35.00

Second printing, 15¢ price, white cover, no ribbon; top information in black, c. 1937 – 1938
SI = 5, $35.00

"Oval" printing with 15¢ price on front cover, c. 1939 – 1940
SI = 3, $10.00

1940s "oval" printing without 15¢ price
SI = 2, $5.00

The next cookbook to be released by the growing company was the *Western Cook Book*, dated Sept. – Oct. 1936 and labeled "Vol. 1 No. 5." The original 15¢ dust jacket has a green color. The *Western Cook Book* is also called *Western Cookery* or *Tempting Western Recipes*. It was edited by Kay Morrow. Like the others in the series, the booklet has 48 pages. This publication is slightly less common than the ones that preceded it, although the demand is somewhat less.

Later copies were made without the dust jacket motif, and in 1940 the 15¢ price tag was removed. Some copies exist from 1936 with "Texas Centennial" markings; theoretically these should sell for more than normal copies.

First printing, 15¢ price, green cover + dust jacket
SI = 4, $25.00

Second printing, 15¢ price, dust jacket does not list Delineator materials inside, c. 1937 – 1938
SI = 3, $20.00

Later printings, no dust jacket , SI = 3, $5.00 – 10.00

The *'Round the World Cook Book* is very interesting as well as being hard to find. First, it is larger and therefore has a 25¢ price tag in the upper right hand corner. Like the others in the series, the '*Round the World Cook Book* was released with a dust jacket (shown). The book is dated "Nov. – Dec. 1936 Vol. 1, No. 6." It also states, "Published on the first of every second month" and lists the POB 915 address in Reading, PA. Recipes from 30 countries are included. This book does not appear to be related to Ida Bailey Allen's booklet of the same title, which had been published in 1934.

First printing, 64 pages, blue dust jacket, lists books available, $50.00

Second printing, 64 pages, blue dust jacket with blank interior, $30.00

Later printing, 48 pages, "Around the World Cook Book," $10.00

Special printing, 48 pages, Kalamazoo, MI, 50th anniversary, $20.00

All SI = 5

1937:

The Cookie Book, dated "Jan. – Feb. 1937 Vol. 2, No. 1," would become one of their most popular booklets. The cover illustration is by H. Charles Kellum, the same man who illustrated the *Southern Cook Book*. Shown is the original edition (with a 15¢ price tag), apparently available until 1940, when it became part of what I call "Series 1."

First printing, dj has boy climbing into cookie jar, $30.00

Second printing, same drawing, no dj, no 15¢ price, $20.00

Third printing, transitional, red cover, c. 1940, $15.00

After this time, the book became part of Series 1, listed below.

All SI = 3

It was in early 1937 that Davidow and company purchased the publishing rights to the Delineator cooking materials. The Great Depression may have been responsible for the changes within Butterick. At any rate, this gave Davidow the opportunity to expand.

In 1937, the first six of the Culinary Arts Press cookbooks were collected together in a box labeled *1500 Recipes From All Over the Globe*. The copies of the books were all "15 cent" cover versions, namely: the fourth or fifth (oval, 15¢) printing of the *Pennsylvania Dutch Cook Book*; the fourth printing of the *Southern Cook Book*; the third printing of the *Chinese Cook Book*; the second printing of the *New England Cook Book*; the second printing of the *Western Cook Book*; and the second printing of the *Around the World Cook Book*.

SI = Box: RARE

*New England Cook Book –
1940s*

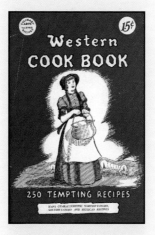

Western Cook Book

'Round the World Cook Book – 1936

Around the World Cook Book –
1951

Cookie Book (The) – 1939

Cookie Book (The) – 1937

A special promotional item was produced for Culinary Arts Press sometime during 1935 – 1936. McKee Glass was the manufacturer of this butter dish which was emblazoned with a metal promotional lid for CAP. These dishes (with the CAP advertising lid) are rare. The company slogan reads: "Attractive Ideas to Make the World a Better Place to Eat in." It is not known how many other advertising items might have been made for CAP.

SI = RARE

The Culinary Arts Press had begun as a publishing outlet for material collected by Leonard S. Davidow. By 1938, CAP was issuing eight cookbooks of its own creation, those listed on pages 129 – 133, plus the *Candy Book*.

In about April 1937, Culinary Arts Press acquired the *Delineator Cook Book* and rights to publish the material contained in the Delineator Service booklets. This quickly made CAP/CAI into one of the largest publishing services devoted to cooking.

Before leaving the Culinary Arts Press material for 1936 – 1937, we must make note of something that might be staggering to CAP/CAI collectors. 1937 copies of most CAP cookbooklets also list the following books as being available. The numbers and the prices are CAP's.

#35. *Cooking for Two* (25¢, all prices include postage)
#36. *Hors D'Oeuvres and Canapes* (25¢)
#37. *Feeding Children* (25¢)
#38. *How to Entertain Six and Eight* (25¢)
#39. *Feeding the Pre-School Child* (25¢)
#40. *Party Sandwiches* (15¢)
#41. *Picnics and Porch Meals* (15¢)
#42. *What to Eat* (20¢)
#43. *Menu Calendar* (35¢)
#44. *Cookery Book* (15¢)
#45. *Recipe Book* (15¢)
#46. *Hot Dishes to Delight Guests* (8¢)
#47. *Sandwiches for All Occasions* (8¢)
#48. *Menu Book* (15¢)
#49. *Table-Made Dishes* (8¢)
#50. *Vitamin Primer* (10¢)
#51. *Appetizing Appetizers* (8¢)
#52. *Candy Cookery* (8¢)
#53. *Sweet Suggestions* (8¢)
#54. *Bridge Luncheon Menus* (15¢)
#55. *Best Cake Recipes* (20¢)
#56. *Best Frozen Dishes* (15¢)
#57. *Cooking for the Crowd* (15¢)
#58. *Best Pickle Recipes* (15¢)
#59. *This is So Good* (15¢)
#60. *Table Settings for Every Occasion* (15¢)
#61. *How to Mix Drinks* (35¢)

To date, no copies of the books at the bottom of page 134 are known, but if they exist, they are reissues of Butterick/Delineator material, since the titles are similar or identical to certain Delineator booklets. The 8¢ books have fewer pages than their 48-page, fifteen-cent counterparts. In the listing, there are also books numbering 73 through 87 which deal with "Homemaking"; books numbering 90 to 101 dealing with "Beauty"; books about "Entertainment" numbering 110 to 149; books about "Gardening" numbering 160 through 189; books about "Sub-Deb" (debutante) numbering 200 through 226; books about "Child Training" numbering 230 through 240; books about "Fashions and Needlecraft" numbering 250 through 282; and books about "Hobbies" numbering 241 through 242 and 283 through 299. Items 300 and 301 are the "Schnitzelbank" posters (which were available in 1935 at least). Items 302 and 303 are posters of "The world's favorite drinking songs." Items 305 and 306 are "Baggage labels from hotels and steamers all over the world." Finally, items 308 through 320 are "Handsome Reproductions of Old Masters for Your Home. Printed on Heavy Paper."

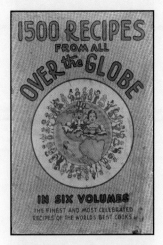

1500 Recipes From All Over the Globe

Except for the posters and labels, the booklets mentioned above were all once part of the Delineator Service series. Again, though, no copies are known to exist with Davidow/Spencer Press/CAP markings, though they were all available through CAP.

1938:

The Candy Book, 48 pages was compiled and edited by S. Claire Sondheim. This was the basis for the larger *Candy Book* that was later issued in CAI's Series 1 and Series 101. However, the first edition of *The Candy Book* does not indicate in the upper right hand corner of the front cover that it is part of a series. Later copies were numbered as part of "Series 1."

Cookie Book (The) – 1939

First printing, no number in upper right hand corner and Culinary Arts blurb at bottom)
SI = 7, $20.00

Woodbacks:

We cannot leave any discussion of the Culinary Arts Press material without talking about the "woodback" editions of their books. Many of the early CAP books (and some 1940 – 1941 CAI books) were available in woodback editions beginning c. 1939 and continuing at least through the 1960s. These feature normal copies (without prices or dust jackets) of their popular cookbooks bound to wooden or false-wood outside covers. Some of the earlier ones (c. 1939) mention that the wood binding was done by "Three Mountaineers." Again we note that all of the "oval" copies of the CAP booklets were made c. 1940 and later (at least to 1948) because they list the set of 20 CAI Series 1 booklets on the back cover. Some of them list later booklets as well. These are also the most common of the series and appear most commonly as woodbacks. However, all of these later editions have random copyright dates, as early as 1935, even though they were actually sold later.

CAP advertising lid

CAP advertising lid

 135

The Candy Book

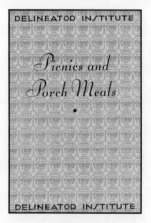

Picnics and Porch Meals

My Favorite Recipe

First printings, original contents, $30.00+ each

Later printings, $15.00 each; *Southern Cookbook* sells for $20.00.

Copies from the 1960s or 1970s sell for less.

The Culinary Arts Institute

As the publishing outlet expanded, other publishers, such as Spencer Press and Consolidated Books, were formed. Spencer Press published mostly literary works, but Consolidated published almost any kind of book. Late in 1938, CAP expanded to become the Culinary Arts Institute, still operated by the same personnel. Most of the CAI material in the years that followed would be published by Consolidated.

Late in 1938, the Culinary Arts Institute issued its first hardback book. While some copies list the correct title, *My Favorite Recipe*, on the cover, others give the title as *World's Best Recipes*. In each case, the book is subtitled "By 500 of the World's Best Cooks." Inside on all copies, the title is shown as *My Favorite Recipe*, with the same subtitle. The title is appropriate, since over 500 housewives each submitted their favorite recipe for inclusion in the book. S. Claire Sondheim is listed as the compiler and editor of the book, for as yet CAI had not chosen a director. 244 pages. Published by Consolidated Book Publishers; printed by Cuneo Press. The book is scarce.
SI = 7, $35.00 – $50.00

1939:

This was an important year in the history of the cookbook publishing company. Ruth Berolzheimer came on board, she being responsible for the Institute's most famous books and booklets. Although Kay Morrow and S. Claire Sondheim had worked extensively on the CAP material, Berolzheimer is listed as the first titled Director. Since some of the CAP material had been taken directly from the Delineator Service booklets, perhaps it was the task of compiling a great deal of all-new material that gave rise to the hiring of a permanent director for the Institute.

The American Woman's Cook Book from 1939 was Berolzheimer's first book as the director of the Institute. The Delineator material was reprinted almost as-is into the *American Woman's Cook Book* under the auspices of Berolzheimer.

Quickly reprinted, there are many editions of this book, including various bindings made for specific companies (Prudence Penny — a person; *Everywoman* magazine; Kenmore (Sears); Readers' Service and certain purposes ("National," "International," "Canadian," and "Victory"). Collecting the book in its various bindings throughout the 1940s can be a pastime all by itself. The Victory editions, for example, feature a dedication to General Douglas McArthur. By 1943, the book was a million seller.

First printing, light green cover, 1939 on front page and copyright page, $30.00
Dust jacket, $20.00

Later printings (1940, 1941, 1942 – 2 printings, 1943, 1944, 1945, 1946, 1948, 1962, 1968, 1971, etc.), $15.00 – 25.00 each, but copies from the 1960s and later generally fetch $5.00 – 10.00.

Victory binding, w/dj and original box, $35.00
Some copies list the publisher as "Garden City;" others list "Consolidated."

World's Best Recipes

Although the first printing of *The American Woman's Cook Book* lists 1939 on both the front page and the copyright page, nearly all editions list the additional date of 1938 on the copyright page, since the material had been purchased and copyrighted in 1938. Also, although the first printing (correctly) lists the copyright dates for *The Delineator Cook Book* as 1928 and 1934, later printings say 1927 instead of 1928. Apparently the copyright was changed to reflect the fact that the *Delineator Cook Book* is an expansion and revision of the *Butterick Book of Recipes and Household Helps* (from 1927). However, quite a few of the sections in the Helps book had already appeared in the 1924 *New Butterick Cook Book*.

Also in 1939, all of the domestic pamphlets from the CAP series were collected into *The United States Regional Cook Book* along with some new material. The book was reissued in 1940 as *The Greater American Cookbook* and again as the *United States Regional Cook Book* in 1947.

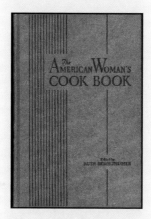

The American Woman's Cook Book – 1939

This may have been adapted to become the *Fifty States Cook Book* (1977), which appeared later. A Prudence Penny binding exists of this book. NOTE: by 1940 the two books above were bound similarly so that they might be sold together. For $7.50, both books could be purchased together, in a cardboard binder, as *The American Encyclopedia of Cooking and Homemaking*.

All editions are SI = 2 – 4

First printing, light green cover, 1939 on front page and copyright page, $30.00
Dust jacket, $20.00

Second printing, white cover with blue print, 1939 on copyright page only, $30.00

Cardboard Housing for American Woman's Cook Book and *United States Regional Cook Book*, with CAI logo, called *The American Encyclopedia of Cooking and Homemaking*, $25.00

Greater American Cookbook, 1940 copyright, $20.00 – 25.00

1947 printing, new blue and yellow cover, or green cover, $20.00; dust jacket, $15.00

The American Woman's
Cook Book – 1943

The American Woman's
Cook Book – 1943

NOTE: The later printings of the *United States Regional Cook Book* have the color photographs in different places in the book, and the credits for these photographs are different.

Checklist

Title	Edition	Value in Mint Condition
☐ *1500 Recipes from All Over the Globe* (box only)	1937	$50.00 (estimate)
☐ American Woman's Cook Book (light green cover)	1939	$30.00
☐ American Woman's Cook Book (original dj)	1939	$20.00
☐ American Woman's Cook Book (later printing)	1940 – 1970	$5.00 – 25.00
☐ American Woman's Cook Book (Victory binding)	1943	$35.00 w/dj & box
☐ American Woman's Cook Book (other special binding)	1940s – 1950s	$20.00
☐ Canadian Woman's Cook Book (American Woman's)	1939 – 1940s	$25.00
☐ The Candy Book (CAP markings)	1938	$20.00
☐ The Candy Book (woodback)	1939	$15.00
☐ Chinese Cook Book (yellow cover)	1936	$35.00
☐ Chinese Cook Book (red/black colors on brown cover)	1936	$30.00 w/dj
☐ Chinese Cook Book (blue cover, 15¢ price)	1937 – 1938	$20.00 – 25.00 w/dj
☐ Chinese Cook Book (blue cover, no price)	1940s	$15.00 – 20.00
☐ Chinese Cook Book (later printing)	1950s – 1970s	$5.00

Checklist

Title	Edition	Value in Mint Condition
❏ *Chinese Cook Book* (woodback)	1939 – 1950s	$15.00 – 30.00
❏ *The Cookie Book* (boy climbing into jar, 15¢ price)	1937	$30.00 w/dj
❏ *The Cookie Book* (boy climbing into jar, no price)	1939 – 1940	$20.00
❏ *The Cookie Book* (red cover)	1940	$15.00
❏ *The Cookie Book* (woodback)	1939 – 1940s	$15.00 – 30.00
❏ Culinary Arts Press butter dish (with lid)	1935 – 1936	$100.00
❏ *Greater American Cook Book* (green cover)	1940	$20.00 – 25.00
❏ *My Favorite Recipe*	1938	$35.00 – 50.00
❏ *New England Cook Book* (white cover, banner at top)	1936	$35.00 w/dj
❏ *New England Cook Book* (white cover, price in black)	1936 – 1937	$35.00 w/dj
❏ *New England Cook Book* (oval printing, 15¢ price)	1937 – 1938	$10.00 w/dj
❏ *New England Cook Book* (common oval printing)	1940s	$5.00
❏ *New England Cook Book* (woodback)	1939 – 1950s	$15.00 – 30.00
❏ *Pennsylvania Dutch Cook Book*	1934	$40.00 w/dj
❏ *Pennsylvania Dutch Cook Book* (lists *Southern Cook Book*)	1935	$35.00 w/dj
❏ *Pennsylvania Dutch Cook Book* (red dress, black 15¢)	1935 – 1936	$35.00 w/dj

The American Woman's Cook Book dust jacket – 1940

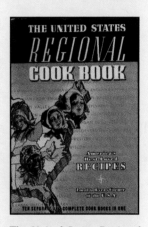

The United States Regional Cook Book dust jacket

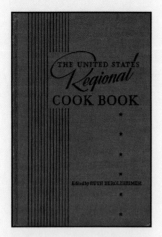

The United States Regional Cook Book – 1939

The United States Regional Cook Book – 1940s

Checklist

Title	Edition	Value in Mint Condition
❏ *Pennsylvania Dutch Cook Book* (green dress)	1936	$30.00 w/dj
❏ *Pennsylvania Dutch Cook Book* (oval 15¢ cover)	1937	$30.00 w/dj
❏ *Pennsylvania Dutch Cook Book* (PA map cover)	1937	$30.00
❏ *Pennsylvania Dutch Cook Book* (common oval print)	1940s	$5.00 – 10.00
❏ *Pennsylvania Dutch Cook Book* (woodback)	1939 – 1950s	$15.00 – 30.00
❏ *'Round the World Cook Book* (blue dj with list)	1936	$50.00 w/dj
❏ *'Round the World Cook Book* (blue dj, no list)	1937 – 1938	$30.00 w/dj
❏ *'Round the World Cook Book* (later printing)	1940s	$10.00
❏ *'Round the World Cook Book* (Kalamazoo printing)	1951	$20.00
❏ *'Round the World Cook Book* (woodback)	c. 1939 – 1940	$30.00
❏ *Southern Cook Book* (family cover)	1935	$35.00 – 40.00 w/dj
❏ *Southern Cook Book* (white woman, banner at top)	1936	$35.00 w/dj
❏ *Southern Cook Book* (white woman, price in black)	1936 – 1937	$25.00 w/dj
❏ *Southern Cook Book* ("mammy" cover, 15¢ price)	1937 – 1938	$15.00 – 20.00 w/dj
❏ *Southern Cook Book* ("mammy" cover, 25¢ price)	1938 – 1939	$15.00 w/dj

Checklist

Title	Edition	Value in Mint Condition
☐ *Southern Cook Book* (no dj)	1940s	$10.00
☐ *Southern Cook Book* (later printing)	1950s – 1970s	$5.00
☐ *Southern Cook Book* (woodback)	1939 – 1940s	$20.00 – 50.00
☐ *United States Regional Cook Book* (light green cover)	1939	$30.00
☐ *United States Regional Cook Book* (original dj)	1939	$20.00
☐ *United States Regional Cook Book* (white/blue cover)	1940s	$30.00
☐ *United States Regional Cook Book* (blue/yellow or green cover)	1947	$20.00
☐ *United States Regional Cook Book* (1947 dj)	1947	$15.00
☐ *United States Regional Cook Book* (special binding)	1940s	$20.00
☐ *Western Cook Book* (green dj, lists other books)	1936	$25.00 w/dj
☐ *Western Cook Book* (Texas Centennial markings)	1936	$50.00 (estimate)
☐ *Western Cook Book* (green dj, no list)	1937 – 1938	$20.00 w/dj
☐ *Western Cook Book*	1940s	$5.00 – 10.00
☐ *Western Cook Book* (woodback)	1939 – 1950s	$15.00 – 30.00
☐ *World's Best Recipes*	1938	$35.00 – 50.00

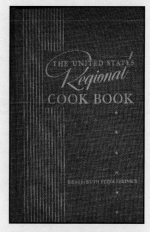

The United States Regional Cook Book – 1947

The American Encyclopedia of Cooking and Homemaking

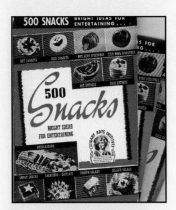

500 Snacks

500 Snacks

1940 – 1941:

The year 1940 was perhaps the most important one for CAI. During 1940 and the years which followed, the Culinary Arts Institute published numerous pamphlets in two related series. One of these series was extremely popular; the other appears to have been moderately popular.

The former series is referred to here as "Series 1" because it started with a pamphlet numbered "1" As far as I can ascertain, the paperback pamphlets cost 15¢ each for most of 1940 – 1941 (although later copies of some books are found with 25¢ prices on the cover), whereas the (rare) spiral hardback copies cost 25¢ each. Some of the spiral hardbacks indicate "25¢" on the covers. The whole series appears to have been produced in spiral hardback, although I know of just 11 titles.

Most of the spiral hardbacks in my possession mention Culinary Arts Press inside. In at least the case of the *Dairy Dishes* book (#18), the SHB copy and PB are dated 1940.

It appears that 12 of the "Series 1" pamphlets were produced in PB in 1940 in various colors. Their color scheme has nothing to do with what printing a pamphlet is. All of the booklets exist in three or more colors — all copyrighted 1940 with few additional distinguishing features. Some copies come with heavy lamination, which others lack.

All true original copies should have an address on the first page on South Dearborn St. Copies made later, from mid-1941, have an address on N. Michigan Ave. Copies made from about early 1942 on have a 25¢ price on the cover. Some of those later covers are slightly different from the two earlier issues.

The 12 original members of Series 1 were:
#1. *500 Snacks*
#2. *500 Delicious Dishes from Leftovers*
#3. *250 Classic Cake Recipes*
#4. *250 Ways to Prepare Poultry*
#5. *250 Superb Pies and Pastries*
#6. *250 Delicious Soups*
#7. *500 Delicious Salads*
#8. *250 Ways to Prepare Meat*
#9. *250 Fish and Seafood Recipes*
#10. *300 Ways to Serve Eggs*
#11. *250 Ways to Serve Fresh Vegetables*
#12. *250 Delectable Desserts*

Their number in the series can be found in the upper right hand corner of the booklet. All 12 of these books are fairly common and sold quite well. The collector should have no trouble acquiring the whole series.

250 Classic Cake Recipes

At least one special printing is known. The special printing has the cover and most contents similar to the common copies. However, the title page lists Frances Troy Northcross, home counselor of the *Washington Times-Herald*, creator of "Radio Recipes," instead of Ruth Berolzheimer and the usual publishing information. The special printing was obviously intended to be available locally via the *Times-Herald*.

Copies sold c. 1941 – 1942 in Nebraska have professionally-made advertising stamped on the back (as though it were part of the cover). That advertisement mentions that the entire set could be had for free from Crete Mills (in Crete, NE) with the purchase of a 50-pound sack of flour. The binder (see below) could also be purchased from Crete Mills for 50¢. Theoretically, these copies could sell for more, although no price difference has been established so far.

Northcross printing, SI = 8, $12.00

Dearborn address, SI = 2, $8.00

N. Michigan address, SI = 2, $6.00

25¢ price, SI = 5, $10.00

SHB, SI = 7, $12.00+

Copies in lesser grades can often be found for $1.00.

In 1940 or early 1941, the thirteenth book in the series must have been produced, because from #14 on, there is an additional name listed in the credits. Note however, that #'s 15, 17, and 18 (at least) are reissues of earlier material.

A set of eight more pamphlets in Series 1 was produced in 1940 – 1941, although some had been published earlier. These second eight are as follows:

#13. *250 Ways of Serving Potatoes*
#14. *500 Tasty Sandwiches*
#15. *250 Ways to Make Candy*
#16. *250 Luscious Refrigerator Desserts*
#17. *250 Cookie and Small Cake Recipes*
#18. *300 Tasty, Healthful Dairy Dishes*
#19. *250 Breads, Biscuits, and Rolls*
#20. *Menus For Every Day of the Year*

These, too, are reasonably easy to find. Collectors should be able to locate copies in various colors.

Northcross printing, SI = 8, $12.00

250 Fish and Sea Food Recipes

Dearborn address

Dearborn address

N. Michigan address

Dearborn address

250 Ways of Serving Potatoes

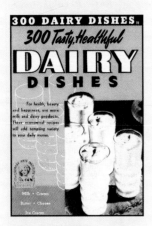

300 Tasty, Healthful Dairy Dishes

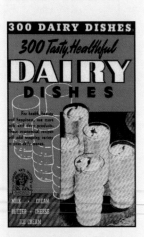

300 Tasty, Healthful Dairy Dishes

Dearborn address, SI = 2, $8.00

N. Michigan address, SI = 2, $6.00

25¢ price, SI = 5, $10.00

SHB, SI = 7, $12.00+

Colors noted in Series 1, apparently published for each title in the series, include: blue; orange; yellow/orange; red; and green. I have seen some in what appears to be brown and some in what appears to be pink (but which may be an off-color red).

In 1941, the 20 Series 1 books were collected into a binder with the title *The Culinary Arts Institute Encyclopedia of Cooking and Homemaking*, apparently superceding the two-volume hardback set with the same name. At some point also, the first 20 were sent out in boxes, with the box being labeled *American Encyclopedia of Cooking and Homemaking*.

Binder: SI = 4, $20.00
Box (blue or red): SI = 7, $25.00

1941 – 1945:

Before the change in address (from S. Dearborn to N. Michigan) came *The Dairy Cook Book*, from 1941. The hardbound book was issued with one of at least six dust jackets, promoting different companies. The original cost was $2.00. *The Dairy Cook Book* is reasonably easy to locate.

Regular copy, SI = 3, $6.00 – 12.00

Special printing: cover reads *The Prairie Farms Dairy Cook Book*, SI = 4, $15.00

Any dust jacket, $10.00

Series 101:

Shortly thereafter, still in 1941, the address change came. The first 20 cookbooks were reissued with the new address. Also, all 20 were reissued into the new "Series 101." At first, Series 101 copies all had similar-looking multicolored covers. Not only did booklets 1 – 20 stay in circulation, but also booklets with numbers higher than 120 began to be issued. Most of these newer copies came without Series 1 counterparts, although 101 – 120 do correspond to numbers 1 – 20. Certain copies numbering higher than 121 mention inside that cookbooks from the two series contain the same recipes, but this was only true for numbers 1 – 101 and 20 – 120. Sometimes the titles on Series 1 and Series 101 booklets are different, but the contents of 1 – 20 and 101 – 120 are identical. The contents of 121 – 129 are unique, since these were entirely new booklets.

Here are titles that I am aware of which number 121 – 129, all of which were issued in 1942:

#121. *The Breakfast and Brunch Book*. Waffle on cover.
#122. *Quick Dinners for the Woman in a Hurry Cook Book*
#123. *How to Feed a Family of 5 on $15.00 a Week*
#124. *250 Ways to Save Sugar*
#125. *Body Building Dishes For Children*; reissued in 1949 as #22.
#126. *Dishes Mother Used to Make*
#127. Not Known
#128. *Meals for Two Cook Book*; reissued in 1949 as #21.
#129. *Sunday Night Suppers*

These books are more difficult to find in general than their lower-numbered counterparts.

Any copy, SI = 4 – 5, $12.00

Victory Series

Also in 1942 – 45, but not part of Series 1 or 101, Consolidated Book Publishers issued a long series of what I have termed "patriotic" booklets. *The Victory Series* is Consolidated's name for this, Series 501. Only certain members of the series had anything to do with cooking. Some of them were collected into hardback books by Consolidated. For example, book 558, *The Bedside Book* (1943) contains a story by J. D. Salinger that was first published in *Collier's* in December of 1942 and then acquired by Consolidated and used also in a hardback collection from 1943, *The Kit Book for Soldiers, Sailors, and Marines*.

Several booklets were issued in the series dealing with cooking during World War II. These are shown in bold face below. At least three of these have the CAI name inside. If you have any information that contributes to a more complete listing, please provide it.

#502. *How to Grow a Victory Garden*, 1942.
#502N. *Vegetable Gardener's Handbook*, 1942.
#505. *First Aid*, 1942. Patriotic cover.
#505N. *What to do Until the Doctor Arrives*, 1942.
#506. *The Wartime Cook Book*, 1942. Patriotic cover.
#509. *Wartime Entertaining*, 1942. Contains menus from the
   Wartime Cook Book. Red cover or yellow/orange cover.
#510. *Victory Canning*, 1942.
#511. *Practical Home Nursing*, 1942. Family on cover.
#511N. *Practical Home Nursing*, 1942. Additional cover description.
#512. *How to Live on a Reduced War Budget*, 1942.
#512N. *How to Cut Your Cost of Living*, 1942. Red cover.
#514. *War Dictionary*, 1942.
#515. *How to Get Added Life Out of Your Car*, 1942.

The Wartime Cookbook, SI = 6, $30.00

Wartime Entertaining, SI = 6, $10.00

Victory Canning, SI = 6, $20.00

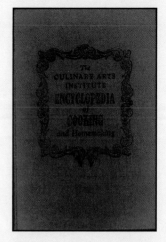

The Culinary Arts Institute Encyclopedia of Cooking and Homemaking

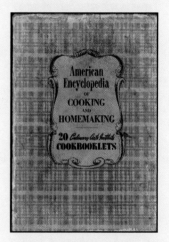

American Encyclopedia of Cooking and Homemaking

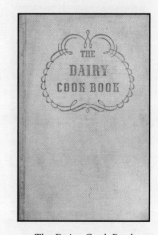

The Dairy Cook Book

The Breakfast and Brunch Book

Quick Dinners for the Woman in a Hurry Cook Book

How to Feed a Family of 5 on $15.00 a Week

Series 551:

As the war neared a close, Series 501 (the Victory Series) came to be used for purposes other than supporting the war effort. In fact, from a certain point on, Series 501 was entirely focused on comic reprints. Series 551 also began in 1942, shortly after the emergence of the *Victory Series*. In 1944, it too tended toward comedy, although some of that comedy was focused on military life. Some of the books in Series 551 are listed below, with those related to cooking in bold face type.

#551. *Cut 20% From Your Food Bill Cook Book,* 1942. The first of two reissues of *The Wartime Cookbook.*
#552. *The A-B-C of Canning,* 1942. A reissue of *Victory Canning.* Green or red cover.
#552N. *The A-B-C of Canning,* 1942. Same as the above book; full color cover.
#558. *The Bedside Book*, 1943. Military/wartime cartoons and stories.
#562. *Photo Crimes*, 1944. Mysteries with photos.
#578. *1000 Games and Stunts,* 1945. Priced at 13¢.
#593. *11 of the World's Great War & Spy Stories*, 1944. Includes one O. Henry story.

Clearly, the 551 series was used later on for items that were not war-related.

Cut 20% from Your Food Bill, SI = 6, $12.00

The A-B-C of Canning (green, red, or full color), SI = 4, $10.00

The 1943 – 1945 "Wartime" issues have different-style covers than #'s 125 – 129 and were probably not considered for collection in a hardbound edition until 1949's encyclopedic cookbooks. These books are numbered 30 – 130 and higher; all of them are scarce. The booklets of which I am personally aware are:

#30. *Military Meals at Home Cook Book*, 1943.
#31. *Meals Without Meat Cook Book*, 1943.
#131N. *Cooling Dishes For Hot Weather Cook Book*, 1943. Apparently reissued into the *Fabulous Foods* (50s) series as #118; same contents as #31.
#34. *American Woman's Food Stretcher Cook Book*, 1943.
#134N. *Family Cook Book*, 1943. Same contents as #34.
#35. *American Woman's 3-Way Meat Stretcher Cook Book*, 1943.
#36. *500 Food-Extender Wartime Recipes*, 1943. This book is shown inside as "1942" because it is a reissue of the *Wartime Cook Book*, which was issued in 1942. At least some of this information, along with book 123, was added to the Victory bindings of the *American Woman's Cook Book.*

Any copy numbered 30 – 130 or higher, SI = 6, $12.00 to $15.00

My estimate of scarcity is as follows:
#'s 1 – 20, flat or glossy covers, Dearborn or Michigan address, each SI = 2
#'s 1 – 20, Northcross printing, each SI = 8

#'s 101 – 120, glossy or flat covers, SI = 3
#'s 121 – 129, all SI = 4 to 5
#127 is not known
#'s 30 – 130 or higher, each SI = 6
#'s 506, 509, 510, 551, each SI = 6
#'s 552, 552N, each SI = 4

The Series 1 pamphlets were reprinted in 1949, 1950, 1951, 1952, 1953, 1954, 1964 (smaller), 1965, and 1969 (smaller), on into the 1970s — at least! Copies from the mid-1970s, containing the same material reworked into "new" pamphlets, were called the *Kitchen Companion* series. Some were also reprinted in other years. A binder, still called *Encyclopedia of Cooking,* was issued in 1949 with the reissued series of 24 books. Value of binder: $15.00.

250 Ways to Save Sugar Cook Book

1948 – 1949:

The next great achievement of the Culinary Arts Institute was *The Encyclopedic Cookbook*, published by Book Production Industries. The original is the 1948 edition; copies can be found in various colors and with either the title on the front or with a cover design of dots. Apparently, none of the pamphlets from the 1930s were reprinted in the cookbook indicating that the material inside was (c) 1940, 1941, 1942, 1943, 1944, and 1945. Therefore, little, if any, of the CAP material was used in compiling the encyclopedic edition.

The cover to the 1949 edition is yellow with black dots. The 1949 edition appears uncommon, although the 1950 (orange) edition is much easier to find. I conclude that sales of the book had begun to escalate by 1950. Although this was not the first thumb-indexed cookbook, the indexing certainly made the book easy to peruse, and the distribution obtained through various CAI outlets was wide. This book was reprinted many times under various names (e.g., *Cooking For Young Homemakers*, 1958) and with different bindings (Norge, 1950). A revised edition was issued in 1964 and again in 1976 (as *The Encyclopedia of Home Cooking*). It was issued in paperback in 1980 and later in 1986; the paperback is still in print. The total number of copies sold must be quite large.

Body Building Dishes For Children Cook Book

Note: Col. Bob Allen, author of *A Guide to Collecting Cookbooks* mentions a 1936 CAP book with the same name which probably reprinted some of the Delineator material. His list indicates that Kay Morrow was the editor, assisted by Pauline Dubin, Hazel Hemminger, and S. Claire Sondheim, 799 pages, CAP, 1936. In the past several years, no copies have surfaced on the Internet. No such book is listed inside the dust jacket of any CAP publication from 1936 – 1937. If the book exists, it should be considered rare.

First printing: SI = 4 (1948), $30.00; dust jacket $10.00

Second printing: SI = 4 (yellow, 1949), $25.00

1950s printings: SI = 2, $12.00 to $15.00

Later printings: $12.00 or less

Dishes Mother Used to Make Cook Book

Meals for Two Cook Book

Sunday Night Suppers Cook Book

The Wartime Cook Book

A lesser-known book, published in 1949, was Ruth Berolzheimer's *What Will We Eat Today?*, subtitled *Pressure Cookery for Every Meal.* Containing a foreword by Kate Smith, the book was written to promote the Ecko Pressure Cooker and was available in hardback and softback editions. 207 recipes. SI = 6 (HB or PB)

Hardback edition (turquoise): SI = 6, $25.00

Softcover edition: SI = 5, $15.00 to $20.00

Reissues of the Series 1 Books:

All of the Series 1 books were reprinted with new covers and with a four-page color centerfold insert. Also in 1949, four more books were taken from other series and added into Series 1. The cookbook that had been known as #20, *Menus For Every Day of the Year* was renumbered as #24, so that it would appear last in the series. A new #20, *Sauces, Gravies, and Dressings,* replaced it. In 1949 and years following, the 24 books were available together as *The Encyclopedia of Cooking.*

The books from 1949 numbering 20 – 24 are:

#20. *Sauces, Gravies, and Dressings*
#21. *Meals for Two* (originally #128)
#22. *Body Building Dishes for Children* (originally #125)
#23. *Facts About Food*
#24. *Menus For Every Day of the Year* (originally #20)

Any 1949 – 1963 reissue of #1 – 24 or #101 – 124, SI = 1, $3.00

Binder for 20 books (1948, blue), SI = 4, $20.00

Binder for 24 books (red, 1949, or white, 1952 or 1953), SI = 2, $15.00

Checklist

Title	Edition	Value in Mint Condition
250 Breads, Biscuits, and Rolls (#19, typical copy)	1941	$6.00 – 8.00
250 Breads, Biscuits, and Rolls (#19, SHB)	1941	$12.00
250 Breads, Biscuits, and Rolls (#119, early reissue)	1943 – 1948	$3.00
250 Classic Cake Recipes (#3, typical copy)	1940	$6.00 – 8.00
250 Classic Cake Recipes (#3, SHB)	1940	$12.00
250 Classic Cake Recipes (#103)	1943 – 1948	$3.00
250 Cookie and Small Cake Recipes (#17, typical copy)	1940	$6.00 – 8.00
250 Cookie and Small Cake Recipes (#17, SHB)	1940	$12.00
250 Cookie and Small Cake Recipes (#117)	1943 – 1948	$3.00
250 Delectable Desserts (#12, typical copy)	1940	$6.00 – 8.00
250 Delectable Desserts (#12, SHB)	1940	$12.00
250 Delectable Desserts (#112)	1943 – 1948	$3.00
250 Delicious Soups (#6, typical copy)	1940	$6.00 – 8.00
250 Delicious Soups (#6, SHB)	1940	$12.00
250 Delicious Soups (#106)	1943 – 1948	$3.00

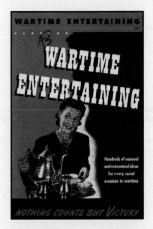

Wartime Entertaining

Victory Canning

How to Live on a Reduced War Budget

How to Cut Your Cost of Living

Cut 20% From Your Food Bill Cook Book

The A-B-C of Canning

Checklist

Title	Edition	Value in Mint Condition
❏ *250 Fish and Seafood Recipes* (#9, typical copy)	1940	$6.00 – 8.00
❏ *250 Fish and Seafood Recipes* (#9, SHB)	1940	$12.00
❏ *250 Fish and Seafood Recipes* (#109)	1943 – 1948	$3.00
❏ *250 Luscious Refrigerator Desserts* (#16, typical copy)	1941	$6.00 – 8.00
❏ *250 Luscious Refrigerator Desserts* (#16, SHB)	1941	$12.00
❏ *250 Luscious Refrigerator Desserts* (#116)	1943 – 1948	$3.00
❏ *250 Superb Pies and Pastries* (#5, typical copy)	1940	$6.00 – 8.00
❏ *250 Superb Pies and Pastries* (#5, SHB)	1940	$12.00
❏ *250 Superb Pies and Pastries* (#105)	1943 – 1948	$3.00
❏ *250 Ways of Serving Potatoes* (#13, typical copy)	1941	$6.00 – 8.00
❏ *250 Ways of Serving Potatoes* (#13, SHB)	1941	$12.00
❏ *250 Ways of Serving Potatoes* (#113)	1943 – 1948	$3.00
❏ *250 Ways to Make Candy* (#15, typical copy)	1940	$6.00 – 8.00
❏ *250 Ways to Make Candy* (#15, SHB)	1940	$12.00
❏ *250 Ways to Make Candy* (#115)	1943 – 1948	$3.00

Checklist

Title	Edition	Value in Mint Condition
❏ *250 Ways to Prepare Meat* (#8, typical copy)	1940	$6.00 – 8.00
❏ *250 Ways to Prepare Meat* (#8, SHB)	1940	$12.00
❏ *250 Ways to Prepare Meat* (#108)	1943 – 1948	$3.00
❏ *250 Ways to Prepare Poultry* (#4, typical copy)	1940	$6.00 – 8.00
❏ *250 Ways to Prepare Poultry* (#4, SHB)	1940	$12.00
❏ *250 Ways to Prepare Poultry* (#104)	1943 – 1948	$3.00
❏ *250 Ways to Save Sugar* (#124)	1942	$12.00
❏ *250 Ways to Serve Fresh Vegetables* (#11, typical copy)	1940	$6.00 – 8.00
❏ *250 Ways to Serve Fresh Vegetables* (#11, SHB)	1940	$12.00
❏ *250 Ways to Serve Fresh Vegetables* (#111)	1943 – 1948	$3.00
❏ *300 Ways to Serve Eggs* (#10, typical copy)	1940	$6.00 – 8.00
❏ *300 Ways to Serve Eggs* (#10, SHB)	1940	$12.00
❏ *300 Ways to Serve Eggs* (#110)	1943 – 1948	$3.00
❏ *500 Delicious Dishes from Leftovers* (#2, typical copy)	1940	$6.00 – 8.00
❏ *500 Delicious Dishes from Leftovers* (#2, SHB)	1940	$12.00

The A-B-C of Canning

Military Meals at Home Cook Book

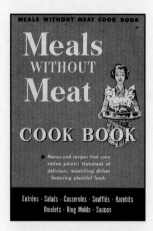

Meals Without Meat Cook Book

Cooling Dishes For Hot Weather Cook Book

Checklist

Title	Edition	Value in Mint Condition
☐ *500 Delicious Dishes from Leftovers* (#102)	1943 – 1948	$3.00
☐ *500 Delicious Salads* (#7, typical copy)	1940	$6.00 – 8.00
☐ *500 Delicious Salads* (#7, SHB)	1940	$12.00
☐ *500 Delicious Salads* (#107)	1943– 1948	$3.00
☐ *500 Food-Extender Wartime Recipes* (#36)	1943	$12.00 – 15.00
☐ *500 Snacks* (#1, typical copy)	1940	$6.00 – 8.00
☐ *500 Snacks* (#1, SHB)	1940	$12.00
☐ *500 Snacks* (#101)	1943 – 1948	$3.00
☐ *500 Tasty Sandwiches* (#14, typical copy)	1941	$6.00 – 8.00
☐ *500 Tasty Sandwiches* (#14, SHB)	1941	$12.00
☐ *500 Tasty Sandwiches* (#114)	1943 – 1948	$3.00
☐ *The A-B-C of Canning* (#552, green or red cover)	1942	$10.00
☐ *The A-B-C of Canning* (#552N, multicolored cover)	1942	$10.00
☐ *American Encyclopedia of Cooking and Homemaking*	1940s	$25.00, box only
☐ *The American Woman's 3-Way Meat Stretcher Cook Book* (#35)	1943	$12.00 – 15.00

Checklist

Title	Edition	Value in Mint Condition
☐ The American Woman's Food Stretcher Cook Book (#34)	1943	$12.00 – 15.00
☐ Body Building Dishes For Children (#125)	1942	$12.00
☐ Breakfast and Brunch Cook Book (#121)	1942	$12.00
☐ Cooling Dishes For Hot Weather (#131N)	1943	$12.00 – 15.00
☐ Culinary Arts Institute Encyclopedia of Cooking and Homemaking	1941 – 1945	$20.00 binder
☐ Cut 20% From Your Food Bill Cook Book (#551)	1942	$12.00
☐ The Dairy Cook Book (regular copy)	1941	$6.00 – 12.00
☐ The Dairy Cook Book (Prairie Farms binding)	1941	$15.00
☐ The Dairy Cook Book (dj)	1941	$10.00
☐ Dairy Dishes (#18, typical copy)	1941	$6.00 – 8.00
☐ Dairy Dishes (#18, SHB)	1941	$12.00
☐ Dairy Dishes (#118)	1943 –1948	$3.00
☐ Dishes Mother Used to Make (#126)	1942	$12.00
☐ Encyclopedia of Cooking	1949 – 1950s	$15.00 binder
☐ The Encyclopedic Cookbook (1st printing)	1948	$30.00

The American Woman's Food Stretcher Cook Book

The Family Cook Book

The American Woman's 3-Way Meat Stretcher Cook Book

500 Food-Extender Wartime Recipes

Encyclopedic Cook Book

Checklist

Title	Edition	Value in Mint Condition
☐ The Encyclopedic Cookbook (dj)	1948	$10.00
☐ The Encyclopedic Cookbook (yellow cover)	1949	$25.00
☐ The Encyclopedic Cookbook (any 1950s printing)	1950s	$12.00 – 15.00
☐ The Encyclopedic Cookbook (later printing)	1960 – 1980	$12.00 or less
☐ The Family Cook Book (#134N)	1943	$12.00 – 15.00
☐ How to Feed a Family of 5 on $15.00 a Week (#123)	1942	$12.00
☐ Meals for Two CB (#128)	1942	$12.00
☐ Meals Without Meat Cook Book (#31)	1943	$12.00 – 15.00
☐ Menus For Every Day of the Year (#20, typical copy)	1941	$6.00 – 8.00
☐ Menus For Every Day of the Year (#20, SHB)	1941	$12.00
☐ Menus For Every Day of the Year (#120)	1943 – 1948	$3.00
☐ Military Meals at Home (#30)	1943	$12.00 – 15.00
☐ Quick Dinners for the Woman in a Hurry (#122)	1942	$12.00
☐ Sunday Night Suppers (#129)	1942	$12.00
☐ Victory Canning (#510)	1942	$20.00

Checklist

Title	Edition	Value in Mint Condition
The Wartime Cookbook (#506)	1942	$30.00
Wartime Entertaining (#509)	1942	$10.00
What Will We Eat Today? (HB)	1949	$25.00 w/dj
What Will We Eat Today? (PB)	1949	$15.00

Any 1949 – 1970s reissue of an earlier booklet, $3.00 or less

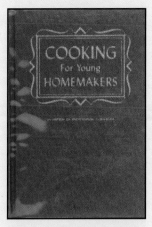

Cooking For Young Home-makers

What Will We Eat Today?

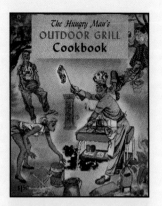

The Hungry Man's Outdoor Grill Cookbook

The Hungarian Cookbook

The Mixer, Hand Mixer, and Blender Cookbook

Spencer Press, who would later issue the *American Peoples Cook Book*, released this plastic-coated 10" x 8" paperback, called *The Hungry Man's Outdoor Grill Cookbook*. Illustrated in color, the book cost $1.50 originally. Among 1950s CAI items, this one is harder to find than most. This book marks Melanie de Proft's appearance as director of CAI, replacing Ruth Berolzheimer, who had served for 15 years.

For Spencer Press, Leonard S. Davidow had been the editor of a 20-volume set called *The World's Greatest Literature* (including Plutarch's Lives and Ralph Waldo Emerson's *Essays*); the set was published by Spencer in 1936 – 1937. In fact, one of those volumes indicates that the pictures were copyrighted by Consolidated Book Publishers. This book marks a return to an association between CAI and Spencer Press.

Davidow, writing from Reading, Pennsylvania, indicated that the company was named after William Augustus Spencer, "a patron of the fine binders of his day," a man who died aboard the Titanic in 1912. Around 1950, Spencer Press again began publishing volumes as they had once done. A multi-volume set called *Landmarks of American History* was part of this new presence. Consolidated continued as publisher, even issuing non-CAI cookbooks, such as *Pillsbury's Best of the Bake-Off* (1959) and the *Good Housekeeping* booklet series (1958) mentioned later in this article. The non-CAI cookbooks mentioned above are also listed on the back of the 1965 edition of the *Pennsylvania Dutch English Dictionary* as being available from Culinary Arts Press!

The Hungry Man's Outdoor Grill Cookbook
SI = 5, $12.00

Cooking Magic (1950s) Series

In 1954, CAI began a new series of pamphlets, starting again with 101. Curiously, the old 101 series was still in print. I have seen early 1950s reprints (which look like the Series 1 reprints) and a 1957 reissue that looks different (see above). This mid-fifties series, though, appears to be largely new— not reprinted from former sources. I will call them the 1950s Series, in order to distinguish them from the earlier two series of pamphlets. There were 24 members of the 1950s Series, as follows:

#101. *Quick Dishes for the Woman in a Hurry*, 332 recipes (styled from the earlier #122)
#102. *The Casserole Cook Book*, 175 recipes
#103. *The French Cook Book*, 141 recipes
#104. *The Chocolate Cook Book*, 218 recipes
#105. *The Lunch Box Cook Book*, 336 recipes
#106. *The Italian Cook Book*, 160 recipes
#107. *Brunch, Breakfast, and Morning Coffee*, 262 recipes

#108. *The Ground Meat Cook Book*, 204 recipes

#109. *Elegant Desserts*, 220 recipes

#110. *The Creole Cook Book*, 201 recipes (originally entitled *The New Orleans Cook Book* in 1954)

#111. *Dishes Children Love*, 264 recipes

#112. *The Gourmet Foods Cook Book*, 152 recipes

#113. *The Scandanavian Cook Book*, 159 recipes

#114. *The Hungarian Cookbook*, 151 recipes

#115. *Entertaining Six or Eight*, 143 recipes

#116. *The Cheese Cook Book*, 179 recipes

#117. *Cooling Dishes for Hot Weather*, 260 recipes (styled from the earlier #131N)

#118. *The New England Cook Book*, 191 recipes

#119. *Sunday Night Suppers*, 161 recipes (styled from the earlier #129)

#120. *The German and Viennese Cook Book*, 147 recipes

#121. *Cooking With Sour Cream and Buttermilk*, 161 recipes

#122. *The Southern and Southwestern Cook Book*, 173 recipes

#123. *Tempting Low Calorie Recipes*, 253 recipes

#124. *The Holiday Cook Book*, 220 recipes

The American Peoples Cookbook

As with the earlier Series 1, the 1950s Series was released in two sets of 12 books, dating from 1954 – 1956. The first 12 were collected into a binder, then all 24 were sold in a boxed set with two binders as *Cooking Magic*.

Unlike previous series, the dates on reissues of the 1950s Series are generally reliable. If a copy states that it was made in 1955, then it was.

Individual booklet, first printing, SI = 3, $8.00

Individual booklet, other 1950s printing, SI = 1 – 2, $4.00

Individual booklet, later printing, $4.00 or less

Binders for 101 – 112, 113 – 124, SI = 3, $15.00

Box for *Cooking Magic* set, SI = 7, $25.00

My Favorite Recipes

The entire set was reissued into the 1970s with *Cooking Magic Series* prominent on the new covers. The latest issue I have seen is from 1975.

From 1954, we have *The Mixer, Hand Mixer, and Blender Cookbook* by the Home Economists of Culinary Arts Institute; published by Spencer Press, Inc., 256 pages. Published in hardback and paperback.

HB, SI = 5, $20.00
PB, SI = 5, $15.00

Box from the *Fabulous Foods Cooking Magic Series*

The American Peoples Cookbook was released in 1956, was published by Spencer Press, and has 600 pages. The recipes were gathered from Sears Book Club members, and so it is possible that the book was marketed through Sears. Although the book seems to

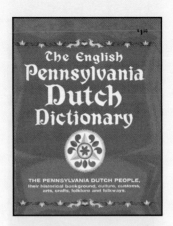

The English Pennsylvania Dutch Dictionary

Low-Carbohydrate Diet Menus and Recipes

The Outdoor Grill Cookbook – 1960.

have been reissued as a whole over the years, material from this cookbook was adapted later (1963 and 1986) into *CAI's Family Home Cook Book*, published by Lexicon Publications.
SI = 4, $15.00

My Favorite Recipes was the name of a 1959 CAI book published under Melanie de Proft by Spencer Press. 320 pages in size. Not easy to find. This book appears to be an abridgement of *The American Peoples Cookbook*.

The book went through a second printing in 1974.
SI = 5, $10.00

1960s – 1970s:

Series 1 and the 1950s Series continued to be reissued, along with some of the more popular Culinary Arts Press books.

In 1960, The Hungry Man's Outdoor Cook Book was reissued with a different name. Measuring 10¼"x 8⅛", *The Master Chef's Outdoor Grill Cook Book* cost $2.00 originally in paperback. 64 pages. Includes color pictures. There was also a hardback version without "Master Chef" in the title, which came out later that year. This spanned 111 pages and was published by Grosset & Dunlap/Castle.

HB, SI = 5, $8.00
PB, SI = 5, $8.00

In 1961, de Proft and the Institute released *The Woman's World Cookbook* (512 pages, hardback). The material comprising this book was taken from *The American Woman's Cook Book*.
SI = 3, $10.00

In 1963, *The American Peoples Cook Book* was reissued as *The Family Home Cook Book*. 632 pages. HB w/dj.
SI = 2, $8.00

In 1965, there was a lone issue of *The English Pennsylvania Dutch Dictionary*. Shown as a recompilation of material from 1941 and 1949, some of this book is new. This first edition was published by the Culinary Arts Press (in Reading, PA) in 1965. A few recipes (from the *Pennsylvania Dutch Cook Book*) are included in this 96-page book authored by Howard Snader.
SI = 5, $10.00

A companion to *The English Pennsylvania Dutch Dictionary* was the *Pennsylvania Dutch People's Cook Book*, which had its first printing in 1968 and its second in 1974. Again the book was published by Culinary Arts Press, and again the book was 96 pages in length. 250 recipes.
SI = 3, $5.00

The following year (1966), *Low-Carbohydrate Diet Menus and Recipes* came out. The softback book cost $1.00 originally and contains information about food cholesterol. It is numbered "A1" in the upper right-hand corner and was part of a series, each containing 64 pages and costing $1.00.
SI = 7, $12.00

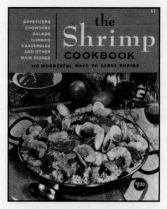

The second part of the same series, numbered "A2," is *The Shrimp Cookbook*. The booklet was authored by Dr. Alex D. Hawkes and consists largely of contributions from his recipe columns in two Florida newspapers. The format of the series is identical to the McCall's series from 1965, which was printed by Advance. Although Advance operated out of Orlando, Florida, they had a mailing address in Chicago. The size, number of pages, paper stock, numbering system, and $1.00 sticker are the same on the CAI "A" series as they are on the McCall's "M" series.
SI = 7, $12.00

The Shrimp Cookbook

In 1968, *The Presidents' Own White House Cookbook* was first released, with recipes up through President Johnson. It was reissued later.
SI = 4, $5.00

That same year, CAI published *The Jewish Woman's Cookbook*, by Sarah Lee Margolis. Contains 275 recipes; 96 pages; softcover. Melanie DeProft is listed as editor-in-chief, but not as Director of CAI. Claire S. Davidow is listed as managing editor. The book is copyrighted to Ann D. Goodman. Although CAI is mentioned as having tested the recipes, the book is shown as being authored by Culinary Arts Press in Reading, Pennsylvania.
SI = 6, $30.00
1976 reprint, $25.00

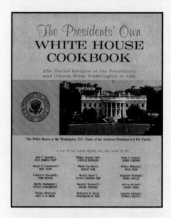

The Presidents' Own White House Cookbook

1971 brought us the first edition of *The American Family Cookbook*. 848 pages. The revised edition of 1974 is shown.

The American Family Home Cookbook was issued in paperback by Simon and Schuster in 1979, with that edition having 832 pages and claiming that over 300,000 copies of the cookbook had been sold. The paperback shows that while the book had been compiled originally by de Proft, it was revised by the staff of CAI after her departure. A new edition in hardback was released in 1985, which also ran 832 pages.
SI = 3 (any edition), $5.00

The New World Encyclopedia of Cooking was first issued in 1972, then reissued in 1973, 1975, and again in 1979. The 832-page book was published in New York and included 800 pages of recipes and 32 pages of nutritional information. Most of this information appears to have been taken from CAI's earlier cookbooks. Hardback with dust jacket. This item has no retail price and was probably a premium available to people who subscribed to the *New World Encyclopedia*. Interestingly, no one is listed as director of the Institute at this time, so it may be the case that Melanie de Proft was no longer with the

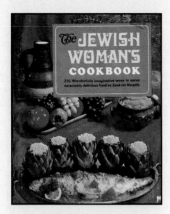

The Jewish Woman's Cookbook

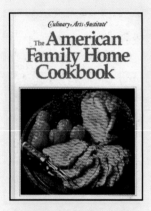

The American Family Home Cookbook

Institute by this time. As a point of note, CAI appears to have published nothing new of its own from this point until 1976 (after Helen Geist had taken over as director).
SI = 5, $20.00

In 1973 *The World's 100 Best Recipes*, by Roland Goock was published — 110 pages in hardback. The book is listed as an English translation of a book published in 1971 in Europe. Large color illustrations. With dust jacket.
SI = 6, $12.00

There is a 1973 issue of the *Encyclopedic Cook Book* that looks like it belongs with the covers to the *Good Housekeeping* series. We know that the *Good Housekeeping* series was also published by Consolidated Book Publishers in 1958. Also, the 1965 issue of *The English Pennsylvania Dutch Dictionary* shows the *Good Housekeeping Series* as available through Culinary Arts Press.

In 1973, there appeared a Nixon edition of The President's Own White House Cookbook (hardback, yellow cover, 255 recipes). A "Bicentennial" edition appeared in 1975, with recipes up through Ford.

The following year, the *Encyclopedia of Nutrition & Cooking* saw print. The 415-page hardback book contained a foreword by Dr. Philip L. White, who was the American Medical Association's director of foods and nutrition and who consulted with CAI on the book. The Encyclopedia appears to have been a giveaway of some sort. Helen Geist is named among the Institute's staff, but no director is named. Published by Grosset & Dunlap, with dust jacket.
SI = 4, $12.00

By this time, the *American Woman's Cook Book* had sold over 8,000,000 copies.

Also in 1974, Culinary Arts Press issued two new books, *The Chinese Cookbook of Many Delights* and *The Hawaiian Cookbook*, each costing $1.50 in softback and being 64 pages in length. The Chinese volume borrowed largely from M. Sing Au's earlier (1936) CAP masterpiece, whereas the Hawaiian volume was authored by Buck Buchwach and Patricia Hunter. The center spread lists the following cookbooks as still available from CAP: *Pennsylvania Dutch Cook Book*, *Southern Cook Book*, *Chinese Cook Book*, *New England Cook Book*, *Pennsylvania Dutch People's Cook Book*, *English Pennsylvania Dutch Dictionary*, and the *Presidents' Own White House Cook Book*. The earlier volumes were 75¢ each, while the newer ones sold for $1.50 each. All 18 of the McCall's series of cookbooks from 1965 are listed as available through Culinary Arts Press (POB 1182 in Reading).

Chinese Cook Book of Many Delights: SI = 5, $8.00

Hawaiian Cook Book: SI = 5, $12.00

Sometime between 1975 and 1977, Consolidated became part of Delair Publishing.

Adventures in Cooking

In 1975 – 1976, the Institute published at least 11 new books. Their director at this time was Helen Geist. These are called the *Adventures in Cooking* series and cost $1.95 each. They were larger (7¹³/₁₆" x 10¼"), 96-page (later 80-page) paperbacks and hardbacks called:

* *The Outdoor Cook Book*, by Barbara MacDonald
* *The Canning and Freezing Cook Book*
* *Wine in Cooking and Dining*
* *The Budget Cook Book*
* *Parties For All Seasons*
* *Crockery Cooking*
* *Polish Cook Book*
* *Bread and Soup Cook Book*
* *Mexican Cook Book*
* *Italian Cook Book*
* *The Cookie Jar*

The New World Encyclopedia of Cooking

At an additional cost ($5.95), the books were available in hardback, although the cost of later hardback copies is $7.95. All of the above were published by Consolidated Book Publishers in Chicago. See below for more members.

Any hardback, SI = 1 – 3, $5.00
Any paperback, SI = 2 – 4, $4.00

The year of the U. S. Bicentennial found CAI releasing *The Encyclopedia of Home Cooking*, published through Banner Press. This 633-page book contains an update for microwave cooking; otherwise it is similar to CAI's earlier material.
SI = 3, $4.00

Encyclopedia of Nutrition & Cooking

1977's *Fifty States Cookbook* measures approximately 8" x 9½" and runs a full 320 pages. Hardback with dust jacket. Is this a recycled version of an earlier cookbook?
SI = 4, $5.00

The *Adventures in Cooking* series continued to add members, some of which were new versions of the 50s Series booklets, including the following:

* *The Complete Book of Creative Crepes* (1977, 96 pages)
* *Nutrition Cook Book* (1977)
* *The Casserole Cook Book* (1980)
* *Caribbean Cook Book* (1980, 96 pages)
* *Cooking With Beer* (1980)
* *Cooking With Cheese* (1982)
* *Wok, Fondue, and Chafing Dish Cook Book* (1982)
* *The Hungarian Cook Book* (1982, 80 pages)
* *The Holiday Cook Book* (1982, 80 pages)
* *The Scandinavian Cook Book* (1982, 80 pages)

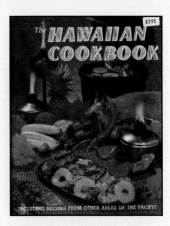

The Hawaiian Cookbook

Bread & Soup Cook Book

* An upscale version of *Quick Dishes for the Woman in a Hurry* (1982 or 1986, 80 pages)
* *German and Viennese Cooking* (1982, 80 pages)
* *The Fish and Shellfish Cook Book* (1983, 80 pages)
* *Cooking For Christmas* (1983, 80 pages)
* *How to Make Candy* (1983, 80 pages)
* *Family Favorites* (1983, 80 pages)

The *Adventures in Cooking* series proved to be CAI's most recent successful series of books for the home kitchen. SI = 1 – 3, $4.00 each.

The Canning and Freezing Cook Book was also made available in trade paperback form in 1976. With an original cost of $1.95, the paperback form was sold through Pocket Books (number 80434). SI = 5, $1.00

In support of T-Fal non-stick cookware, CAI issued *The T-Fal Cookbook* in 1976. The 48-page booklet details various ways in which their non-stick pans can be used with ease to create interesting meals. The French company T-Fal (or Tefal) invented non-stick cookware in 1955. More information about the company can be found on their website at www.T-Fal.com. SI = 6, $1.00

Also in connection with another company (and again in 1976), CAI released *Toastmaster System III Oven Broiler Cook Book*. The "oven broiler" was what we call today a toaster oven. Although the cover shows a $1.95 price tag, the book was probably given away with the purchase of either of two models of Toastmaster. The book comes with a letter insert from the Toastmaster company introducing the book. 64 pages. SI = 5, $1.00

In conjunction with Coca-Cola, the Culinary Arts Institute (under Helen Geist) released a series of 60 recipe cards in 1978. The 60 cards are grouped into categories of 10 recipes each. Measuring 5" x 4", every one of the recipes either uses Coca-Cola or "goes good with Coke." Some Coke recipe card collections are housed in tins; this one was housed in a red box. SI = 6, $40.00 – 50.00

CAI closed out the 1970s by continuing to focus on their *Adventures in Cooking* series. Even so, 1979 saw the publication of a premium item. As a giveaway with Crisco cooking oil, CAI produced the *Salad Lover's Cookbook*. The 6" x 9" softback had 48 pages and approximately 60 salad recipes. SI = 4, $3.00 or less

1980 – Present

Cooking French the New Way, by Sue Spitler, leads off CAI in the 80s. The book is 96 pages in length and appears in their larger paperback style. Also available in hardback with dust jacket.
SI = 4 (HB or PB), $3.00

The Cake Decorating Book came out in 1981 and featured 80 pages of illustrated ideas. This appears to have accompanied *The Baking Book*, by Lloyd Moxon, a 255-page masterpiece that was released that same year.
SI = 3, $3.00

Modern Promotions released this book of *Alltime Favorite Recipes* in 1981. The softback book was priced at $8.95 originally and contained "over 1001" recipes. Sixteen pages are in color. 379 pages, Delair.
SI = 3, $5.00

1001 Kitchen Favorites also came out in 1981. The 384-page book appears to connect with *Alltime Favorite Recipes*.
SI = 3, $5.00

The Canadian Family Cookbook was also released in 1981, weighing in at a whopping 832 pages. Contains recipes from each Canadian province.
SI = 6, $6.00

Delair released *The Kitchen Treasury* in 1981, containing over 2,000 recipes from around the U. S. and the world. 384 pages, probably overlapping their other early 80s publications.
SI = 5, $3.00

Following up on *Alltime Favorite Recipes*, Modern Promotions released *1001 Great Recipes From Around the World* in 1982. The softback book was also priced at $8.95 originally. 379 pages, Delair.
SI = 4, $5.00

1982 saw CAI co-publish *Duncan Hines' Baking With American Dash*, published by Cy DeCosse Creative in Minneapolis. A ring binder with 272 numbered pages, plus dividers.
SI = 4, $3.00

The Culinary Arts Institute Cookbook appears to share a lot with the *Encyclopedic Cookbook*, although the *Encyclopedic Cookbook* was still in print in paperback as of 1988. This 799-page book (from 1985) was also reprinted in 1989.
SI = 4, $10.00

CAI's American Family Home Cook Book, from 1986, contains some material from *The American Peoples Cook Book*. The remainder of the material may be new. 608 pages in hardback, the volume contains a section on microwave cooking. Published by Lexicon Publications of New York. No Director is mentioned for the Institute, but Donald D. Wolf is editorial director of the volume.
SI = 4, $5.00

The Cookie Jar

The Chinese Cookbook of Many Delights

Toastmaster System III Oven Broiler Cookbook

The Kitchen Treasury Series was released in 1987. This contained several 80-page hardback books, including *Old Fashioned Favorites*. Published by Lexicon Publications. Apparently rehashed versions of earlier material, most of it from the *Kitchen Treasury* book (1981). SI = 3, $3.00 each

Checklist

Title	Edition	Value in Mint Condition
❑ *The American Peoples Cookbook*	1956	$15.00
❑ *Brunch, Breakfast, and Morning Coffee* (#104)	1954 – 1956	$4.00 – 8.00
❑ *The Casserole Cook Book* (#102)	1954 – 1956	$4.00 – 8.00
❑ *The Cheese Cook Book* (#116)	1955 – 1956	$4.00 – 8.00
❑ *The Chocolate Cook Book* (#104)	1954 – 1956	$4.00 – 8.00
❑ *Cooking Magic* (two binders)	1956	$15.00
❑ *Cooking Magic* (box)	1956	$25.00
❑ *Cooking With Sour Cream and Buttermilk* (#121)	1954 – 1956	$4.00 – 8.00
❑ *Cooling Dishes for Hot Weather* (#117)	1955 – 1956	$4.00 – 8.00
❑ *The Creole Cook Book* (#110)	1955 – 1956	$4.00 – 8.00
❑ *Dishes Children Love* (#111)	1954 – 1956	$4.00 – 8.00
❑ *Elegant Desserts* (#109)	1954 – 1956	$4.00 – 8.00
❑ *English Pennsylvania Dutch Dictionary*	1965	$10.00

Checklist

Title	Edition	Value in Mint Condition
☐ *Entertaining Six or Eight* (#115)	1955 – 1956	$4.00 – 8.00
☐ *The Family Home Cook Book*	1963	$8.00 w/dj
☐ *The French Cook Book* (#103)	1954 – 1956	$4.00 – 8.00
☐ *The German and Viennese Cook Book* (#120)	1955 – 1956	$4.00 – 8.00
☐ *The Gourmet Foods Cook Book* (#112)	1954 – 1956	$4.00 – 8.00
☐ *The Ground Meat Cook Book* (#108)	1954 – 1956	$4.00 – 8.00
☐ *The Holiday Cook Book* (#124)	1955 – 1956	$4.00 – 8.00
☐ *The Hungarian Cook Book* (#114)	1955 – 1956	$4.00 – 8.00
☐ *The Hungry Man's Outdoor Grill Cookbook*	1953	$12.00
☐ *The Italian Cook Book* (#106)	1954 – 1956	$4.00 – 8.00
☐ *The Jewish Woman's Cookbook*	1968	$30.00
☐ *Low-Carbohydrate Diet Menus and Recipes* (A1)	1966	$12.00
☐ *The Lunch Box Cook Book* (#105)	1954 – 1956	$4.00 – 8.00
☐ *The Master Chef's Outdoor Grill Cook Book*	1960	$8.00
☐ *The Master Chef's Outdoor Grill Cook Book*	1960	$8.00
☐ *The Mixer, Hand Mixer, and Blender Cookbook* (HB)	1954	$20.00

Coca-Cola card

Alltime Favorite Recipes

Checklist

	Title	Edition	Value in Mint Condition
☐	*The Mixer, Hand Mixer, and Blender Cookbook* (PB)	1954	$15.00
☐	*My Favorite Recipes*	1959	$10.00
☐	*The New England Cook Book* (#118)	1955 – 1956	$4.00 – 8.00
☐	*The New Orleans Cook Book* (#110)	1954	$4.00 – 8.00
☐	*Pennsylvania Dutch People's Cook Book*	1968	$5.00
☐	*The President's Own White House Cookbook*	1968	$5.00
☐	*Quick Dishes for the Woman in a Hurry* (#101)	1954 – 1956	$4.00 – 8.00
☐	*The Scandanavian Cook Book* (#113)	1955 – 1956	$4.00 – 8.00
☐	*The Shrimp Cookbook* (A2)	1966	$12.00
☐	*The Southern and Southwestern Cook Book* (#122)	1955 – 1956	$4.00 – 8.00
☐	*Sunday Night Suppers* (#119)	1955 – 1956	$4.00 – 8.00
☐	*Tempting Low Calorie Recipes* (#123)	1955 – 1956	$4.00 – 8.00
☐	*The Woman's World Cookbook*	1961	$10.00

See above listings for books published after 1969.

Any reissue of an earlier booklet $3.00 or less

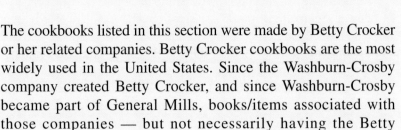
The cookbooks listed in this section were made by Betty Crocker or her related companies. Betty Crocker cookbooks are the most widely used in the United States. Since the Washburn-Crosby company created Betty Crocker, and since Washburn-Crosby became part of General Mills, books/items associated with those companies — but not necessarily having the Betty Crocker name — are also listed in this section. Since Washburn-Crosby's first cookbook was an issue of one of Maria Parloa's cookbooks, that book is also listed in this section.

Cookbooks, booklets, and pamphlets listed in this section and in those that follow will be listed in a narrative format that follows chronologically. Certain abbreviations will occasionally appear:

HB — hardback — stiff covers, pages usually bound via stitching

SHB — spiral hardback — stiff covers, pages bound with a metal spiral or plastic comb

PB — paperback — soft covers, pages bound by stitching or stapling

SPB — spiral paperback — soft covers, pages bound with a metal spiral or plastic comb

RB — ring binder

PAM — pamphlet — a single sheet, which may be folded; no staples

The Scarcity Index, referred to in the listings by the initials SI, is described in more detail in this book's introduction on page 7.

The value given is for a copy in Near Mint condition. For values in lower grades, consult the section in this book on grading on page 6.

The three sections comprising this section cover material as follows:
Washburn-Crosby and related cookbooks, 1880 – 1926
General Mills – Betty Crocker cookbooks, 1928 – 1952
General Mills – Betty Crocker cookbooks, 1953 – 1969

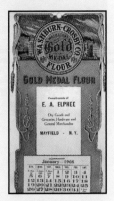

Gold Medal advertising calendar

Washburn-Crosby "Yuco" cereal trade card

Gold Medal advertising booklet for ordering products

Washburn, Crosby Merchant Millers

Miss Parloa's New Cook Book and Marketing Guide

Miss Parloa's New Cook Book – 1880

According to the General Mills website, Cadwallader C. Washburn founded the Minneapolis Mill Company in 1856, thinking to lease power rights along the Mississippi River to millers. He bought the land owned by a failed Minneapolis mill in 1866, spending $100,000 to construct a new, modern mill on the site. Although people called the mill "Washburn's folly" and believed that no mill so large should have been constructed so far west, Washburn believed that there would be demand for midwestern wheat. By 1874, he had the capital to construct yet another, larger mill — the Washburn "A" Mill. Following the usual practice of labeling mills according to size, the 1866 mill was relabeled the "B" Mill. In ten years' time, Washburn's flour was winning awards at the Centennial Exposition.

In September 1877, he partnered with his brother and John Crosby, forming the Washburn-Crosby Company, but tragedy struck almost immediately. An explosion leveled the "A" Mill and five other buildings on May 2, 1878, temporarily crippling production. Bringing in safer new equipment, the mill was rebuilt, this time including the steel rollers that made their mill the world's first automated mill. The "A" Mill reached a capacity of 5,500 barrels of flour per day — foremost among mills until the advent of Pillsbury's own "A" Mill in 1881.

Two years later (1880), the miller competed in the International Millers' Exposition in Cincinnati, sweeping the competition and prompting Washburn-Crosby to label their flour "best in the world." The company picked up three medals at the expo, with their highest quality Superlative flour coming away with the gold medal. About two months after the victory on June 8, some sacks of the Washburn-Crosby flour began to go out renamed as Gold Medal Flour in honor of their outstanding achievement. The name took over, and the flour became one of the industry standards.

1880:

Miss Parloa's New Cook Book and Marketing Guide is the earliest known cooking publication that had a relationship to Washburn-Crosby. The 1880 hardback edition of Maria Parloa's book was quickly reprinted with an almost identical cover. Maria Parloa had become an important figure in the sphere of homemaking and cooking. After publishing the *Appledore Cook Book* (1872), in 1876 she began giving public lectures and offered her first courses in "Domestic Science" at Lasell Seminary. The following year, she lectured in Boston, and the idea occurred to her to start a cooking school. In 1878, the Boston Cooking School was created, under the auspices of the Woman's Educational Association. Miss Parloa was one of the two first directors of the school. After the publication of her *Miss Parloa's New Cook Book*, her name became a household word among those interested in cookery. She is considered to be the person who popularized tomato soup. Walter Baker & Co., manufacturers of chocolate, also engaged the services of Miss Parloa in contributing recipes to their *Choice Recipes* pamphlets.

1926:

What Every Woman Should Know About Baking
    Subtitled *The New Meaning of Flour*
    6¼" x 5"
    Features the Betty Crocker signature; written "by" Betty Crocker.
    The front cover appears to be the first attempt at depicting Betty in
    any booklet. The same portrait had already appeared in advertising.
    12 pages, SI = 6 , $15.00

Wheat and Flour

Late 1920s:

Gold Medal Home Service recipe box
These boxes were very popular and came out in several styles
throughout the years:

* Wooden box; information in gold on front of lid; inside of lid
shows several bags of flour and other items labeled "Gold Medal
Foods" (c. 1924 – 1928)

* Wooden box; information in gold on front of lid; inside of lid
shows one bag of flour with new slogan: "Kitchen-Tested" (c. 1928)

* Wooden box; information on sticker on front of box; inside of lid
shows woman in the kitchen (1929 – early 1930s)

* Metal box; information on sticker on front of box (1930s)

*The Story of Wheat from
Seed to Flour*

The earlier cards have a logo that reads "Eventually... why not now"
in the upper left corner. The metal box was reproduced somewhat
recently. A Gold Medal "Products Control" box of professional
recipes also exists, probably c. 1930.
SI = 5, $15.00 – $30.00 each

Directions for Making a Standard American Loaf of Bread
    This larger pamphlet came out at about the same time as the recipe
    boxes were first issued. The Gold Medal logo still features the
    "Eventually" slogan prominently, and the company is still listed as
    Washburn-Crosby (rather than General Mills).
    SI = 8, $5.00

Unknown Time:

Gold Medal Sandwich Book
    Dedicated to the Earl of Sandwich
    3" x 5"; contains 100 recipes for sandwiches
    Published by Washburn-Crosby, so it predates General Mills.
    36 pages, SI = 6, $12.00

Gold Medal Home Service
recipe box

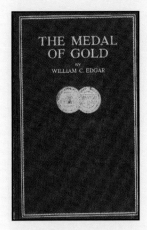

The Medal of Gold

What Every Woman Should Know About Baking

Checklist

Title	Edition	Value in Mint Condition
☐ Best for Every Purpose	1921	$5.00
☐ Directions for Making a Standard American Loaf of Bread	1920s	$5.00
☐ Gold Medal Flour Cook Book	1904	$75.00
☐ Gold Medal Flour Cook Book (1904 Christmas)	1904	$100.00
☐ Gold Medal Flour Cook Book (Christmas reissue)	1970s	$4.00
☐ Gold Medal Flour Cook Book	1908	$35.00
☐ Gold Medal Flour Cook Book	1909	$25.00
☐ Gold Medal Flour Cook Book	1910	$25.00
☐ Gold Medal Flour Cook Book	1916	$25.00
☐ Gold Medal Flour Cook Book	1917	$20.00
☐ Gold Medal Flour — Eventually, Why Not Now?	1916	$12.00
☐ Gold Medal Home Service recipe box (with cards)	Any edition	$15.00 – 30.00
☐ Gold Medal Sandwich Book	unknown	$12.00
☐ A Good Bread Recipe	1916	$15.00
☐ How a Well Bred Maid Makes Well Made Bread	1911	$20.00
☐ How About Sweet Potato Pie?	c. 1910	$20.00
☐ Miss Parloa's New Cook Book and Marketing Guide	1880	$50.00
☐ Miss Parloa's New Cook Book and Marketing Guide	1880s	$40.00

Checklist

Title	Edition	Value in Mint Condition
❏ *Miss Parloa's New Cook Book* (any copy)	1880	$75.00
❏ *Miss Parloa's New Cook Book* (reprint)	1970s – 1980s	$3.00
❏ *'Tis Well to Remember Men Like Bread*	1911	$20.00
❏ *Washburn's Best Cook Book*	1888	$125.00
❏ *Washburn, Crosby Co. Flour Mills*	1893	$50.00
❏ *Washburn-Crosby Co.'s New Cook Book*	1894	$75.00
❏ *What Every Woman Should Know About Baking*	1926	$15.00

Directions for Making a Standard American Loaf of Bread

The Gold Medal Sandwich Book

How to "Simplify" Your Baking

15 Ways to a Man's Heart

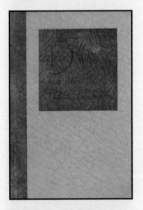

Betty Crocker's 101 Delicious Bisquick Creations

Betty Crocker's $25,000 Recipe Set

1928:

This year Washburn-Crosby joined several other millers in collecting together to form General Mills.

1929:

How to "Simplify" Your Baking
The information contained in the booklet (along with recipes) indicates that baking is "simplified" when flour is used that has been tested in kitchens as well as laboratories. "Kitchen-tested" was an expression that would become synonymous with Gold Medal Flour. The last page in the booklet contains the sketch of Betty that was used in the 1926 booklet and has a coupon that would enable someone to obtain a wooden box and recipe cards from General Mills for one dollar. The first page shows the original Betty Crocker signature.
16 pages, SI = 8, $10.00

1931:

The highly popular "fast cooking" Bisquick was introduced this year. A General Mills executive, Carl Smith, learned from a railroad cook that a biscuit dough could be created which could be stored and made to order quickly. The chemists at General Mills discovered how to turn the cook's idea into a pre-packaged mix, and Bisquick emerged. Bisquick was promoted from the start by various means, including a tin recipe file from 1931. That file was reproduced in 1981 at the 50th anniversary of Bisquick.

1932:

15 Ways to a Man's Heart
Shows two slightly different versions of the Betty Crocker signature. The facial portrait that appeared in the 1926 pamphlet is shown here with a signature across it.
HB, 24 pages, SI = 8, $15.00

1933:

Betty Crocker's 101 Delicious Bisquick Creations
This first Bisquick cookbook emerged in 1933, to be followed by many others. Bisquick was promoted as "Smart, Simple, Sure," and the popularity of the product indicates that most people agreed with that assessment. This booklet was also the first of at least three to feature recipes and testimonials from famous people. Among those represented here are Mary Pickford and Claudette Colbert.
32 pages, SI = 2, $6.00

Betty Crocker's $25,000 Recipe Set
A spiral-bound collection of recipes from famous chefs, kitchen-tested and adapted for American kitchens by the Gold Medal Home Service department.
60 pages, SI = 4, $20.00

Also in 1933, Wheaties became known as the "Breakfast of Champions," as the product began to sponsor baseball games. The slogan first appeared on a sign at a ball park, but the association of Wheaties with sports — and the slogan — has been part of advertising legend ever since.

1934:

New Party Cakes for All Occasions
Sponsored by Softasilk. Includes the "Queen of Hearts" cake, which is pictured on the front cover. Booklet number 765.
24 pages, SI = 6, $15.00

Vitality Demands Energy
Subtitled "109 Smart New Ways to Serve Bread"
As with the Bisquick booklets, this bread book features testimonials from celebrities, including Emily Post. The foreword also displays a drawing of Betty Crocker herself. This is a hardback version of the following paperback.
100 pages, SI = 9, $25.00

Vitality Demands Energy
Subtitled "109 Smart New Ways to Serve Bread"
As with the Bisquick booklets, this bread book features testimonials from celebrities, including Emily Post. The foreword also displays a drawing of Betty Crocker herself.
100 pages, SI = 4, $5.00

From 1934 until 1942, Bisquick and Wheaties ran an advertising promotion that involved Shirley Temple. Buy the General Mills product, and send in coupons for cobalt blue Shirley Temple tumblers and pitcher. Although not rare, these are collectible in excellent condition.

1935:

Let the Stars Show You How to Take a Trick a Day with Bisquick
The "stars" included several of the most famous people of the day, including Clark Gable and of course Betty Crocker.
41 pages, SI = 3, $5.00

The 1932 flatware pattern "Friendship," made by Wm. Rogers & Son (Oneida) was also available by this time through Gold Medal Flour, Wheaties, Softasilk, and Bisquick coupons as "Medality." Coupons were available in small recipe pamphlets that retailed for 15¢ each. These coupons were the precursor to the later Betty Crocker points. These pamphlets included such titles as *Foods Men Rave About* and *Foods Men Hurry Home For* and feature a drawing of Betty Crocker. These sell for about $1.00 each now.

1936:

Betty Crocker's 15 Prize Recipes
Subtitled "Favorites of Each Year — 1921 to 1936"
Celebrating the 15th anniversary of Betty Crocker.
PAM, SI = 5, $5.00

New Party Cakes for All Occasions

Vitality Demands Energy

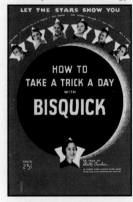

Let the Stars Show You How to Take a Trick a Day with Bisquick

Betty Crocker's 15 Prize Recipes

Foods Men Rave About

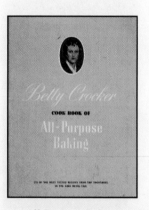

The Story of Fifty Hymns

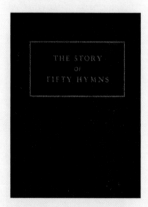

All-Purpose Baking

Meal Planning on a Limited Budget

1939:

The Story of Fifty Hymns
Black and gold cover. Contains the lyrics and stories behind 50 of the hymns that were sung on the "Hymns of All Churches" radio program, which was sponsored by General Mills since its inception in 1934. The booklet contains one new recipe by Betty Crocker, the favorite cake recipe of the radio program's director, Joe Emerson.
121 pages, SI = 7, $6.00

1942:

All-Purpose Baking
Gold cover; 25¢. This was a very popular booklet.
100 pages, SI = 2, $3.00

Meal Planning on a Limited Budget
Subtitled "Nutrition for Defense"
A black and white booklet with tips on saving food money. Features the (original) Betty Crocker signature on the front cover. Prepared prior to food rationing but issued afterward.
Contains a rubber stamping indicating new bread standards for the coming year of 1943.
16 pages, SI = 7, $20.00

1943:

Your Share
5¼"x 8"
Talks about how to save dairy products, fat, and reduce the consumption of rationed foods.
48 pages, SI = 1, $2.00

c. 1945:

Betty Crocker "Double-Quick" Method Gold Medal Cakes
No date, but is part of the series inaugurated by the *New Method* cakes booklet on page 179. Contains a color center spread. Mentions what to do in case sugar is in low supply.
100 pages, SI = 6, $10.00

1946:

Oneida began offering their "Queen Bess" pattern of flatware in conjunction with General Mills' new promotion, which consisted of including points along with Betty Crocker products, which could be redeemed for premiums. The points idea became so popular that it is still used today.

A new portrait of a more mature Betty Crocker was commissioned. The official rendering was painted by Haddom H. Sundblom in oil on canvas. Also that year, a new signature came into use. In the second signature, the shape of the "B" is quite different, with a straight left side. (See the cookbook photos for details).

Betty Crocker "New Method" Gold Medal Cakes
　No date, but appears to precede the booklet that follows. Contains recipes that answer requests made of Betty during the course of her radio show.
　100 pages, SI = 8, $12.00

New Betty Crocker Method Recipes
　Subtitled "New Magic in Cake-Making"
　Two printings are known. One printing has the subtitle against a red background, and the other (shown) has the subtitle written on a black background.
　32 pages, SI = 4, $6.00

Betty Crocker Method Streamlined Recipes
　Another booklet promoting the easier method.
　11 pages, SI = 7, $5.00

1947:

The Betty Crocker Guide to Pressure Cooking
　The manual for the GM PressureQuick saucepan.

Toast: "The Betty Crocker Way"
　The instruction manual for the GM Automatic Toaster.

1948:

Chiffon Cake Recipes
　About 5½" x 9"
　According to one report, the chiffon cake was a specialty item until Betty Crocker released this cookbook in 1948. The booklet was popular.
　20 pages, SI = 3, $8.00
　There is also a one-page handout promoting the Chiffon booklet that contains a few recipes.

Betty Crocker Picture Cooky Book
　Another popular release from Betty, containing recipes that were well-used in the kitchen.
　48 pages, SI = 4, $8.00

Specialty Breads
　Contains professional bread recipes.
　144 pages, SPB, SI = 7, $12.00

1949:

Cooking for Fifty
　Features recipes for large groups: camps; socials; school lunches; etc.
　34 pages, SI = 6, $8.00

1950:

Betty Crocker's Picture Cook Book
　Red cover; first printing does not mention printing info.
　Betty Crocker's first comprehensive cookbook was available in both hardback and ringbound editions. The binder format proved to be

Your Share

Betty Crocker "Double-Quick" Method Gold Medal Cakes

New Betty Crocker Method Recipes

New Betty Crocker Method Recipes

 179

Betty Crocker Picture
Cooky Book – 1948

Specialty Breads

Cooking for Fifty

Chiffon Cake Recipes

more popular. The recipes were so useful that the book became available in at least nine printings from 1950 to 1956.
SI = 2, RB or HB, $40.00

Betty Crocker's Picture Cook Book, Limited Special Edition
Multicolored blue cover; first printing so indicates.
This is a deluxe format version of the popular *Picture Cook Book*. Each of these copies was given away and inscribed to someone. The inscription page was signed in pen with a Betty Crocker signature.
448 pages, SI = 7, $50.00

A Gift You Bake is From the Heart
121 recipes
8 pages, SI = 9, $8.00

1951:

Betty Crocker's Cake Mix Magic
Five binder holes
8 recipes and gift-wrapping suggestions.
28 pages, SI = 7, $12.00

1952:

So You're Serving a Crowd
A booklet of recipes adapted for larger groups.
50 pages, SI = 8, $15.00

Checklist

Title	Edition	Value in Mint Condition
❑ *15 Prize Recipes*	1936	$5.00
❑ *15 Ways to a Man's Heart*	1932	$15.00
❑ *All-Purpose Baking*	1942	$3.00
❑ *Betty Crocker Method Streamlined Recipes*	1946	$5.00
❑ *Betty Crocker Picture Cooky Book*	1948	$8.00
❑ *Betty Crocker's 101 Delicious Bisquick Creations*	1933	$6.00

Checklist

Title	Edition	Value in Mint Condition
☐ Betty Crocker's $25,000 Recipe Set	1933	$20.00
☐ Betty Crocker's Picture Cook Book	1950	$40.00
☐ Betty Crocker's Picture Cook Book (Ltd. Special Ed.)	1950	$50.00
☐ Cake Mix Magic	1951	$12.00
☐ Chiffon Cake Recipes	1948	$8.00
☐ Cooking for Fifty	1949	$8.00
☐ "Double-Quick" Method Gold Medal Cakes	c. 1945	$10.00
☐ A Gift You Bake is From the Heart	1950	$8.00
☐ How to "Simplify" your Baking	1929	$10.00
☐ Let the Stars Show You How to Take a Trick a Day with Bisquick	1935	$5.00
☐ Meal Planning on a Limited Budget	1942	$20.00
☐ New Betty Crocker Method Recipes	1946	$6.00
☐ "New Method" Gold Medal Cakes	1946	$12.00
☐ New Party Cakes for All Occasions	1934	$15.00
☐ So You're Serving a Crowd	1952	$15.00
☐ Specialty Breads	1948	$12.00
☐ The Story of Fifty Hymns	1939	$6.00
☐ Vitality Demands Energy (HB)	1934	$25.00
☐ Vitality Demands Energy (PB)	1934	$5.00
☐ Your Share	1943	$2.00

Betty Crocker's Picture Cook Book

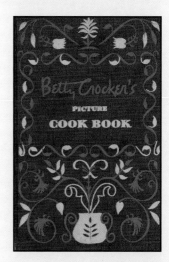

Betty Crocker's Picture Cook Book, Limited Special Edition

Betty Crocker's Cake Mix Magic

Betty Crocker's Junior Baking Book

Betty Crocker's Good and Easy Cook Book

My Betty Crocker Notebook

Gold Medal Jubilee Select Recipes

1953:

Mirro Aluminum made the Junior Baking Kit, which included the following cookbooks:

Betty Crocker's Junior Baking Book
6" x 9"
An introduction to baking for children. Blue or white cover.
16 pages, SI = 6, $8.00

Notes from the Betty Crocker Kitchen
No date, but since the transitional signature (straight-sided "B") is found on the cover, the booklet must have been issued between 1946 and 1954.
12 pages, SI = 8, $3.00

1954:

In conjunction with the introduction of two Betty Crocker cake mixes, Mirro Aluminum released two cake pans, engraved with slogans introducing the mixes.

A new Betty Crocker signature emerged this year, with a "B" that sported an extension on the left side at the top. Notice that the crossbar of the two "t's" extends over the "y" in "Betty."

Betty Crocker's Good and Easy Cook Book
6" x 8"
White cover with block background.
256 pages, SHB, $1.00 original price

Issued in at least 8 printings, then reissued in 1962 as the *New Good & Easy Cook Book*, with a pentagram trivet and different food on the cover and 196 pages.

Good & Easy Cook Book, SI = 1, $15.00
New Good & Easy Cook Book, SI = 1, $8.00

The spiral hardback series was extremely popular. General Mills (Betty Crocker) released several books in the coming years in the small format, then revamped the entire series beginning in 1963 in a newer large format. The series continued to add members, finally being incorporated into other series in 1970.

Mid – Late 1950s:

My Betty Crocker Notebook
Dividers and blank pages
6" x 8"
Intended for use at home, the pages are simply white paper, but the dividers have recipes printed on them.
RB, SI = 6, $20.00

 182

1955:

Gold Medal Jubilee Select Recipes
6" x 10"
49 pages, SI = 3, $6.00

1956:

Betty Crocker's Picture Cook Book
A new and revised edition. Issued in at least 4 printings. Hardbound (less common) or ringbound (more common)
472 pages, HB, SI = 3, $60.00
472 pages, RB, SI = 2, $60.00

Betty Crocker's Bisquick Cook Book
6" x 8"
26 pages, SI = 2, $3.00

1957:

Betty Crocker's Cook Book for Boys and Girls
6" x 8"
White cover with children.
191 pages, SHB, $1.00 original price

Issued in at least six printings, then reissued in 1965 as the *New Boys and Girls Cook Book*, with a yellow cover and 156 pages.

Cook Book for Boys and Girls, SI = 1, $20.00
New Boys and Girls Cook Book, SI = 1, $8.00

Betty Crocker's Pie Parade
Three binder holes
38 pages, SI = 4, $8.00

Betty Crocker's Softasilk Special Occasion Cakes
Pink cover
32 pages, SI = 2, $3.00

Betty Crocker's Bisquick Party Book
6" x 8"
24 pages, SI = 3, $3.00

Betty Crocker Invites you to Enjoy Music for Cake 'N Coffee Time
45 RPM record, with picture sleeve and coupon insert
RCA SP-45-29
Back of sleeve features four short recipes.
SI = 7, $20.00

Betty Crocker's Cooky Carnival
Three binder holes
Multicolored cover; contains recipes from the *Picture Cook Book*.
40 pages, SI = 3, $12.00

Betty Crocker's Bisquick Cook Book – 1956

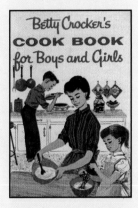

Betty Crocker's for Boys and Girls Cook Book – 1957

Betty Crocker's New Boys and Girls Cook Book – 1965

Betty Crocker's Softasilk Special Occasion Cakes

 183

Betty Crocker's Bisquick Party Book

Cake 'N Coffee Time

Betty Crocker's Cooky Carnival

Betty Crocker's Dinner for Two Cook Book

1958:

Betty Crocker's Dinner for Two Cook Book
6" x 8"
Cover shows blue and white dinnerware and food.
Issued in at least four printings, then reissued in 1964 as the *New Dinner for Two Cook Book*, with 156 pages and a cover showing candles.

Dinner for Two, 207 pages, SHB, SI = 1, $12.00
New Dinner For Two, SHB, SI = 1, $6.00

How to Have the Most Fun With Cake Mixes
5½" x 8"
25¢ cover price
Introduces four Betty Crocker frosting mixes. Date is approximate.
34 pages, SI = 2, $3.00

Betty Crocker's Frosting Secrets
Subtitled "Fun With Frostings"
24 pages, SI = 2 , $3.00

Betty Crocker's Holiday Almanac
7" x 10", w/binder holes
Contains several holiday recipes. All pulp paper; no slick cover.
8 pages, SI = 6, $2.00

1959:

Betty Crocker's Guide to Easy Entertaining
6" x 8"
Cover looks like needlepoint.
Known in at least two printings.
176 pages, SHB, SI = 1, $6.00

133 Quicker Ways to Homemade...With Bisquick
26 pages, SI = 5, $3.00

Betty Crocker's Frankly Fancy Foods Recipe Book
Five binder holes
28 pages, SI = 4, $6.00

12 Spectacular Television Treats
Magazine insert with two coupons and recipes.
Contains ads for seven shows sponsored by General Mills.
6 pages, SI = 4, $1.00

Late 1950s:

Breads You Bake ... With Yeast
Five binder holes
12 pages, SI = 5, $2.00

1960:

Betty Crocker's Party Book
6" x 8"
Cover shows a party.
Known in at least two printings.
176 pages, SHB, SI = 2 – 3, $8.00

All-American Favorite Recipes
Subtitled "With Mazola Corn Oil and Gold Medal Flour"
Five binder holes
20 pages, SI = 4, $3.00

1961:

Outdoor Cook Book
White cover with tree. At least four printings exist.
Reissued in 1967 as the *New Outdoor Cook Book*, with a red cover and 156 pages.

A Bantam Books paperback edition of this book and nine others in the series was published in June of 1976.
Either edition, 176 pages, SHB, SI = 2, $6.00

Betty Crocker's New Picture Cook Book
At least three printings exist of each version.
455 pages, RB (more common) or HB (less common)
SI = 1, $75.00

Betty Crocker's Bake Up a Story
Package insert
Includes such unforgettable items as "Magic Carpet Cookies," "Camelot Cookies," "Jack-be-nimble Date Cake," and "Tom Thumb Pizzas." Uses the earlier Betty Crocker signature, where the crossbar of the T's extends over the "Y." That fact, and the number on the back cover date this pamphlet earlier than 1963. The pamphlet itself is undated.
20 pages, SI = 4, $3.00

1962:

Betty Crocker's Cooking Calendar
Multicolored cover
176 pages, SHB, SI = 3, $5.00

Betty Crocker's Talking Recipes
33⅓ RPM records for the blind, with titles in braille.
3 LP's, SI = 8, $30.00

1963:

Betty Crocker's Cooky Book
Red cover. Large size. At least 16 printings exist.
The tenth printings (from 1970 on) have different covers than the first nine.
156 pages, SHB, SI = 1, $30.00 (early printing)

Betty Crocker's New Dinner for Two Cook Book

How to Have the Most Fun With Cake Mixes

Betty Crocker's Holiday Almanac

133 Quicker Ways to Homemade...With Bisquick

Betty Crocker's Frankly Fancy Foods Recipe Book

12 Spectacular Television Treats

Betty Crocker's Party Book

All-American Favorite Recipes

The above book features a new Betty Crocker signature, which looks very similar to the earlier one, except that the crossbar for the two T's does not extend over the "y" in "Betty." That new signature is also different from the one currently in use.

Betty Crocker's Merry Makings
Subtitled "*Fun Foods for Happy Entertaining*"
Cover has a blue-violet background and multicolored drawing.
Date is approximate.
 24 pages, SI = 4, $3.00

1964:

Betty Crocker's Parties for Children
Pink cover. Large size. At least two printings exist.
163 pages, SHB, SI = 1, Value: $6.00

Bisquick Cook Book
6" x 8". Several printings exist.
112 pages, SHB, SI = 2, $6.00

Festive Fixins With a Foreign Flair
Package insert
This was Betty Crocker's holiday insert from 1964, containing Christmas recipes from around the world.
24 pages, SI = 5, $3.00

1965:

Betty Crocker's Dinner in a Dish Cook Book
Large size. Also available in hardback.
Several printings exist.
152 pages, SHB, SI = 2, $4.00

Honey, That's Delicious
Red embossed cover
16 pages, PB, SI = 7, $6.00

Holidays on Parade
Package insert.
This, the holiday insert for 1965, for the first time includes recipes made with Peter Pan peanut butter, which had been introduced by General Mills during the year. Also contains a coupon good for 7¢ off of any Peter Pan peanut butter purchase.
24 pages, SI = 5, $3.00

1966:

Betty Crocker's Cake and Frosting Mix Cookbook
Large size
Cover pictures cakes; one chocolate cake says "Tex" in the icing.
144 pages, SHB, SI = 3, $3.00

Betty Crocker's Holiday Heritage
 This holiday booklet for 1966 features "heritage" sections from the
 East, Midwest, Southwest, and South, along with a section of cookies.
 16 pages, SI = 4, $3.00

Holiday Recipes and Ideas for the 12 Days of Christmas
 16 pages, SI = 4, $2.00

1967:

Betty Crocker's Hostess Cook Book
 Large size
 168 pages, SHB, SI = 2, $6.00

So Quick with New Bisquick
 Cover pictures waffles and pancakes.
 120 pages, SI = 3, $3.00

42 Hot Potato Ideas
 White and multicolored cover, featuring spoon logo.
 16 pages, SI = 6, $3.00

1968:

Betty Crocker's Pie and Pastry Cook Book
 Large size
 160 pages, SHB, SI = 2, $6.00

TV Cooking Capers
 Orange cover with drawing of a fox. Has earlier signature with cross-
 bars extending over the "y" in "Betty."
 10 pages, SI = 3, $1.00

Holiday Hostess "Can Do" Recipes
 16 pages, SI = 6, $1.00

1969:

Betty Crocker's Cookbook
 Red cover or trade paperback with white cover. May be found with
 or without insert from Sears. At least 22 printings exist.
 HB or RB, SI = 1, $50.00 (early copy)

Betty Crocker's Ways With Hamburger
 28 pages, HB, SI = 5, $3.00

Betty Crocker's Ways With Chicken
 Light blue cover with drawing of a chicken.
 Printed by Golden Press.
 24 pages, SI = 5, $3.00

Betty Crocker's Kitchen Gardens
 Includes sections on planting and harvesting herbs and vegetables —
 and of course their uses in recipes.
 170 pages, HB, SI = 5, $5.00

*Betty Crocker's Outdoor
Cook Book – 1961*

*Betty Crocker's New Outdoor
Cookbook*

*Betty Crocker's New Picture Cook
Book*

Betty Crocker's Bake Up a Story

 187

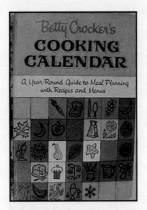

Betty Crocker's Cooking Calendar

Betty Crocker's Talking Recipes

Betty Crocker's Cooky Book – 1963

Betty Crocker's Merry Makings

Betty Crocker's Cakes Kids Love
Quite a few recipes for cakes in interesting shapes and decorations. 24 pages, SI = 4, $3.00

Checklist

Title	Edition	Value in Mint Condition
❑ *12 Spectacular Television Treats*	1959	$1.00
❑ *133 Quicker Ways to Homemade... With Bisquick*	1959	$3.00
❑ *42 Hot Potato Ideas*	1967	$3.00
❑ *All-American Favorite Recipes*	1960	$3.00
❑ *Bake Up a Story*	1961	$3.00
❑ *Betty Crocker's Bisquick Cook Book*	1956	$3.00
❑ *Betty Crocker's Cookbook* (RB or HB, early edition)	1969	$50.00
❑ *Betty Crocker's New Picture Cook Book* (RB or HB)	1961	$75.00
❑ *Betty Crocker's Picture Cook Book* (RB or HB)	1956	$60.00
❑ *Bisquick Cook Book*	1964	$6.00
❑ *Bisquick Party Book*	1957	$3.00
❑ *Breads You Bake ... With Yeast*	c. 1959	$2.00
❑ *Cake and Frosting Mix Cookbook*	1966	$3.00
❑ *Cake 'N Coffee Time* (45 RPM record, with sleeve)	1957	$20.00
❑ *Cakes Kids Love*	1969	$3.00
❑ *Cook Book for Boys and Girls*	1957	$20.00
❑ *Cooking Calendar*	1962	$5.00
❑ *Cooky Book*	1963	$15.00 – 30.00

Checklist

	Title	Edition	Value in Mint Condition
☐	*Cooky Carnival*	1957	$12.00
☐	*Dinner for Two Cook Book*	1958	$12.00
☐	*Dinner in a Dish Cook Book*	1965	$4.00
☐	*Festive Fixins With a Foreign Flair*	1964	$3.00
☐	*Frankly Fancy Foods Recipe Book*	1959	$6.00
☐	*Frosting Secrets*	1958	$3.00
☐	*Gold Medal Jubilee Select Recipes*	1955	$6.00
☐	*Good and Easy Cook Book*	1954	$15.00
☐	*Guide to Easy Entertaining*	1959	$6.00
☐	*Holiday Calendar*	1958	$2.00
☐	*Holiday Heritage*	1966	$3.00
☐	*Holiday Hostess "Can Do" Recipes*	1968	$1.00
☐	*Holiday Recipes and Ideas for the 12 Days of Christmas*	1966	$2.00
☐	*Holidays on Parade*	1965	$3.00
☐	*Honey, That's Delicious*	1965	$6.00
☐	*Hostess Cookbook*	1967	$6.00
☐	*How to Have the Most Fun With Cake Mixes*	1958	$3.00
☐	*Junior Baking Book* (blue or white cover)	1953	$8.00
☐	*Junior Baking Kit* (complete, w/box)	1953	$75.00
☐	*Kitchen Gardens*	1969	$5.00
☐	*Merry Makings*	1963	$3.00

Betty Crocker's Parties for Children

The Bisquick Cook Book – 1964

Festive Fixins With a Foreign Flair

"Honey, That's Delicious!"

Betty Crocker's Holidays on Parade

Betty Crocker's Holiday Heritage

Holiday Recipes and Ideas for the 12 Days of Christmas

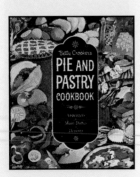
Betty Crocker's Pie and Pastry Cook Book – 1968

Checklist

Title	Edition	Value in Mint Condition
❑ *My Betty Crocker Notebook*	1954 – 1960	$20.00
❑ *New Boys and Girls Cook Book*	1965	$8.00
❑ *New Dinner for Two Cook Book*	1964	$6.00
❑ *New Good and Easy Cook Book*	1962	$8.00
❑ *New Outdoor Cook Book*	1967	$6.00
❑ *Notes from the Betty Crocker Kitchen*	1953	$3.00
❑ *Outdoor Cook Book*	1961	$6.00
❑ *Parties for Children*	1964	$6.00
❑ *Party Book*	1960	$8.00
❑ *Pie and Pastry Cookbook*	1968	$3.00
❑ *Pie Parade*	1957	$8.00
❑ *So Quick with New Bisquick*	1967	$3.00
❑ *Softasilk Special Occasion Cakes*	1957	$3.00
❑ *Talking Recipes*	1962	$30.00
❑ *TV Cooking Capers*	1968	$1.00
❑ *Ways With Chicken*	1969	$3.00
❑ *Ways With Hamburger*	1969	$3.00

The cookbooks listed in this section were made by the Pillsbury Flour Mills or related companies. Largely due to the immensely popular Pillsbury Bake-Offs which began in 1949, Pillsbury's cookbooks are widely used and collected in the United States.

Cookbooks, booklets, and pamphlets listed in this section and in those that follow will be listed in a narrative format that follows chronologically. Certain abbreviations will occasionally appear:

HB — hardback — stiff covers, pages usually bound via stitching

SHB — spiral hardback — stiff covers, pages bound with a metal spiral or plastic comb

PB — paperback — soft covers, pages bound by stitching or stapling

SPB — spiral paperback — soft covers, pages bound with a metal spiral or plastic comb

RB — ring binder

PAM — pamphlet — a single sheet, which may be folded; no staples

1880s "Merchant Millers" package insert

The Scarcity Index, referred to in the listings by the initials SI, is described in more detail in this book's introduction on page 7.

The Value given is for a copy in Near Mint condition. For values in lower grades, consult the section in this book on grading on page 6.

Early Pillsbury trade card

The four divisions comprising this section cover material as follows:
Pillsbury cookbooks, 1900 – 1940
Pillsbury cookbooks, 1941 – 1957
Pillsbury cookbooks, 1958 – 1969
Pillsbury Bake-Off cookbooks, 1950 and beyond

1890s Pillsbury trade card

1890s Pillsbury trade card

Pillsbury Vitos cereal ad

Pillsbury's Vitos Recipe and Household Expense Book

Flour Recipes, Saint Louis Exposition (World's Fair)

A Little Book for a Little Cook

Charles A. Pillsbury bought the Minneapolis Flour Mill in 1869, renovating it and converting it to the Pillsbury Mill. At the time, the mill was capable of producing 150 barrels of flour per day. C. A. Pillsbury & Co. was organized a year later. Immediately profitable, the Pillsbury operation began to expand. Pillsbury began to make use of the latest processes for refining and purifying flour. His confidence in the fineness of his flour was demonstrated by his marking it (beginning in 1872) with four X's: at the time, the finest flour was described as XXX, but Pillsbury honestly believed his flour to be finer than the others. Customers made "Pillsbury's BEST" a household term. In 1881, the "A" mill was completed, and although most operations worldwide were producing under 500 barrels per day, the Pillsbury operation set production records at over 5,000 barrels per day. The "B" mill had actually been constructed earlier (in 1866, by Taylor Brothers), but Pillsbury did not acquire it until later. By 1887, the Pillsbury operation was the largest in the world, and by 1925, the "A" mill's capacity had expanded to 17,500 barrels per day, with the mills as a whole producing up to 42,000 barrels.

In 1889, the operation (along with other mills) was purchased and became part of the Pillsbury-Washburn Company, Ltd., a new British company. Charles A. Pillsbury remained involved until near the time of his death in 1899.

1900:

Pillsbury's first baking contest was held in 1900. According to Pillsbury publications and the original ad shown, the prizes from that contest totaled a mere $680.00. Vitos had been introduced in 1897 as a breakfast food. The cereal rapidly became so popular that other companies copied it. Vitos later became known as "Pillsbury's Wheat Cereal."

Pillsbury's Vitos Recipe and Household Expense Book
5" x 6¾"
A collection of 86 recipes and a table for writing in one's "household expenses." Subtitled "The Vitos Cook Book," this appears to have been Pillsbury's first cookbook. Advertisements from 1900 such as the one shown indicate that the booklet was available for free from grocers who marketed Vitos.
36 pages, SI = 8, $75.00

Pillsbury attended the 1900 Paris Exposition, which commenced in April. There were 76,000 exhibitors during the event, which attracted over 50 million people. According to an article in the May 1900, issue of *Overland Monthly*, although the United States was not alloted any more space than the European nations, one goal of the American exhibit was to display for the first time the raw products, manufacturing processes, and finished products side by side. Pillsbury was awarded a gold medal in 1901 for its part in the exhibition.

1904:

This triumph was followed in 1904 by representation in the Saint Louis Exposition (World's Fair), where Pillsbury was awarded three grand prizes. Pillsbury had a small pamphlet prepared, which was handed out during the exhibition in St. Louis.

Flour Recipes
by Fannie Farmer, Isabel Howard Neff, Myra Russell Garrett, et al.
Original price: free
Contents compiled for the 1904 World's Fair in St. Louis. The recipes inside are made with Pillsbury's Best Flour and with Vitos.
This booklet was handed out at the World's Fair, as indicated on the back cover. Copies were made available to retailers immediately after the fair as well.
32 pages, SI = 7, $50.00

A Book for a Cook

Resulting from the demand for recipes, Pillsbury was determined to publish a booklet based on the recipes that were on display at the exhibition. Two books surfaced the following year.

Made in Minneapolis

1905:

A Little Book for a Little Cook
by L. P. Hubbard
Pillsbury's first children's cookbook, released at the same time as their general cookbook. This smaller paperback advertises that when children have mastered the recipes contained in it, they should consider sending in 10¢ for the complete *Book for a Cook*.
28 pages, SI = 8, $75.00

A Book for a Cook
by L. P. Hubbard
Original price: 10¢
Contents compiled by Nellie Duling Gans for the 1904 World's Fair in St. Louis.
This book was available for free by sending in coupons from certain magazines.
128 pages, SI = 5, $40.00

The Pillsbury Cook Book – 1911

Nellie Duling Gans was the director of the Chicago Cooking College from 1887 to 1915. The Northwestern Yeast Company employed her services in 1890 to compile their book, *Good Bread — How to Make It*. Gans used Pillsbury's Best Flour exclusively at the 1904 World's Fair and took the grand prize. She adapted her prize-winning recipes for home use, resulting in *A Book for a Cook*. Gans also published the *Rex Beef Extract* booklet for the Cudahy Packing Company (Omaha, NE) in 1905. Rex also produced bacon, ham, and other meats; one of their mottos was "The Taste Tells." In fact, their "Extract of Beef" won several awards in competition. Gans also submitted the recipes for Jell-O's second advertising booklet, *Jell-O, The Dainty Dessert*, first available that same year.

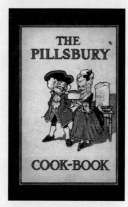
The Pillsbury Cook-Book – 1914

Family of Foods

*Pillsbury's Health Bran —
Ask Your Grocer*

What He Told Her

Pillsbury's Best flour ad

c. 1905 – 1908:

Made in Minneapolis
This pamphlet asks rhetorically on the back cover whether there is a man in America who isn't proud when his wife can bake a good loaf of bread. Inside, it advertises *A Book for a Cook* and gives recipes for bread, biscuits, cake, and pie crust.
PAM, SI = 8, $5.00

The year 1908 was not a good one. With a banking panic going on in the U. S., Pillsbury-Washburn was forced into receivership, showing a loss for the first eight months of the year. The mills closed temporarily (although the "A" mill was out for less than three days). An operating company was established that became (in 1909) the Pillsbury Flour Mills Company. This operating company gained authority over the flour mills later that year and began to pull Pillsbury out of debt.

1911:

The Pillsbury Cook Book
6" x 9¼"
Front page pictures Pillsbury's "A" mill.
Last page is a "pass" allowing a free tour of the Pillsbury flour mill.
126 pages, SI = 5, $30.00

This year, the "A" mill was reinforced structurally and a flour laboratory was constructed on the top floor of the Pillsbury headquarters. The "A" mill had suffered from dry rot and general use, but the reinforcements (which took two years) kept the mill in working order for many years.

1913:

The Pillsbury Cook Book
"A" mill photo and "pass," 1911
126 pages, SI = 4, $20.00

1914:

The Pillsbury Cook Book
First cover: picture of Pillsbury's "A" mill, 1911.
126 pages, SI = 3, $20.00

Second cover: colonial couple; "Cook-Book" is hyphenated.
126 pages, SI = 3, $20.00

The colonials came to be used in Pillsbury advertising, at least until 1930. "Little Nick" was the name associated with the male character. One book places the introduction of the characters as early as 1910.

The "Cook-Book" came in a brown envelope with "From the Pillsbury Flour Mills Company, Minneapolis, Minn." in large letters across the front. No value has yet been established for the envelope, nor an SI rating.

This year, the combined output for all of the mills in Minneapolis reached a record total of 18,541,650 barrels.

In 1919, Pillsbury redesigned their boxed products to emphasize that the company was producing a "family of foods." The new design, found on the cookbook also beginning in 1924 contained a red and white swirl.

c. 1919 – 1920:

Pillsbury's Health Bran — Ask Your Grocer
When the "family of foods" concept was first marketed, Pillsbury's Health Bran was introduced in this little booklet that was also included with copies of *Pillsbury's Cook Book* in 1920. The booklet describes Health Bran as, among other things, "a mild laxative."
12 pages, SI = 7, $8.00

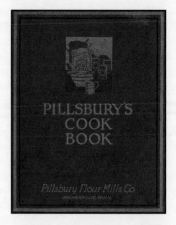

Pillsbury's Cook Book – 1921

What He Told Her
One side of the brochure contains a story ad for Pillsbury's Best Flour and picture ads for the flour, Pillsbury's Best Cereal, and Pillsbury's Health Bran. The other side consists of five recipes.
The drawing of Pillsbury's Wheat Cereal depicts the earlier style Vitos box, not the newer "swirl" design.
10 pages, PAM, SI = 7, $10.00

1920:

Pillsbury's Cook Book
Reissue of the earlier book with the same title.
SI = 5, $25.00

The Story of Flour

1921:

Pillsbury's Cook Book
Softcover
Inset drawing of flour bags and mixing bowl on cover.
96 pages, SI = 5, $30.00

1922:

In 1922, Pillsbury added a mill in Atchison, Kansas. With the addition of another mill in Buffalo (NY) in 1923, Pillsbury's capacity for flour production increased to 42,000 barrels per day. By this time, the "A" mill had expanded to include a South "A" mill, a rye mill, and large grain elevators (capable of holding four million bushels of grain). This area came to be called the East Side Milling District.

The Story of Flour
Includes a fold-out diagram of the "A" mill operation.
Reissued in 1928.
Reissued again (SB) in 1940.
28 pages, HB, SI = 6, $15.00

(Buy this Flour Because)
Pillsbury's Best

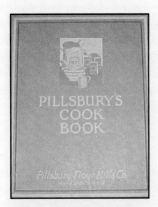

*Pillsbury's Cook Book –
1923*

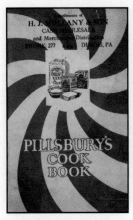

*Pillsbury's Cook Book –
1924*

Pillsbury's Household Manual

(Buy this Flour Because) Pillsbury's Best
>Dated September 1922. Apart from cosmetic changes, this pamphlet was reprinted in 1927 and called "One of the Family." "Form 924."
>10 pages, PAM, SI = 7, $6.00

1923:

Pillsbury's Cook Book
>8" x 10"
>Inset drawing of flour bags and mixing bowl on cover.
>Historical information updated.
>Earlier issues had string hole (in upper left corner), whereas this issue does not.
>75 pages, SI = 5, $20.00

1924:

Pillsbury's Cook Book
>Red and white swirl cover.
>Note: This is the same design that adorned the Pillsbury boxed products of the period, beginning in 1919.
>48 pages, SI = 5, $20.00

1925:

Pillsbury's Household Manual
>by Mary Ellis Ames
>Includes a chapter of recipes.
>7½" x 9"
>78 pages, SI = 6, $50.00

1926:

50 Prize-Winning Recipes for Pillsbury's Health Bran
>Reissued in 1929 as *Recipes for Pillsbury's Wheat Bran*, noting the change in product name.
>16 pages, SI = 4, $6.00

15 Prize-Winning Recipes for Pillsbury's Health Bran
>3" x 6"
>An abridged form of the above booklet.
>"Form 766"
>12 pages, SI = 5, $3.00

1927:

Pillsbury's Cook Book
>5" x 8", as 1924 issue.
>48 pages, SI = 3, $15.00

One of the Family
>Depicts Pancake Flour, Farina, and Health Bran on the back.
>"Form 924." Apart from cosmetic changes, this is a reprint of the "Buy this Flour" pamphlet from 1922.
>8 pages, fold-out PAM, SI = 7, $6.00

100 Delicious Foods from 4 Basic Recipes
Brown front cover with woman baking.
About 6" x 5"
Back cover has slogan, "One of the Family"
30 pages, SI = 7 , $20.00

1929:

Pillsbury's Cook Book
5" x 7½", as 1924 issue.
48 pages, SI = 3, $15.00

15 Prize Winning Recipes for Pillsbury's Wheat Bran
An abridged form of the booklet first put out in 1926 (see above) and reissued in 1929.
SI = 7, $3.00

15 Prize Winning Recipes for Pillsbury's Health Bran

Also in 1929, Pillsbury began to sponsor radio shows. Certain programs were popular enough that booklets and premiums were published which promoted not only the shows but also Pillsbury. Finally, Pillsbury's Cake Flour was introduced this year.

Early 1930s:

New Recipes for Pillsbury Cake Flour
by Ida Bailey Allen, author of cooking booklets for Beech-Nut (1923), Coca-Cola (1932), Karo Corn Syrup (1927), and several of her own cookbooks. She was a radio personality and was the founder of the Radio Home-Makers' Club.
10 pages, SI = 8, $10.00

Pillsbury's Best Flour: Flavor, Economy, Sure
Featuring "Little Nick"
Fold-out PAM, SI = 7, $3.00

One of the Family – 1922

1932:

15 Wonderful Recipes Inside — Look!
This pamphlet featuring "Little Nick" has drawings of several Pillsbury products, including Pillsbury's Cake Flour.
PAM, SI = 7, $3.00

1933:

Balanced Recipes
Aluminum, spiral bound. $1.25 original cost
224 recipe cards, SI = 2, $25.00

Mary Ellis Ames, director of the Pillsbury Cooking Service, offered her own cooking program on CBS radio. In the years that followed, "Cooking Close-Ups" was aired on both Wednesday and Friday mornings.

One of the Family – 1927

100 Delicious Foods from 4 Basic Recipes

Pillsbury's Best Flour: Flavor, Economy, Sure

Balanced Recipes

Twenty-One Successful Little Dinners
> by Mary Ellis Ames (director)
> Advertises the *Balanced Recipes* book.
> Released through Pillsbury's Cooking Service.
> 48 pages, SI = 6, $15.00

c. 1934:

Pillsbury's New Cookery Ideas
> Numbered "No. 12 of a series." Contains a coupon good for 25¢ off of *Balanced Recipes*.
> 14 pages, fold-out PAM, SI = 7, $3.00

Good Things to Eat
> 5¼" x 8¼"
> Twelve recipes. What makes this booklet unique is the fact that alternate pages are in Hebrew. The book includes a recipe for "Sabbath Twists" and was marketed to Jewish customers.
> 16 pages, SI = 8, $50.00

1934 – 1946:

Cookery Club Bulletins
> Numbers 1 through 18 plus Christmas 1934 bulletin are known.
> For a 10¢ membership rate per three-month period, anyone could join Pillsbury's Cookery Club and receive three bulletins. These booklets were hole-punched so that they could be inserted into the *Balanced Recipes* book.
>
> A silver (paper) cover resembling the aluminum cover of *Balanced Recipes* was made to contain them and was available from the club for 10¢.
> SI = 6, $3.00 (each)

c. 1936:

15 Delightful New Recipes You Will Want to Try
> by Mary Ellis Ames
> 6 pages, PAM, SI = 6, $2.00

Checklist

	Title	Edition	Value in Mint Condition
☐	*100 Delicious Foods from 4 Basic Recipes*	1927	$20.00
☐	*15 Delightful New Recipes You Will Want to Try*	1936	$2.00

Checklist

Title	Edition	Value in Mint Condition
☐ *15 Prize Winning Recipes for Pillsbury's Health Bran*	1926	$3.00
☐ *15 Prize Winning Recipes for Pillsbury's Wheat Bran*	1929	$3.00
☐ *15 Wonderful Recipes Inside — Look!*	1932	$3.00
☐ *50 Prize Winning Recipes for Pillsbury's Health Bran*	1926	$6.00
☐ *50 Prize Winning Recipes for Pillsbury's Wheat Bran*	1929	$6.00
☐ *Balanced Recipes*	1933	$25.00
☐ *A Book for a Cook*	1905	$40.00
☐ *(Buy this Flour Because) Pillsbury's Best*	1922	$6.00
☐ *Cookery Club Bulletin*	1934 – 1936	$3.00 each
☐ *Flavor, Economy, Sure*	1930s	$3.00
☐ *Flour Recipes*	1904	$50.00
☐ *Good Things to Eat*	1934	$50.00
☐ *A Little Book for a Little Cook*	1905	$75.00
☐ *Made in Minneapolis*	1905 – 1908	$5.00
☐ *New Cookery Ideas*	c. 1934	$3.00
☐ *New Recipes for Pillsbury Cake Flour*	1930s	$10.00
☐ *One of the Family*	1927	$6.00
☐ *The Pillsbury Cook Book*	1911	$30.00
☐ *The Pillsbury Cook Book*	1913	$20.00

Pillsbury's New Cookery Ideas

Good Things to Eat

Pillsbury's Cookery Club Bulletins

Pillsbury's Cookery Club Bulletins

15 Delightful New Recipes You Will Want to Try

Checklist

Title	Edition	Value in Mint Condition
❑ The Pillsbury Cook Book (either cover)	1914	$20.00
❑ Pillsbury's Cook Book	1920	$25.00 – 30.00
❑ Pillsbury's Cook Book	1921	$30.00
❑ Pillsbury's Cook Book	1923	$20.00
❑ Pillsbury's Cook Book	1924	$20.00
❑ Pillsbury's Cook Book	1927	$15.00
❑ Pillsbury's Cook Book	1929	$15.00
❑ Pillsbury's Health Bran — Ask Your Grocer	1919 – 1920	$8.00
❑ Pillsbury's Household Manual	1925	$50.00
❑ The Story of Flour	1922	$15.00
❑ Twenty-One Successful Little Dinners	1933	$15.00
❑ Vitos Recipe and Household Expense Book	1900	$75.00
❑ What He Told Her	1919 – 1920	$10.00

1941:

Let's Bake!
by Mary Ellis Ames
Subtitled "A Handbook of Baking;" the inside title is "Your Guide to Better Baking"
96 pages, SB, SI = 4, $5.00

Let's Bake!

1942:

Fightin' Food
Talks about cooking nutritious meals and how flour is an important tool during wartime. See also the "Student Edition" of 1943.
36 pages, SI = 6, $25.00

c. 1942 – 1943:

Pillsbury's 40 War Time Recipes
Pillsbury customers were feeling the pinch to conserve, and so the company provided this booklet. Not only do these recipes help to conserve sugar and butter, but wheat and lard as well!
24 pages, SI = 6, $20.00

Fightin' Food

1943:

Fightin' Food
"Student Edition"
Talks about rationing and how flour is an important nutritive tool during wartime.
13 pages, three binder holes, SI = 6, $20.00

Ann Pillsbury's Sugar-Shy Recipes
8 pages

Ann Pillsbury's Meat Miser Magic
8 pages

Choice Ann Pillsbury Wheat Emergency Recipes
8 pages

The above three pamphlets have similar black-and-white cover designs. Each of them features wartime versions of "regular" recipes.
SI = 8, $6.00 each

The Three "Rs" of Wartime Baking
Subtitled: *"Ration, 'Richment, and Recipes"*
by Mary Ellis Ames
6" x 5"
SI = 7, $12.00

Pillsbury's 40 War Time Recipes

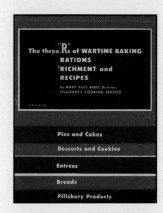

The Three "Rs" of Wartime Baking

Pillsbury's Diamond Anniversary Recipes

Cookin' Up Kitchen Dates

Higher, Finer Textured, Better Tasting Cakes

Sugar 'n Spice and Everything Nice

1944:

Pillsbury's Diamond Anniversary Recipes
11" x 8½"
Available free from magazines.
Ann Pillsbury was a fictitious character created for marketing purposes. Ann Pillsbury essentially represented the members of the Pillsbury home service department.
32 pages, SI = 4, $8.00

Cookin' Up Kitchen Dates
Booklet for teenagers.
Lists the "seven" basic food groups.
24 pages, SI = 6 , $12.00

In September, the company name was changed from Pillsbury Flour Mills Company to Pillsbury Mills, Inc.

1945:

Higher, Finer Textured, Better Tasting Cakes
Subtitled: "with Sno-Sheen"
16 pages, SI = 6, $10.00

Sugar 'n Spice and Everything Nice
Folder number 41 in a series from the Pillsbury home service department, this one contains five dessert recipes.
Form 10-299
SI = 8, $15.00

The Talking Millstones
by Camilla Wing
A history of the milling of flour.
Illustrated by Henry C. Pitz
78 pages, SI = 5, $15.00

Baking is Fun...the Ann Pillsbury Way
The first printing from 1945 has a pink cover. The second printing, from 1946, has a blue cover and a different central photo. That second printing features "streamlined" quick-mix and no-knead recipes found in the booklet below. This booklet was reissued in 1948.
64 pages, SI = 7, $12.00 (first or second printing)

Bake the No-Knead Way: Ann Pillsbury's Amazing Discovery
Only copyright is 1945.
Shipped in red and white envelope.
64 pages, SI = 3, $6.00

1946:

Bake the No-Knead Way: Ann Pillsbury's Amazing Discovery
Second copyright. First copyright is 1945.
Reissue of the above booklet.
64 pages, SI = 2, $2.00

1948:

Tasty Talk, by Ann Pillsbury
This original *Tasty Talk* booklet gave rise to a series of short pamphlets, all of them called *Ann Pillsbury's Tasty Talk*. These newsletters were subtitled differently, depending upon their content. Known subtitles include "Fun With Cookies," "Fun With Breads," and "Easy Tricks for Picnic and Patio Fun." Since the introductions to the recipes themselves refer to the early Bake-Offs, the *Tasty Talk* newsletters were issued c. 1958 – 1959.
6 pages, SI = 7, $8.00

Baking is Fun
This is the 1948 reissue of the earlier booklets (1945, 1946).
64 pages, SI = 3, $3.00

Adventures in Cake Craft, by Ann Pillsbury
40 pages, SI = 3, $3.00

1949:

Globe A-1 Biscuit Book
20 pages, SI = 7, $3.00

1950:

Ann Pillsbury's Baking Book
A Pocket Book paperback edition, number 789.
Reprinted in 1951, 1954, 1959, and again in 1961.
Also available in hardback through A.S. Barnes & Co.; also 361 pages.
361 pages, HB, SI = 6, $20.00
361 pages, PB, SI = 3, $6.00

c. 1950:

12 New Cake Recipes
Subtitled: "Made With Pillsbury's Sno-Sheen Cake Flour"
PAM, SI = 7, $3.00

Pillsbury's Ten Thousand Dollar Bakery Formula Book
gold cover
Contains 121 "formulas" (recipes)
SB, SI = 6 – 7, $20.00

1952:

Kate Smith Chooses Her 55 Favorite Cake Recipes
by Ann Pillsbury
64 pages, SI = 2, $1.00

Ann Pillsbury's $200,000 Prize Winning Cook Book
Published by Fawcett at 75¢, #171.
Contains recipes from the first three Grand National Bake-Offs.
144 pages, SI = 6, $20.00

The Talking Millstones

Baking is Fun...the Ann Pillsbury Way – 1946

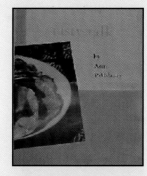

Tasty Talk, by Ann Pillsbury

Tasty Talk, by Ann Pillsbury — Fun With Breads

Baking is Fun...the Ann Pillsbury Way – 1948

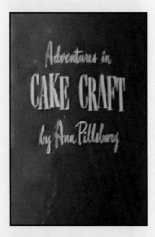

Adventures in Cake Craft, by Ann Pillsbury

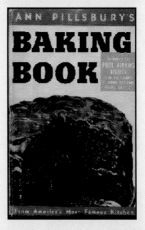

Ann Pillsbury's Baking Book

Pillsbury's Ten Thousand Dollar Bakery Formula Book

300 Pillsbury Prize Recipes
>Published by Dell (#D112) at 35¢.
>Contains recipes from the first three Grand National Bake-Offs.
>383 pages, SI = 4, $6.00

1954:

Cakes
>Professional package for bakers using Pillsbury products in cooking.
>Photocopies of typed recipes in a light blue binder.
>Contains one recipe from the 5th Grand National Bake-Off.
>SI = 8, $12.00

Ann Pillsbury's New Cook Book
>Fawcett Publications #226.
>9½" x 6"
>Pillsbury had already published their Bake-Off materials in experimental formats. This cookbook contains the "100 prize-winning recipes" from the 5th Grand National Bake-Off, but the format and publisher were similar to the $200,000 *Prize Winning Cook Book* from 1952. 75¢ (paper) or $2.00 (hardback) cover price.
>144 pages, HB, SI = 9 , $25.00
>144 pages, PB, SI = 7, $10.00

1955:

Pillsbury's Prize Winning Cook Book
>Fawcett Publications, "How to" series #265.
>9½" x 6"
>Pillsbury had already published their Bake-Off materials in experimental formats. This cookbook contains the "100 prize-winning recipes" from the 6th Grand National Bake-Off, but the format and publisher were similar to the $200,000 *Prize Winning Cook Book* from 1952. 75¢ (paperback) or $2.00 (hardback) cover price.
>144 pages, HB, SI = 8, $25.00
>144 pages, PB, SI = 6, $8.00

Pillsbury's Prize Winners
>All Baked With French's Spices and Extracts
>Contains those recipes from the 6th Grand National Bake-Off that were prepared with French's seasonings.
>PAM, SI = 5, $1.00

New Horizons in Baking
>Sold to professional bakers. Contains recipes for rolls, cakes, donuts, and biscuits.
>Small three-ring binder.
>153 pages (including 8 dividers), SI = 6, $20.00

1957:

Fun Filled Butter Cookie Cookbook
>Book mentions the 7th Grand National Bake-Off
>15¢ original price.
>48 pages, SI = 3, $1.00

Checklist

Title	Edition	Value in Mint Condition
☐ *12 New Cake Recipes*	c. 1950	$3.00
☐ *$200,000 Prize Winning Cook Book*	1952	$20.00
☐ *300 Pillsbury Prize Recipes*	1952	$6.00
☐ *40 War Time Recipes*	1942 – 1943	$20.00
☐ *Adventures in Cake Craft*	1948	$3.00
☐ *Ann Pillsbury's Baking Book* (HB)	1950	$20.00
☐ *Ann Pillsbury's Baking Book* (PB)	1950	$6.00
☐ *Ann Pillsbury's Meat Miser Magic*	1943	$6.00
☐ *Ann Pillsbury's New Cook Book* (HB)	1954	$25.00
☐ *Ann Pillsbury's New Cook Book* (PB)	1954	$10.00
☐ *Ann Pillsbury's Sugar-Shy Recipes*	1943	$6.00
☐ *Baking is Fun*	1948	$3.00
☐ *Baking is Fun...the Ann Pillsbury Way* (pink cover)	1945	$12.00
☐ *Baking is Fun...the Ann Pillsbury Way* (blue cover)	1946	$12.00
☐ *Bake the No-Knead Way: Ann Pillsbury's Amazing Discovery*	1945	$6.00
☐ *Bake the No-Knead Way: Ann Pillsbury's Amazing Discovery*	1946	$2.00
☐ *Cakes*	1954	$12.00
☐ *Choice Ann Pillsbury Wheat Emergency Recipes*	1943	$6.00

Kate Smith Chooses her 55 Favorite Cake Recipes

Ann Pillsbury's $200,000 Prize Winning Cook Book

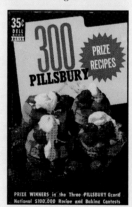

300 Pillsbury Prize Recipes

Cakes

Ann Pillsbury's New Cook Book

Pillsbury's Prize Winning Cook Book

Pillsbury's Prize Winners — Were All Baked With French's Spices and Extracts

New Horizons in Baking

Checklist

Title	Edition	Value in Mint Condition
❑ Cookin' Up Kitchen Dates	1944	$12.00
❑ Diamond Anniversary Recipes	1944	$8.00
❑ Fightin' Food	1942	$25.00
❑ Fightin' Food (Student Edition)	1943	$20.00
❑ Fun Filled Butter Cookie Cookbook	1957	$1.00
❑ Globe A-1 Biscuit Book	1949	$3.00
❑ Higher, Finer Textured, Better Tasting Cakes	1945	$10.00
❑ Kate Smith Chooses her 55 Favorite Cake Recipes	1952	$2.00
❑ Let's Bake!	1941	$5.00
❑ New Horizons in Baking	1955	$20.00
❑ Prize Winners ... French's Spices and Extracts	1955	$1.00
❑ Prize Winning Cook Book (HB)	1955	$25.00
❑ Prize Winning Cook Book (PB)	1955	$8.00
❑ Sugar 'n Spice and Everything Nice	1945	$15.00
❑ The Talking Millstones	1945	$15.00
❑ Tasty Talk	1948	$8.00
❑ Tasty Talk (magazine)	1958 – 1959	$8.00 each
❑ Ten Thousand Dollar Bakery Formula Book	c. 1950	$20.00
❑ The Three "Rs" of Wartime Baking	1943	$12.00

1958:

Pillsbury's Best New Butter Cookie Cookbook
> Vol. II
> Yellow cover
> 20¢ original price
> 48 pages, SI = 2, $5.00

Best One-Dish Meals Cookbook
> Mentions 9th Bake-Off
> No cover price; used as a premium
> 54 pages, binder holes, SI = 2, $3.00

1959:

Best Loved Foods of Christmas
> Mentions 10th Bake-Off
> 25¢ original price
> 66 pages, binder holes, SI = 3, $3.00

Best of the Bake-Off Collection
> 1,000 recipes; a collection from the first ten Bake-Offs
> Published by Consolidated Book Publishers
> Regular edition has a slick white/multicolored cover; deluxe edition
> has a rough stock tan cover with gold print.
> 608 pages, HB w/dj, SI = 3, $20.00 (regular edition)
> 608 pages, HB w/dj, SI = 6, $25.00 (deluxe edition)

4 Wonderful Short-Cut Breads
> Possibly 1959, since states "from Pillsbury's Best Bake-Off Collection."
> No price on cover.
> 40 pages, binder holes, SI = 3, $3.00

Cool Ideas Cookbook
> Probably from 1959, since it states "from Pillsbury's Best Bake-Off
> Collection."
> No price on cover. Copies exist with or without a "Best of the Bake-
> Off" ribbon printed on the front cover.
> 33 pages, binder holes, SI = 4, $5.00

Butter Cookie Cookbook, Vol. III
> 20¢ original price
> red cover
> 48 pages, binder holes, SI = 2, $5.00

1960s:

Pillsbury's 24 Meat 'N Potato Ideas
> by Ann Pillsbury
> 22 pages, SI = 5, $3.00

*Pillsbury's Best New
Butter Cookie Cookbook*

Best One-Dish Meals Cookbook

Best Loved Foods of Christmas

Best of the Bake-Off Collection

4 Wonderful Short-Cut Breads

Cool Ideas Cookbook

Any Time Quick Bread Ideas
   14 pages, SI = 6, $3.00

Sweet 10 Calorie-Slim Recipes (from Pillsbury)
   c. 1961
   64 pages, SI = 8, $5.00

   This was reissued in 1967 as *Calorie-Slim Recipes* costing 50¢.
   SI = 5, $3.00

1961:

Fabulous Pies
   No price on cover
   24 pages, binder holes, SI = 3, $5.00

Butter Cookie Booklet
   Contains 25 recipes from Pillsbury's "Best of the Bake-Off Collection."
   6" x 5"
   24 pages, SI = 5, $3.00

In 1961, Pillsbury purchased an artificial sweetener business and began to market "Sweet 10," which became one of the most popular sweeteners on the market. From 1964 through 1969, Pillsbury sold "Funny Face" drink mix, which was similar to Kool Aid but which used Sweet 10. The original Sweet 10 was withdrawn in 1969 (due to an FDA ban of its formula), and Funny Face was reformulated to use saccharine. Funny Face continued to be popular throughout the 1970s, although reduced sales in the late 1970s caused Pillsbury to sell the product to Brady Enterprises in 1980.

1963:

The Pillsbury Family Cook Book
   Large size, regular bound, original cost $4.95
   RB, original cost $5.95
   575 pages, SI = 1, $50.00 (first printing)

   Reissued in 1969, $20.00
   Reissued again in 1970, $20.00
   Reissued again in 1973 as *The New Pillsbury Family Cook Book*, $35.00

Early 1960s:

Gift Box Butter Cookies
   Presents on cover
   32 pages, SI = 5, $3.00

Fancy Free Entertaining
   Drawing of woman and party symbols on cover.
   16 pages, SI = 7, $3.00

Pillsbury's Best Gravy Cookbook
> Shaped like Pillsbury's all-purpose flour shaker.
> hard stock
> 8 pages, SI = 8, $20.00

Hot Roll Mix Baking Book
> Large blue Pillsbury logo.
> 64 pages, binder holes, SI = 4, $6.00

Baking Like Mommy
> pulp paper cover
> SI = 7, $12.00

1965:

The Pillsbury Doughboy, more formally "Poppin' Fresh," made his television debut in a commercial for Pillsbury's crescent rolls. Within a few years, he highlighted the cover of the Bake-Off cookbook series. Before long, he was everyone's favorite baking advertisement. These days, he even has his own website.

Butter Cookie Cookbook, Vol. III

"Do-It-Together" Butter Cookies
> Contains cookie recipes and decorating ideas.
> 30 pages, SI = 3, $3.00

1966:

The Convenience Cookbook
> 69¢ original price, so probably 1966.
> Refrigerated food recipes
> SI = 3, $2.00

1967:

Time Saver Cook Book
> 79¢ original price; later used as a giveaway.
> 100 pages, SI = 1 or 2, $2.00

The Pillsbury Family Cook Book

1968:

Bake-Off Dessert Cookbook
> No cover price; used as a premium.
> 144 pages, HB, SI = 2, $2.00

Bake-Off Breads Cookbook
> $3.95 original price
> 145 pages, HB, SI = 3, $3.00

Bake-Off Main Dish Cookbook
> $3.95 original price
> 143 pages, HB, SI = 1, $2.00

Pillsbury's Best Gravy Cookbook

Hot Roll Mix Baking Book

Baking Like Mommy

Bake-Off Cookie Book
$3.95 original price; also used as a premium.
143 pages, HB, SI = 2, $4.00

1969:

A Treasury of Bake Off Favorites
98¢ original price
96 pages, PB, SI = 2, $2.00

Sweet 'N Thin Cook Book
98¢ original price
64 pages, PB, SI = 3, $3.00

Pillsbury's Meat Cookbook
98¢ cover price
80 pages, PB, SI = 3, $3.00

Pillsbury's Soup & Salad Cookbook
98¢ cover price
80 pages, PB, SI = 3, $3.00

Pillsbury's Vegetable Cookbook
98¢ cover price
80 pages, PB, SI = 3, $3.00

Checklist

Title	Edition	Value in Mint Condition
❑ *24 Meat 'N Potato Ideas*	1960s	$3.00
❑ *Any Time Quick Bread Ideas*	1960s	$3.00
❑ *Bake-Off Breads Cookbook*	1968	$3.00
❑ *Bake-Off Cookie Book*	1968	$4.00
❑ *Pillsbury's Bake Off Dessert Cook Book*	1968	$2.00
❑ *Bake-Off Main Dish Cookbook*	1968	$2.00
❑ *Baking Like Mommy*	c. 1965	$12.00
❑ *Best Loved Foods of Christmas*	1959	$3.00
❑ *Best of the Bake-Off Collection* (regular)	1959	$20.00

Checklist

Title	Edition	Value in Mint Condition
☐ *Best of the Bake-Off Collection* (deluxe)	1959	$25.00
☐ *Best One-Dish Meals Cookbook*	1958	$3.00
☐ *Butter Cookie Booklet*	1961	$3.00
☐ *Butter Cookie Cookbook Vol. III*	1959	$5.00
☐ *Calorie-Slim Recipes*	1967	$3.00
☐ *The Convenience Cookbook*	1966	$2.00
☐ *Cool Ideas Cookbook*	1959	$5.00
☐ *"Do-It-Together" Butter Cookies*	1965	$3.00
☐ *Fabulous Pies*	1961	$5.00
☐ *Fancy Free Entertaining*	c. 1964	$3.00
☐ *Gift Box Butter Cookies*	c. 1964	$3.00
☐ *Gravy Cookbook*	c. 1965	$20.00
☐ *Hot Roll Mix Baking Book*	c. 1963	$6.00
☐ *Meat Cookbook*	1969	$3.00
☐ *Pillsbury's Best New Butter Cookie Cookbook, Vol. II*	1958	$5.00
☐ *The Pillsbury Family Cook Book* (first edition, HB or RB)	1963	$50.00
☐ *The Pillsbury Family Cook Book* (later edition)	1960s	$20.00
☐ *The Pillsbury Family Cook Book* (*The New*)	1973	$35.00
☐ *Short-Cut Breads*	1959	$3.00

Time Saver Cook Book

A Treasury of Bake Off Favorites

Pillsbury's Bake Off Dessert Cook Book

Checklist

Title	Edition	Value in Mint Condition
☐ *Soup & Salad Cookbook*	1969	$3.00
☐ *Sweet 10 Calorie-Slim Recipes* (from Pillsbury)	c. 1961	$5.00
☐ *Sweet 'N Thin Cook Book*	1969	$3.00
☐ *Time Saver Cook Book*	1967	$2.00
☐ *A Treasury of Bake Off Favorites*	1969	$2.00
☐ *Vegetable Cookbook*	1969	$3.00

Pillsbury Bake-Off Cookbooks
1950 and Beyond

Beginning at least in 1900, Pillsbury had hosted several Bake-Off contests of smaller scope before attempting to create the national event that would come to be synonymous with the Pillsbury name. According to information gathered from the Bake-Off booklets, the Grand National Recipe and Baking Contest held on December 13, 1949, was intended to be a one-time only event. Plastic tokens were issued advertising the event in New York's famed Waldorf-Astoria Hotel, for which there was a tremendous turnout. Afterwards, many people began to write to Pillsbury, asking that the recipes from the Bake-Off be published in a booklet. The event had been the first baking event of national scope, and the Bake-Off booklets wound up being Pillsbury's most popular cooking booklets. Most booklets have an SI of 2 and sell for $3.00.

All Bake-Off booklets have 96 interior pages unless specified.

#1. Issued in 1950, no cover price, formally titled *100 Prize-Winning Recipes*. The $50,000.00 prize-winner was entitled "No-Knead Water-Rising Twists." The prize was won by Mrs. Ralph E. Smafield.
SI = 3, $125.00

#2. 1951, 100 pages; 25¢ price begins. The $25,000.00 first prize was won by Mrs. Peter Wuebel for her "Orange Kiss-Me Cake."
SI = 3, $12.00

#3. 1952. The $25,000.00 first prize was awarded to Mrs. Samuel P. Weston's "Starlight Double-Delight Cake."
SI = 3, $4.00

#4. 1953; smaller size begins. The winner this time was Mrs. Peter S. Harlib, who created "Snappy Turtle Cookies."

#5. 1954, 98 pages. The additional two pages consisted of an entry form for the next Bake-Off. The winner, entitled "My Inspiration Cake," was baked by Mrs. Bernard Kanago.

#6. 1955, 98 pages. Mrs. Bernard A. Koteen contributed "Open Sesame Pie," which won the $25,000.00 award.

#7. 1956. "Ring-a-Lings," created by Bertha (Mrs. Henry) Jorgensen took first prize this time.

#8. 1957. Mrs. Hildreth H. Hatheway's "California Casserole" was the hit of the day, and she was the grand prize winner this year.

#9. 1958. The Grand National winner was Mrs. Gerda Roderer, who brought her "Accordion Treats" when she immigrated from France.

Plastic advertising token from the first national Bake-Off

100 Prize-Winning Recipes, 1st Edition

100 Prize-Winning Recipes, 2nd Edition

100 Prize-Winning Recipes, 3rd Edition

*100 Prize-Winning Recipes,
4th Edition*

*100 Prize-Winning Recipes,
5th Edition*

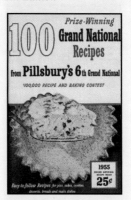

*100 Prize-Winning Recipes,
6th Edition*

*100 Prize-Winning Recipes,
7th Edition*

#10. 1959, 106 pages; larger size with binder holes begins. Dorothy DeVault took home the $25,000.00 prize for her "Spicy Apple Twists."

#11. 1960, 102 pages. The proud winner was Eunice Surles, whose "Mardi Gras Party Cake" was judged worthy of the grand prize.

#12. 1961. "Dilly Casserole Bread," cooked up by Leona Schnuelle, took the prize this time.

#13. 1962; 35¢ cover price begins.

#14. 1963. My personal favorite from all the Bake-Offs is Mrs. Erwin Smogor's "Apple Pie '63." It's one yummy recipe, well-deserving of the $25,000.00 award.

#15. 1964. Mrs. Roman Walilko took the grand prize this time for her "Hungry Boys' Casserole," a delicious main dish.

#16. 1965; 50¢ cover price. This time, the prize went to 17-year-old Janis Boykin. Her "Peacheesy Pie" had been developed for school and was worth $25,000.00.

#17. 1966; no binder holes from here on; 50¢ cover price. Billed as *Busy Lady Bake-Off Recipes*, the book marked a change for Pillsbury. Now, the recipes were streamlined, making them easier for unskilled cooks to make. "Golden Gate Snack Bread" took the prize this time, given to Mrs. John Petrelli.

#18. 1967; 79¢ cover price. The Bake-Offs now rewarded shortcuts, allowing baking mixes and refrigerated dough. Categories for these shortcuts were announced for 1968.

#19. 1968; 98¢ cover price begins. The cover features Mrs. Debora L. Keenan's "Coffee Scotch Whip Pie."

#20. 1969. Mrs. Edna M. Holmgren took home the grand prize. Her "Magic Marshmallow Crescent Puffs" were billed as being "ready to serve in just 30 minutes."

The Bake-Offs have continued as a Pillsbury tradition since 1949, although since 1976 they have been held biannually instead of every year. When Pillsbury began to issue their *Classic* magazine series, the Bake-Off publication became a regular part of that series — beginning in 1982. As the Bake-Off became the Quick & Easy Bake-Off, it became an indicator of changes in American society. Through the year 2000, here is the list of Bake-Off booklets available. Although certain modern issues tend to be slightly less common than the earlier ones, typically, they are not collected.

#21. 1970

#22. 1971; $1.00 cover price

#23. 1972; 89¢ cover price

#24. 1973; 89¢ cover price

#25. 1974; 89¢ cover price

#26. 1975; 99¢ cover price

#27. 1976; 99¢ cover price

#28. 1978; $1.29 cover price

#29. 1980; $1.59 cover price

#30. 1982, *Classic #14*

#31. 1984, *Classic #38*; 112 pages; $2.25 cover price

#32. 1986, *Classic #62*; $2.25 cover price

#33. 1988, *Classic #86*; $2.25 cover price

#34. 1990, *Classic #110*; 104 pages; $2.50 cover price

#35. 1992, *Classic #134*; $2.50 cover price

#36. 1994, *Classic #157*; 104 pages; $2.75 cover price

#37. 1996, *Classic #181*; 124 pages; $2.75 cover price

#38. 1998, *Classic #205*; 120 pages; $2.75 cover price

#39. 2000, *Classic #229*; 116 pages; $2.75 cover price

100 Prize-Winning Recipes, 8th Edition

100 Prize-Winning Recipes, 9th Edition

100 Prize-Winning Recipes, 10th Edition

100 Prize-Winning Recipes, 11th Edition

100 Prize-Winning Recipes,
12th Edition

Note about Scarcity: All of the Bake-Off booklets are common. The first booklet has SI = 3. The 8th – 12th booklets have SI = 2. The others have SI = 1. The first few booklets are more desirable than the later ones and therefore have higher values, despite their being relatively common. All books from the late 1960s on are assumed to be common in higher grades.

100 Prize-Winning Recipes,
13th Edition

100 Prize-Winning Recipes,
16th Edition

100 Prize-Winning Recipes,
17th Edition

100 Prize-Winning Recipes,
18th Edition

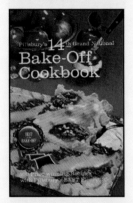

100 Prize-Winning Recipes,
14th Edition

100 Prize-Winning Recipes,
19th Edition

100 Prize-Winning Recipes,
20th Edition

100 Prize-Winning Recipes,
15th Edition

BIBLIOGRAPHY

Historical information published in *The Story of Flour*, Pillsbury, 1922, and *The Story of a Pantry Shelf*, Butterick Publishing, 1925, contributed to this book. Thanks also to Sue Erwin for her assistance and her faithful devotion to the cause of Pillsbury collecting.

Information from *Delineator* magazine (04-1937 – 05- 1937) was used in the CAP section.

The Medal of Gold, by William Edgar, Bellman, 1925, was a source for the history of Washburn-Crosby Co.

A Growing College: Home Economics at Cornell University, by Rose, Stocks, and Whittier, published by the NY State College of Human Ecology, 1969.

The Story of a Pantry Shelf, Butterick, 1925.

CONCLUSIONS

If you own any cookbooks, booklets, pamphlets, or other recipe items that are not listed in this book and that were made by Pillsbury or Betty Crocker (Washburn-Crosby, General Mills) before 1970, or by the Culinary Arts Institute (CAP, or Butterick/Delineator), please contact the author of this book, as I would very much like to provide complete listings. Also, if you own any "older" general cookbooks (1920 or earlier) that you would like to see mentioned in a future edition of this book, please contact me.

Frank Daniels

1375 Mill Street

Ely, NV 89301

EgwEimi@aol.com

A "cookbook book" would be incomplete if it were not also a cookbook. So, here are a few recipes from this author's own kitchen that I hope you will enjoy.

HERETIC'S CHINESE CHILI

Ingredients:

1 lb. boneless, skinless chicken breast
1 lb. small shrimp, cooked, de-veined
½ large Spanish (yellow) onion
1 lg. can (28 oz.) stewed whole (or sliced) tomatoes
1 can Del Monte Mexican style tomatoes
1 can mixed Chinese vegetables, cooked (or cook your own)
1 can bean sprouts, cooked (or cook your own), about 1 oz.
dark brown sugar, to taste
red wine vinegar, about 4 fl. oz.
Soy Vay brand Veri Veri Teriyaki Sauce
about 2 fl. oz. Sweet and Sour dinner sauce
about 1 tsp. Mexican oregano
about 1 tsp. paprika
about ½ clove minced garlic
3 Tbsp. chili powder
4 oz. sliced fresh mushrooms, and some margarine
1 thick slice Velveeta mexican cheese spread
1 Tbsp. Chinese mustard
½ green bell pepper
spicy pepper (optional, to taste)
¼ carrot, sliced thin (optional)
1 jalapeno or other spicy pepper, sliced (optional)
soy sauce (to taste)
1 package dried Chinese noodles

Directions:

Slice the bell pepper into small pieces. Brown chicken breast, and cook bell pepper in skillet (about 15 min. total). Slice the onion into small pieces, and add it after about ten minutes. After another five minutes, saute the mushrooms in margarine in a separate pan. Drain chicken fat from main pan, and put chicken, peppers, mushrooms, and onion into two-quart saucepan. Add tomatoes. Stir together. Cook on medium setting.

Now add the chili powder, oregano, garlic, and paprika — one by one, stirring after each. Add the Teriyaki sauce, and stir. Add the brown sugar, vinegar, and sweet & sour sauce, and stir. Add soy sauce, and stir. Taste: if too sour, add more brown sugar; if too sweet, add more Teriyaki sauce or vinegar. Add more chili powder if desired.

Now add all remaining ingredients except for noodles.

Bring the whole mixture to a boil, using medium heat, stirring about once every 5 – 10 minutes. Taste and adjust. Separately, prepare the Chinese noodles as indicated on the package. Serve chili over the noodles.

Serves about 8 people.

HOT DOG CHILI CASSEROLE

Ingredients:

1 pckg. kosher hot dogs (8)
½ large Spanish (yellow) onion
1 large can (28 oz.) crushed tomatoes
2 cans Del Monte mexican style tomatoes
1 can hot chili beans
1 can black beans
½ oz. dark brown sugar
½ Tbsp. red wine vinegar
1 Tbsp. Mexican oregano
1 tsp. paprika
¼ clove minced garlic
½ Tbsp. chili powder
½ can jumbo/colossal black olives, pitted
½ jar (4½ oz.) sliced or whole mushrooms
1 thick slice Velveeta mexican cheese (mild or hot)
cayenne pepper (optional, to taste)
salt (to taste)
½ bag tortilla chips (for thickening)

Directions:

Set hot dogs to broil in oven. While they are cooking, slice onion and cook in skillet (about 5 minutes). Put onion into casserole dish. Add crushed tomatoes, Mexican tomatoes, and all beans. Stir together. Turn hot dogs as necessary. Remove hot dogs when cooked (not burned), and cut them lengthwise once and widthwise into fourths. Add hot dogs to casserole dish.

Now add the chili powder, oregano, garlic, and paprika. Stir in. Add the vinegar and stir. Add the brown sugar and stir. Taste: if too sour, add more brown sugar; if too sweet, add more vinegar. Add more chili powder if desired.

Slice the black olives, then add all remaining ingredients except for chips. Crush about half of the chips, and stir them in. Put the remaining chips on top of the dish, covered with a thin layer of the sauce.

Bake at 350 degrees until the chips on the top have begun to brown and the casserole is fairly solid but still moist. Serve while hot.

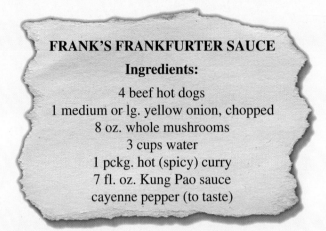

FRANK'S FRANKFURTER SAUCE

Ingredients:

4 beef hot dogs
1 medium or lg. yellow onion, chopped
8 oz. whole mushrooms
3 cups water
1 pckg. hot (spicy) curry
7 fl. oz. Kung Pao sauce
cayenne pepper (to taste)

Directions:

Slice hot dogs into small pieces, and chop onions. Cook in deep skillet on medium high heat until onions are browning. Add water and bring to a boil. Add curry and stir until it is dissolved. Add other ingredients and cook for about 5 minutes. Makes a good baked potato topping.

SPICY SPAM PIZZA

Ingredients:

1 ready-made pizza crust (or you can toss your own)
1½ oz. Newman's Own Bombolina spaghetti sauce or Bandito salsa
shredded mozzarella cheese and shredded cheddar, enough to cover
3 Tbsp. Chinese Chili sauce
2 tsp. cayenne pepper
2 tsp. Chinese mustard
a few drops of mexican hot sauce
several jalapeno peppers, sliced across ("salsa style")
Spam

Directions:

Preheat oven to about 425 degrees (or as shown on pizza crust package).

While oven is preheating, mix all ingredients (except Spam, peppers, and crust) in a mixing bowl until it looks reasonably blended. This will make the sauce.

Lay out pizza crust on pizza pan or cookie sheet.

Spread out sauce on pizza crust, with a thin layer, until nearly all of surface is covered.

Put as much cheese on the pizza as you desire. Cheese should cover all the sauce.

Cut Spam into small portions. Thin squares, ½ inch by ½ inch, work really well. Spread out Spam slices onto pizza. Spread out pepper slices onto pizza.

Place pizza in oven and cook until the crust is starting to brown and the cheese is all melted (about 15 minutes). Serve hot, while singing the "Spam" song from Monty Python.

Notes:

For those who are not fond of spiced ham, fear not: the pizza will not taste like you might imagine.

DOLLS, FIGURES & TEDDY BEARS

6315	**American Character Dolls**, Izen	$24.95
6317	**Arranbee Dolls**, The Dolls that Sell on Sight, DeMillar/Brevik	$24.95
2079	**Barbie Doll** Fashion, Volume I, Eames	$24.95
4846	**Barbie Doll** Fashion, Volume II, Eames	$24.95
6319	**Barbie Doll** Fashion, Volume III, Eames	$29.95
6022	The **Barbie Doll** Years, 5th Ed., Olds	$19.95
5352	Coll. Ency. of **Barbie** Doll Exclusives & More, 2nd Ed., Augustyniak	$24.95
5904	Collector's Guide to **Celebrity Dolls**, Spurgeon	$24.95
5599	Collector's Guide to **Dolls of the 1960s and 1970s**, Sabulis	$24.95
6030	Collector's Guide to **Horsman Dolls**, Jensen	$29.95
6224	**Doll Values**, Antique to Modern, 7th Ed., Moyer	$12.95
6033	**Modern Collectible Dolls**, Volume VI, Moyer	$24.95
5689	**Nippon Dolls** & Playthings, Van Patten/Lau	$29.95
5365	**Peanuts Collectibles**, Podley/Bang	$24.95
6336	Official **Precious Moments** Collector's Guide to Company Dolls, Bomm	$19.95
6026	**Small Dolls** of the 40s & 50s, Stover	$29.95
5253	Story of **Barbie**, 2nd Ed., Westenhouser	$24.95
5277	**Talking Toys** of the 20th Century, Lewis	$15.95
2084	**Teddy Bears**, Annalee's & Steiff Animals, 3rd Series, Mandel	$19.95
4880	World of **Raggedy Ann** Collectibles, Avery	$24.95

TOYS & MARBLES

2333	Antique & Collectible **Marbles**, 3rd Ed., Grist	$9.95
5900	Collector's Guide to **Battery Toys**, 2nd Edition, Hultzman	$24.95
4566	Collector's Guide to **Tootsietoys**, 2nd Ed., Richter	$19.95
5169	Collector's Guide to **TV Toys** & Memorabilia, 2nd Ed., Davis/Morgan	$24.95
5593	Grist's Big Book of **Marbles**, 2nd Ed.	$24.95
3970	Grist's Machine-Made & Contemporary **Marbles**, 2nd Ed.	$9.95
6128	**Hot Wheels**, The Ultimate Redline Guide, 1968 – 1977, Clark/Wicker	$24.95
5830	**McDonald's** Collectibles, 2nd Edition, Henriques/DuVall	$24.95
1540	**Modern Toys**, 1930–1980, Baker	$19.95
6237	**Rubber Toy Vehicles**, Leopard	$19.95
6340	**Schroeder's Collectible Toys**, Antique to Modern Price Guide, 9th Ed.	$17.95
5908	**Toy Car** Collector's Guide, Johnson	$19.95

FURNITURE

3716	American **Oak** Furniture, Book II, McNerney	$12.95
1118	Antique **Oak** Furniture, Hill	$7.95
3720	Collector's Ency. of **American** Furniture, Vol. III, Swedberg	$24.95
5359	Early **American** Furniture, Obbard	$12.95
3906	**Heywood-Wakefield** Modern Furniture, Rouland	$18.95
6338	**Roycroft** Furniture & Collectibles, Koon	$24.95
6343	**Stickley Brothers** Furniture, Koon	$24.95
1885	**Victorian** Furniture, Our American Heritage, McNerney	$9.95
3829	**Victorian** Furniture, Our American Heritage, Book II, McNerney	$9.95

JEWELRY, HATPINS, WATCHES & PURSES

4704	Antique & Collectible **Buttons**, Wisniewski	$19.95
6323	**Christmas Pins**, Past & Present, 2nd Edition, Gallina	$19.95
4850	Collectible **Costume Jewelry**, Simonds	$24.95
5675	Collectible **Silver Jewelry**, Rezazadeh	$24.95
3722	Collector's Ency. of **Compacts**, Carryalls & Face Powder Boxes, Mueller	$24.95
4940	**Costume Jewelry**, A Practical Handbook & Value Guide, Rezazadeh	$24.95
5812	Fifty Years of Collectible **Fashion Jewelry**, 1925 – 1975, Baker	$24.95
6330	**Handkerchiefs**: A Collector's Guide, Guarnaccia/Guggenheim	$24.95
1424	**Hatpins** & Hatpin Holders, Baker	$9.95

5695	**Ladies' Vintage Accessories**, Bruton	$24.95
1181	**100 Years of Collectible Jewelry**, 1850 – 1950, Baker	$9.95
6337	**Purse Masterpieces**, Schwartz	$29.95
4729	**Sewing Tools** & Trinkets, Thompson	$24.95
6038	**Sewing Tools** & Trinkets, Volume 2, Thompson	$24.95
6039	Signed Beauties of **Costume Jewelry**, Brown	$24.95
6341	Signed Beauties of **Costume Jewelry**, Volume II, Brown	$24.95
5620	Unsigned Beauties of **Costume Jewelry**, Brown	$24.95
4878	Vintage & Contemporary **Purse Accessories**, Gerson	$24.95
5696	Vintage & Vogue Ladies' **Compacts**, 2nd Edition, Gerson	$29.95
5923	**Vintage Jewelry** for Investment & Casual Wear, Edeen	$24.95

ARTIFACTS, GUNS, KNIVES, TOOLS, PRIMITIVES

6021	**Arrowheads** of the Central Great Plains, Fox	$19.95
1868	**Antique Tools**, Our American Heritage, McNerney	$9.95
5616	Big Book of **Pocket Knives**, Stewart	$19.95
4943	Field Gde. to Flint **Arrowheads** & Knives of the N. American Indian, Tully	$9.95
3885	**Indian Artifacts** of the Midwest, Book II, Hothem	$16.95
4870	**Indian Artifacts** of the Midwest, Book III, Hothem	$18.95
5685	**Indian Artifacts** of the Midwest, Book IV, Hothem	$19.95
6132	**Modern Guns**, Identification & Values, 14th Ed., Quertermous	$14.95
2164	**Primitives**, Our American Heritage, McNerney	$9.95
1759	**Primitives**, Our American Heritage, 2nd Series, McNerney	$14.95
6031	Standard **Knife** Collector's Guide, 4th Ed., Ritchie & Stewart	$14.95
5999	**Wilderness** Survivor's Guide, Hamper	$12.95

PAPER COLLECTIBLES & BOOKS

5902	**Boys' & Girls' Book** Series, Jones	$19.95
5153	Collector's Guide to **Children's Books**, 1850 to 1950, Volume II, Jones	$19.95
1441	Collector's Guide to **Post Cards**, Wood	$9.95
5926	**Duck Stamps**, Chappell	$9.95
2081	Guide to Collecting **Cookbooks**, Allen	$14.95
2080	Price Guide to **Cookbooks** & Recipe Leaflets, Dickinson	$9.95
3973	**Sheet Music** Reference & Price Guide, 2nd Ed., Pafik & Guiheen	$19.95
6041	Vintage **Postcards** for the Holidays, Reed	$24.95

GLASSWARE

5602	Anchor Hocking's **Fire-King** & More, 2nd Ed.	$24.95
6321	**Carnival Glass**, The Best of the Best, Edwards/Carwile	$29.95
5823	Collectible **Glass Shoes**, 2nd Edition, Wheatley	$24.95
6325	Coll. **Glassware** from the 40s, 50s & 60s, 7th Ed., Florence	$19.95
1810	Collector's Ency. of **American Art Glass**, Shuman	$29.95
6327	Collector's Ency. of **Depression Glass**, 16th Ed., Florence	$19.95
1961	Collector's Ency. of **Fry Glassware**, Fry Glass Society	$24.95
1664	Collector's Ency. of **Heisey Glass**, 1925 – 1938, Bredehoft	$24.95
3905	Collector's Ency. of **Milk Glass**, Newbound	$24.95
5820	Collector's Guide to **Glass Banks**, Reynolds	$24.95
6454	**Crackle Glass** From Around the World, Weitman	$24.95
6125	**Elegant Glassware** of the Depression Era, 10th Ed., Florence	$24.95
6334	Ency. of **Paden City Glass**, Domitz	$24.95
3981	Evers' Standard **Cut Glass** Value Guide	$12.95
6462	Florence's **Glass Kitchen Shakers**, 1930 – 1950s	$19.95
5042	Florence's **Glassware Pattern** Identification Guide, Vol. I	$18.95
5615	Florence's **Glassware Pattern** Identification Guide, Vol. II	$19.95
6142	Florence's **Glassware Pattern** Identification Guide, Vol. III	$19.95
4719	**Fostoria**, Etched, Carved & Cut Designs, Vol. II, Kerr	$24.95
6226	**Fostoria** Value Guide, Long/Seate	$19.95

5899	**Glass** & Ceramic **Baskets**, White	$19.95
6460	**Glass Animals**, Second Edition, Spencer	$24.95
6127	The **Glass Candlestick** Book, Vol. 1, Akro Agate to Fenton, Felt/Stoer	$24.95
6228	The **Glass Candlestick** Book, Vol. 2, Fostoria to Jefferson, Felt/Stoer	$24.95
6461	The **Glass Candlestick** Book, Vol. 3, Kanawha to Wright, Felt/Stoer	$29.95
6329	**Glass Tumblers**, 1860s to 1920s, Bredehoft	$29.95
4644	**Imperial Carnival Glass**, Burns	$18.95
5827	**Kitchen Glassware** of the Depression Years, 6th Ed., Florence	$24.95
5600	Much More Early American **Pattern Glass**, Metz	$17.95
6133	**Mt. Washington Art Glass**, Sisk	$49.95
6136	Pocket Guide to **Depression Glass** & More, 13th Ed., Florence	$12.95
6448	Standard Ency. of **Carnival Glass**, 9th Ed., Edwards/Carwile	$29.95
6449	Standard **Carnival Glass** Price Guide, 14th Ed., Edwards/Carwile	$9.95
6035	Standard Ency. of **Opalescent Glass**, 4th Ed., Edwards/Carwile	$24.95
6241	Treasures of **Very Rare Depression Glass**, Florence	$39.95

POTTERY

4929	**American Art Pottery**, Sigafoose	$24.95
1312	**Blue & White Stoneware**, McNerney	$9.95
4851	Collectible **Cups & Saucers**, Harran	$18.95
6326	Collectible **Cups & Saucers**, Book III, Harran	$24.95
6344	Collectible **Vernon Kilns**, 2nd Edition, Nelson	$29.95
6331	Collecting **Head Vases**, Barron	$24.95
1373	Collector's Ency. of **American Dinnerware**, Cunningham	$24.95
4931	Collector's Ency. of **Bauer Pottery**, Chipman	$24.95
5034	Collector's Ency. of **California Pottery**, 2nd Ed., Chipman	$24.95
3723	Collector's Ency. of **Cookie Jars**, Book II, Roerig	$24.95
4939	Collector's Ency. of **Cookie Jars**, Book III, Roerig	$24.95
5748	Collector's Ency. of **Fiesta**, 9th Ed., Huxford	$24.95
3961	Collector's Ency. of **Early Noritake**, Alden	$24.95
3812	Collector's Ency. of **Flow Blue China**, 2nd Ed., Gaston	$24.95
3431	Collector's Ency. of **Homer Laughlin China**, Jasper	$24.95
1276	Collector's Ency. of **Hull Pottery**, Roberts	$19.95
5609	Collector's Ency. of **Limoges Porcelain**, 3rd Ed., Gaston	$29.95
2334	Collector's Ency. of **Majolica Pottery**, Katz-Marks	$19.95
1358	Collector's Ency. of **McCoy Pottery**, Huxford	$19.95
5677	Collector's Ency. of **Niloak**, 2nd Edition, Gifford	$29.95
5564	Collector's Ency. of **Pickard China**, Reed	$29.95
5679	Collector's Ency. of **Red Wing Art Pottery**, Dollen	$24.95
5618	Collector's Ency. of **Rosemeade Pottery**, Dommel	$24.95
5841	Collector's Ency. of **Roseville Pottery**, Revised, Huxford/Nickel	$24.95
5842	Collector's Ency. of **Roseville Pottery**, 2nd Series, Huxford/Nickel	$24.95
5917	Collector's Ency. of **Russel Wright**, 3rd Editon, Kerr	$29.95
5921	Collector's Ency. of **Stangl Artware**, Lamps, and Birds, Runge	$29.95
3314	Collector's Ency. of **Van Briggle Art Pottery**, Sasicki	$24.95
5680	Collector's Guide to **Feather Edge Ware**, McAllister	$19.95
6124	Collector's Guide to **Made in Japan Ceramics**, Book IV, White	$24.95
1425	**Cookie Jars**, Westfall	$9.95
3440	**Cookie Jars**, Book II, Westfall	$19.95
6316	Decorative **American Pottery & Whiteware**, Wilby	$29.95
5909	**Dresden Porcelain** Studios, Harran	$29.95
5918	Florence's Big Book of **Salt & Pepper Shakers**	$24.95
6320	Gaston's **Blue Willow**, 3rd Edition	$19.95
2379	Lehner's Ency. of **U.S. Marks** on Pottery, Porcelain & China	$24.95
4722	**McCoy Pottery**, Collector's Reference & Value Guide, Hanson/Nissen	$19.95
5913	**McCoy Pottery**, Volume III, Hanson & Nissen	$24.95
6333	**McCoy Pottery Wall Pockets** & Decorations, Nissen	$24.95
6135	**North Carolina Art Pottery**, 1900 – 1960, James/Leftwich	$24.95
6335	Pictorial Guide to **Pottery & Porcelain Marks**, Lage	$29.95
5691	**Post86 Fiesta**, Identification & Value Guide, Racheter	$19.95

1670	**Red Wing Collectibles**, DePasquale	$9.95
1440	**Red Wing Stoneware**, DePasquale	$9.95
6037	**Rookwood Pottery**, Nicholson & Thomas	$24.95
6236	**Rookwood Pottery**, 10 Yrs. of Auction Results, 1990 – 2002, Treadway	$39.95
1632	**Salt & Pepper Shakers**, Guarnaccia	$9.95
5091	**Salt & Pepper Shakers** II, Guarnaccia	$18.95
3443	**Salt & Pepper Shakers** IV, Guarnaccia	$18.95
3738	**Shawnee Pottery**, Mangus	$24.95
4629	Turn of the Century **American Dinnerware**, 1880s–1920s, Jasper	$24.95
5924	**Zanesville Stoneware** Company, Rans, Ralston & Russell	$24.95

OTHER COLLECTIBLES

5916	Advertising **Paperweights**, Holiner & Kammerman	$24.95
5838	Advertising **Thermometers**, Merritt	$16.95
5898	Antique & Contemporary **Advertising Memorabilia**, Summers	$24.95
5814	Antique **Brass & Copper** Collectibles, Gaston	$24.95
1880	Antique **Iron**, McNerney	$9.95
3872	Antique **Tins**, Dodge	$24.95
4845	Antique **Typewriters & Office Collectibles**, Rehr	$19.95
5607	Antiquing and Collecting on the **Internet**, Parry	$12.95
1128	**Bottle** Pricing Guide, 3rd Ed., Cleveland	$7.95
6345	**Business & Tax Guide** for Antiques & Collectibles, Kelly	$14.95
6225	Captain John's **Fishing Tackle** Price Guide, Kolbeck/Lewis	$19.95
3718	Collectible **Aluminum**, Grist	$16.95
6342	Collectible **Soda Pop** Memorabilia, Summers	$24.95
5060	Collectible **Souvenir Spoons**, Bednersh	$19.95
5676	Collectible **Souvenir Spoons**, Book II, Bednersh	$29.95
5666	Collector's Ency. of **Granite Ware**, Book 2, Greguire	$29.95
5836	Collector's Guide to **Antique Radios**, 5th Ed., Bunis	$19.95
3966	Collector's Guide to **Inkwells**, Identification & Values, Badders	$18.95
4947	Collector's Guide to **Inkwells**, Book II, Badders	$19.95
5681	Collector's Guide to **Lunchboxes**, White	$19.95
4864	Collector's Guide to **Wallace Nutting Pictures**, Ivankovich	$18.95
5683	**Fishing Lure** Collectibles, Vol. 1, Murphy/Edmisten	$29.95
6328	**Flea Market Trader**, 14th Ed., Huxford	$12.95
6227	**Garage Sale & Flea Market Annual**, 11th Edition, Huxford	$19.95
4945	**G-Men and FBI Toys** and Collectibles, Whitworth	$18.95
3819	**General Store** Collectibles, Wilson	$24.95
5912	The **Heddon Legacy**, A Century of Classic **Lures**, Roberts & Pavey	$29.95
2216	**Kitchen Antiques**, 1790–1940, McNerney	$14.95
5991	**Lighting Devices** & Accessories of the 17th – 19th Centuries, Hamper	$9.95
5686	**Lighting Fixtures** of the Depression Era, Book I, Thomas	$24.95
4950	The **Lone Ranger**, Collector's Reference & Value Guide, Felbinger	$18.95
6028	Modern **Fishing Lure** Collectibles, Vol. 1, Lewis	$24.95
6131	Modern **Fishing Lure** Collectibles, Vol. 2, Lewis	$24.95
6322	Pictorial Guide to **Christmas Ornaments** & Collectibles, Johnson	$29.95
2026	**Railroad** Collectibles, 4th Ed., Baker	$14.95
5619	**Roy Rogers and Dale Evans** Toys & Memorabilia, Coyle	$24.95
6339	**Schroeder's Antiques** Price Guide, 22nd Edition	$14.95
5007	**Silverplated Flatware**, Revised 4th Edition, Hagan	$18.95
6239	**Star Wars** Super Collector's Wish Book, 2nd Ed., Carlton	$29.95
6139	Summers' Guide to **Coca-Cola**, 4th Ed.	$24.95
6324	Summers' Pocket Guide to **Coca-Cola**, 4th Ed.	$12.95
3977	Value Guide to **Gas Station** Memorabilia, Summers & Priddy	$24.95
4877	Vintage **Bar Ware**, Visakay	$24.95
5925	The Vintage Era of **Golf Club** Collectibles, John	$29.95
6010	The Vintage Era of **Golf Club** Collectibles Collector's Log, John	$9.95
6036	Vintage **Quilts**, Aug, Newman & Roy	$24.95
4935	The W.F. Cody **Buffalo Bill** Collector's Guide with Values	$24.95

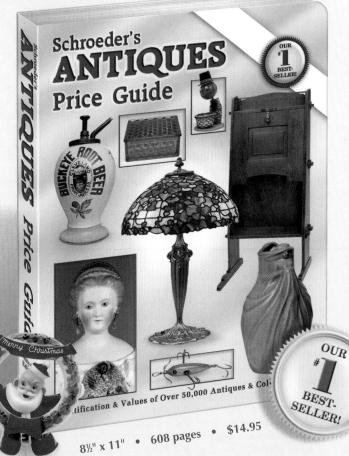

Strang S, Strang P: Questions posed to hospital chaplains by palliative care patients, *J Palliat Med* 5:857, 2002.

Tornstam L: Gerotranscendence: a theoretical and empirical exploration. In Thomas LE, Eisenhandler SA, editors: *Aging and the religious dimension*, Westport, CT, 1994, Greenwood Publishing Group.

Tornstam L: Gerotranscendence: a theory about maturing into old age, *J Aging Identity* 1:37–50, 1996.

Tornstam L: *Gerotranscendence: a developmental theory of positive aging*, New York, 2005, Springer.

Touhy T: Nurturing hope and spirituality in the nursing home, *Holist Nurs Pract* 15:45–56, 2001a.

Touhy T: Touching the spirit of elders in nursing homes: ordinary yet extraordinary care, *Int J Human Caring* 6:12–17, 2001b.

Touhy T, Brown C, Smith C: Spiritual caring: end of life in a nursing home, *J Gerontol Nurs* 31:27–35, 2005.

Touhy T, Zerwekh J: Spiritual caring. In Zerwekh J, editor: *Nursing care at the end of life: palliative care for patients and families*, Philadelphia, 2006, FA Davis.

Wikstrom B: Older adults and the arts, *J Gerontol Nurs* 30:30–36, 2004.

Baltes P, Smith J: New frontiers in the future of aging: from successful aging of the young old to the dilemmas of the fourth age, *Gerontology* 49:123–125, 2003.

Baltes P, Smith J: The fascination of wisdom: its nature, ontogeny, and function, *Perspect Psychol Sci* 3:56–62, 2008.

Bell V, Troxel D: Spirituality and the person with dementia: a view from the field, *Alzheimers Care Q* 2:31–45, 2001.

Bernstein A: *Spirituality and aging: Looking at the big picture*, Aging Well, 2009. http://todaysgeriatricmedicine.com/news/septstory1.shtml. Accessed July 2014.

Cherry K, Marks L, Benedetto T, et al: Perceptions of longevity and successful aging in very old adults, *J Relig Spiritual Aging* 25(4):288–310, 2013.

Cohen G: Research on creativity and aging: the positive impact of the arts on health and illness, *Generations* 30:7, 2006.

Cortes T: *The state of healthy aging*, April 4, 2013. http://hartfordinstitute.wordpress.com/2013/04/04/the-state-of-healthy-aging. Accessed August 2014.

Cousins N: *Anatomy of an illness*, New York, 1979, Norton.

Crowther MR, Parker MW, Achenbaum WA, et al: Rowe and Kahn's model of successful aging revisited: positive spirituality—the forgotten factor, *Gerontologist* 42:613–620, 2002.

Delgado C: Sense of coherence, spirituality, stress and quality of life in chronic illness, *J Nurs Sch* 39(3):229–234, 2007.

Donley R: Spiritual dimensions of health care: nursing's mission, *Nurs Health Care* 12:178–183, 1991.

Dyess S, Chase S: Caring for adults with a chronic illness through communities of faith, *Int J Hum Caring* 14(4):38–44, 2010.

Dyess S, Chase S, Newlin K: State of research for faith community nursing 2009, *J Relig Health* 49:188–199, 2010.

Edlund B: Revisiting spirituality in aging, *J Gerontol Nurs* 40(7):4–5, 2014.

Erikson EH: *Childhood and society*, ed 2, New York, 1963, Norton.

Gaskamp C, Sutter R, Meraviglia M, et al: Evidence-based guideline: promoting spirituality in the older adult, *J Gerontol Nurs* 32:8–13, 2006.

Goldberg B: Connection: an exploration of spirituality in nursing care, *J Adv Nurs* 27:836–842, 1998.

Grudzen M, Soltys FG: Reminiscence at end of life: celebrating a living legacy, *Dimensions* 7(3):4, 5, 8, 2000.

Gueldner S: Sustaining expression on identity in older adults, *J Gerontol Nurs* 33:3–4, 2007.

Haugan G: Nurse-patient interaction is a resource for hope, meaning in life and self-transcendence in nursing home patients, *Scand J Caring Sci* 28:74–88, 2014.

Heriot C: Spirituality and aging, *Holist Nurs Pract* 7:22–31, 1992.

Hodge D, Bonifas R, Chou R: Spirituality and older adults: ethical guidelines to enhance service provision, *Adv Soc Work* 11(1), 2010.

Hooyman N, Kiyak A: *Social gerontology: a multidisciplinary perspective*, Boston, 2005, Pearson.

Hudson F: *The adult years: mastering the art of self-renewal*, San Francisco, 1999, Jossey-Bass.

Killick J: *You are words*, London, 1997, Hawker.

Killick J: *Openings*, London, 2000, Hawker.

Killick J: *Dementia: You and yours (Radio transcript)*, 2005.

Killick J: *Dementia diary*, London, 2008, Hawker.

Kimble M: A personal journey of aging: the spiritual dimension, *Generations* 17(2):27–28, 1993.

Koenig HG, Brooks RG: Religion, health and aging: implications for practice and public policy, *Public Policy Aging Rep* 12:13–19, 2002.

Kohlberg L, Power C: Moral development, religious thinking and the question of a seventh stage. In Kohlberg L, editor: *The philosophy of moral development*, vol 1, San Francisco, 1981, Harper & Row.

Kuhn M: Advocacy in this new age, *Aging* 3:297, 1979.

Larson R: Building intergenerational bonds through the arts, *Generations* 30:38, 2006.

Leetun M: Wellness spirituality in the older adult, *Nurse Pract* 21:60, 65–70, 1996.

Lowry LW, Conco D: Exploring the meaning of spirituality with aging adults in Appalachia, *J Holist Nurs* 20:388–402, 2002.

Lustbader W: Conflict, emotion and power surrounding legacy, *Generations* 20:54–57, 1996.

Macrae J: Nightingale's spiritual philosophy and its significance for modern nursing, *Image J Nurs Sch* 27:8–10, 1995.

Martsolf D, Mickley J: The concept of spirituality in nursing theories: differing world views and extent of focus, *J Adv Nurs* 27:294–303, 1998.

Maslow A: Creativity in self-actualizing people. In Anderson H, editor: *Creativity and its cultivaton*, New York, 1959, Harper & Row.

Maslow A: *Religions, values and peak-experiences*, New York, 1970, Viking Press.

Metcalf CW: *Lighten up (Audiotape)*, Niles, IL, 1993, Nightingale Conant.

Meyer CL: How effectively are nurse educators preparing students to provide spiritual care? *Nurse Educ* 28(4):185–190, 2003.

Newberg AB, Wintering N, Khalsa DS, et al: Meditation effects on cognitive function and cerebral blood flow in subjects with memory loss: a preliminary study, *J Alzheimers Dis* 20:517–226, 2010. doi: 10.3233/JAD-2010-1391.

Newman MA: *Health as expanding consciousness*, ed 2, New York, 1994, National League for Nursing Press.

O'Brien ME: *Spirituality in nursing: standing on holy ground*, Boston, 2003, Jones & Bartlett.

O'Connor P: Hope: a concept for home care nursing, *Home Care Provid* 1:174–179, 1996.

Parisi J, Rebok G, Carlson M, et al: Can the wisdom of aging be activated and make a difference socially? *Educ Gerontol* 35:867–879, 2009.

Peck R: Psychological developments in the second half of life. In Anderson J, editor: *Psychological aspects of aging*, Washington, DC, 1955, American Psychological Association.

Perlstein S: Creative expression and quality of life: a vital relationship for elders, *Generations* 30:5–6, 2006.

Powers B, Watson N: Spiritual nurturance and support for nursing home residents with dementia, *Dementia* 10(1):59–80, 2011.

Puchalski C, Romer A: Taking a spiritual history allows clinicians to understand patients more fully, *J Palliat Med* 3:129–137, 2000.

Reed PG: Toward a nursing theory of self-transcendence: deductive reformulation using developmental theories, *ANS Adv Nurs Sci* 13:64–77, 1991.

Reichstadt J, Sengupta G, Depp C, et al: Older adults' perspective on successful aging: qualitative interviews, *Am J Geriatr Psychiatry* 18(7):567–575, 2010.

Rowe JW, Kahn RL: *Successful aging*, New York, 1998, Pantheon–Random House.

Sarton M: *At seventy: a journal*, New York, 1984, Norton.

Scott-Maxwell F: *The measure of my days*, New York, 1968, Knopf.

Soeken K, Carson V: Responding to the spiritual needs of the chronically ill, *Nurs Clin North Am* 22:603–611, 1987.

Steeves R, Kahn D: Experience of meaning in suffering, *Image J Nurs Sch* 19:114–116, 1987.